Communication Centers and Oral Communication Programs in Higher Education

Communication Centers and Oral Communication Programs in Higher Education

Advantages, Challenges, and New Directions

Edited by
Eunkyong L. Yook and Wendy Atkins-Sayre

LEXINGTON BOOKS
Lanham • Boulder • New York • Toronto • Plymouth, UK

Published by Lexington Books
A wholly owned subsidiary of The Rowman & Littlefield Publishing Group, Inc.
4501 Forbes Boulevard, Suite 200, Lanham, Maryland 20706
www.rowman.com

10 Thornbury Road, Plymouth PL6 7PP, United Kingdom

British Library Cataloguing in Publication Information Available

Library of Congress Cataloging-in-Publication Data
Communication centers and oral communication programs in higher education:
advantages, challenges, and new directions / Eunkyong Lee Yook
    p. cm.
  Summary: "Communication Centers and Oral Communication Programs in Higher
Education, edited by Eunkyong L. Yook and Wendy Atkins-Sayre reveals vital
information that is of theoretical and practical importance to higher education
administrators, educators, and communication centers directors and staff. It is the first
book to be published on communication centers"—Provided by publisher.
  Includes bibliographical references and index.
    1.   Communication—Study and teaching (Higher)—United States. 2.   Oral
        communication—Study and teaching (Higher)—United States. 3.   College
        dropouts—United States—Prevention.   I. Atkins-Sayre, Wendy, 1972- II. Title.
        P91.5.U5Y66 2012
        302.20711—dc23   2011050015

        ISBN: 978-0-7391-6816-5 (cloth : alk. paper)
        ISBN: 978-0-7391-8462-2 (pbk. : alk. paper)
        ISBN: 978-0-7391-7358-9 (electronic)

Printed in the United States of America

Thank you to our families, Ken, Chan, and Hewon Yook, as well as Ward, Gillian, and Owen Sayre. Without your understanding this book would not exist.

Contents

Part IV: New Directions in Consultant Training

ix

Foreword

The Communication Centers Movement in Higher Education

Beth Von Till

The editors, Esther Yook and Wendy Atkins-Sayre, have assembled an impressive collection of articles devoted to the growth and development of communication centers. Whether they support courses in oral communication or communication across the curriculum programs, communication centers have proven themselves to be invaluable in contributing to student success, retention, and graduation by providing pedagogical support for students. This book represents the best in current theory, but also best practices from a wide variety of sizes and types of colleges and universities. More importantly, the contents represent a body of knowledge made possible by the ten-year growth of a remarkable association of professional educators.

Communication centers grew out of research on the efficacy of timely feedback for student speeches. As video cameras and playback devices became more affordable, the lack of class time for feedback became less of an issue and trained tutors could provide student speakers with opportunities for review and improvement. Many labs and centers that began in the 1980s and early 1990s started in small spaces with limited equipment, some literally starting in closets. Other centers were well equipped but often fell victim to budget constraints. Panels of programs about communication centers appeared periodically at regional and national conventions, but there was no concerted effort for professional growth.

I have been involved with communication centers since 1987 when Jo Sprague, president of Western Speech Communication Association (1986) decided that San Jose State University needed a speech lab to support students enrolled in basic oral communication courses. We developed self-paced modules, offered workshops and videotaped feedback sessions, and provided one-on-one tutoring assistance. We rolled equipment into a classroom around other classes to create a temporary center with limited hours. A year later I was asked to direct the Communication Studies Lab. Over time, larger spaces, more equipment, and greater integration with the Communication Studies Department and other programs eventually led to a center that became a point of pride for the entire university.

This development was not a unique situation; likewise, some communication centers were flourishing while other institutions were exploring the possibility of starting their own centers. It was also not uncommon for communication center directors to be waging a struggle for survival when funding got scarce. Space was often limited, equipment was expensive, and staffing was an issue. What was missing was a larger conversation that addressed reoccurring issues, a sharing of research and best practices, and a sense of professionalism that extended beyond a few campuses.

In 2001, two remarkable events occurred organized by two visionary women. These events would have a profound effect on communication centers across the United States by bringing together directors from well-established communication centers or labs. The first of these was a conference organized by Linda Hobgood at the University of Richmond. This was the first "Excellence at the Center" conference in what was to become a yearly event, and was the seed that led to the start of two national organizations. Professor Hobgood felt that there must be other directors who would like to gather to discuss the scholarship of learning and communication centers, initially expecting only 15 people to attend. When over 60 people registered to attend, she knew that she had struck a sympathetic chord. To quote Robert Weiss in the May 2001 issue of the *Speaking Across the Curriculum Newsletter*, "Communication laboratories, which are designed to provide opportunities for students to enhance their communication participation, make vital contributions to speaking across the curriculum programs." This conference brought many of us to the larger conversation that had been missing.

The second important event occurred later that year when Sherry Morreale, then the Associate Director of the National Communication Association, organized a summer conference, titled "Engaging 21st Century Communication Students," in Washington, D.C. One of the "seven strands" of focus was devoted to communication centers. Invited contributors for each strand reviewed different operational models, development of new programs, and methods of assessment. One of the editors, Esther Yook, and I had the privilege of attending, along with Linda Hobgood, Marlene Preston, and others. Dr. Morreale intended that the materials generated from the summer strands would be archived and that presenters would serve as resource people for anyone interested in starting or rethinking existing communication centers. The conference yielded a wealth of information and interest such that Sherry Morreale encouraged us to form a group and petition to become a section of the National Communication Association.

The following fall, we all met at the annual National Communication Association convention in Atlanta and began the process of forming what was to become the communication centers section of NCA. This proposal was approved in the fall of 2002 at the annual conference in New Orleans. The members decided to also retain the more informal association, now called the National Association of Communication Centers (NACC) for the purpose of continuing the series of "Excellence at the Center" yearly mini-conferences.

Prior to 2001, communication center directors did not have many opportunities to share best practices or encourage research and professionalism. There were certainly occasional presentations at national and regional conferences, but few ongoing efforts at maintaining a professional dialogue. After 2001, there were yearly "Excellence at the Center" conferences at Butler, the University of Colorado at Colorado Springs, the University of Mary Washington, the University of Nebraska—Omaha, the University of North Carolina—Greensboro, De-Pauw University, and again at the University of Richmond in 2011 for the tenth anniversary. In addition, the communication centers section of NCA offered panels at each of the annual conventions. The luxury of twice-yearly meetings has produced strong professional and personal bonds and brought new participants into the discussion. Several impressive new programs have begun and new champions will continue the success of the communication centers movement.

A number of people have been involved in the process of establishing this forum of ideas for communication center directors. Many of these ideas were a direct result of meetings of like-minded scholars at NCA and NACC. I hope that this book will encourage many more voices to contribute to this area of scholarly collaboration, rich with potential, to propel our understanding of the various aspects of communication centers in higher education even further. I am sure that you will enjoy the contributions contained in this marvelous collection.

Preface

Eunkyong L. Yook and Wendy Atkins-Sayre

The communication centers movement is a relatively recent phenomenon in higher education, emerging in the late eighties, compared to its writing center counterpart. These centers support communication department or across-the-curriculum programs as higher education rightly focuses more attention on the field of communication. Since the movement's inception, communication centers have grown and become more sophisticated, center leaders have continued to organize professionally (as Beth Von Till discussed in the foreword), and scholarship on communication centers has developed, as evidenced by this collection of essays.

But communication centers are complicated in many ways. These centers are both for students and of students, in that students comprise the majority of the staff. Communication centers are both part of courses and separated from courses, freeing the student to explore communication outside of the classroom and separated from their discipline. The centers both teach communication skills, but also use communication skills in the difficult task of peer tutoring, thus granting peer tutors an enhanced learning experience. As any communication center director has discovered, it takes a great deal of training and careful direction to pull something like this together. Thus, this edited volume goes beyond the basics of setting up a communication center (although we are still in need of more published work in this area) and pushes the reader to think about the issues that emerge once the furniture is purchased, the paint is dry, and the staff members are hired.

Creating a communication center is a significant task, necessitating a vision for the center, significant funding and campus support, physical space, and much more. However, the steadily increasing numbers of communication centers in U.S. institutions of higher learning is a distinct sign that this movement is robust. Over 70 centers exist and are affiliated with the National Association of Communication Centers. The Ivy League universities, campuses that have traditionally shied away from the communication studies discipline, are also following suit, with Stanford University and the University of Pennsylvania establishing vibrant communication centers on their campuses. Even business schools are establishing communication centers developed solely for their students, realizing that students need more than just content knowledge in accounting or business management to get an edge in the job market and to communicate effectively on the job.

From this emerging and complex academic movement comes the idea for this edited volume. It addresses a variety of communication center and general oral communication program issues that will appeal to newcomers to the field, as well as those who currently oversee a center or program. The essays address theoretical issues, covering topics such as the importance of communication centers to higher education, the effects of communication centers on retention, critical thinking at the center, ethics, and different approaches for teaching communication. But the book also discusses praxis, exploring ideas about center set-up and use of space, staff training, technology applications, and campus advertising and outreach. The primary goal of this collection is to organize our cutting-edge knowledge of the theory and empirical research about communication centers so as to be of practical use to peer tutors and directors, both those new to the study of communication centers and those who are seasoned experts. An additional goal is to introduce administrators and those interested in higher education to the potential value of communication centers to higher education. Finally, this book also has a heuristic goal: to engender more research about communication centers that can inform our theory and application of the topic even further.

Specifically, the first part of the book, "Benefits to Higher Education," explains how communication centers play a vital role on campus and their links to significant and timely issues in higher education such as retention, critical thinking, liberal arts curricular goals, student empowerment, and student growth. In this section Eunkyong Yook, in her essay, "Communication Centers and Retention in Higher Education: Is There a Link?" compares institutions of higher education that provide communication centers with their peer institutions that do not have communication centers and finds that those with communication centers, *et ceteris paribus*, have a significantly higher level of six-year persistence rates. In another chapter, "Speaking Our Minds: Communication Centers and Critical Thinking," Wendy Atkins-Sayre proposes that communication centers can play an important role in enhancing critical thinking, thus extending classroom learning. In Corey Liberman's chapter, "Communication Centers and Liberal Arts Education: Problems and Possibilities Associated with Cross-disciplinary Engagements," he explores the place of communication centers in a liberal arts education, concluding that there are both benefits to this type of learning environment, as well as challenges specific to the liberal arts campus. In their chapter, "The Communication Center: A Critical Site of Intervention for Student Empowerment," Sandra Pensoneau-Conway and Nick Romerhausen argue that communication centers not only enhance the learning taking place in the classroom, but also contribute to student empowerment by engaging in truly student-centered and student-driven pedagogical encounters. Finally, in her chapter, "The Role Becomes Them: Examining Communication Center Alumni Experiences," Susan Wilson shares the results of a survey of communication center alumni, presenting first-hand testimonies from former tutors of the enduring positive effects of their undergraduate experiences as communication center consultants, including an enhancement of their own educational experience.

The second part of the volume, "Challenges to Today's Centers," looks at specific problems that centers face in attempting to serve higher education. In their chapter, "Ethics and the Communication Center: Chameleon or Tortoise?" Eunkyong Yook, Anand Rao, and Sarah Wilde discuss the dilemma of maintaining a focus on the rhetorical traditions of the communication field while assisting students to tailor their presentations to their disciplinary expectations. Deanna Dannels and Amy Housley Gaffney, in "The Blind Leading the Blind? An Ethnographic Heuristic for Communication Centers," propose an ethnographic approach for communication centers to learn the disciplinary expectations of the students who seek assistance at the center. Exploring one specific discipline, Trudy Bayer and Karen Curto describe a case study of a "communication intervention" for biology students at their institution in their chapter titled, "Learning to Tell What You Know: A Communication Intervention for Biology Students." Turning to the problem of recruiting center users, Jennifer Butler Ellis and Rose Clark-Hitt, in "Using Theory and Research to Increase Student Use of Communication Center Services," suggest formative research alternatives that will serve as a basis for crafting optimally effective messages for different campuses. Finally, in "Focusing on Faculty: The Importance of Faculty Support to Communication Center Success," Michael King and Wendy Atkins-Sayre delve more specifically into a study of faculty motivators for suggesting the use of the center to their students, making suggestions based on their research for more carefully targeting faculty.

The third part of the book, "Alternative Models for Communication Centers," contains new ideas to implement at the center. These are innovative conceptual developments in the field of communication center research that encourage the reader to think in novel ways about the interface between space configuration and student collaboration, strategies for assessing and implementing methods of maximizing student utilization of communication centers, as well as how to combine resources at a time of budgetary constraint. In "Communication Center Ethos: Remediating Space, Encouraging Collaboration," Russell Carpenter and Shawn Apostel make a compelling argument for the effect of space and collaborative work on the center's ethos, suggesting ways to enhance this collaborative environment in all centers. In her chapter, "The Combined Centers Approach: How Speaking and Writing Centers Can Work Together," Casey Malone Maugh argues that a combined approach to a center, integrating both writing and speaking services, provides a coherent template for enhanced interaction with faculty and students, efficient use of student consultants, and a holistic approach to written and oral communication for campuses with limited resources. The next three chapters explore alternatives for using technology in communication centers. Luke LeFebvre, in "Course Management Systems: Creating Alternative Avenues for Student Access of Communication Centers," explores alternatives for the use of computer mediated communication in communication centers, specifically outlining ways that centers can incorporate course management systems (such as Blackboard, WebCT, and Moodle) into center offerings. Reflecting the current trends in online service, Lynn Cooper discusses one center's move to a completely online tutoring system, providing a conceptual model of an online communication center, in her chapter titled, "Virtual Communication Centers: A Resource for Building Oral Competency." In her chapter on computer mediated communication (CMC) in communication centers, "The Implementation of Computer Mediated Communication in Communication Centers," Alyssa Davis argues that implementing CMC in communication centers, while presenting some challenges, helps to enhance the services offered by extending the way peer tutors can help speakers from solely face-to-face interaction to the widely growing area of Internet communication.

In the fourth section, "New Directions in Consultant Training," various practical issues of communication center staff training are highlighted. Training of communication center staff is vital to not only a center's success but also to the success of the clients they serve. After all, a center is only as good as the competence of the staff members, which is dependent on effective training. In their chapter on technology training, "Technology Tutoring: Communication Centers Take the Lead," Michelle Moreau and Paige Normand suggest a template for training staff on new technology issues that often arise at communication centers. Through specific scenarios, staff can learn how to guide the learner to understand presentation software through the skilled use of questions. "Using Empathetic Listening to Build Client Relationships at the Center," by Kimberly Cuny, Sarah Wilde, and Alexandra Vizzier Stephenson, seeks to show how peer-to-peer tutoring incorporates empathetic listening to build lasting relationships between peers, i.e., between staff and their speaker-clients. Finally, the chapter by Rhonda Troillett and Kristen McIntyre, "Best Practices in Communication Center Training and Training Assessment," explores how current communication centers' staffs are trained and evaluated to identify potential best practices in communication center staff training and assessment.

Taken together, it is our hope that this collection of essays promotes discussion about best practices for the center and perhaps motivates further research into the obstacles that communication centers face in attempting to enhance the college experience. Communication centers are complicated beasts, but it is that complexity that both creates challenges and also provides for such exhilarating opportunities.

In wrapping up this project, we are certain that this could not have happened without two motivating factors. First, we have experienced many of these benefits, challenges, and creative new directions for centers first hand as we were fortunate enough to direct centers on our campuses (University of Mary Washington, Agnes Scott College, and University of Southern Mississippi). To all of the administrators who supported our endeavors there and the student workers who made the centers function so beautifully, we thank you. Second, the growth of such a supportive and creative community in the National Association of Communication Centers (NACC) has motivated much of the writing that is included in this volume and is certain to continue to push the envelope in research in this area. We are hard pressed to find another group of scholars so eager to help each other out and so capable of having so much fun while doing substantive work. Sincere thanks go to our colleagues and friends in the NACC who have motivated the creation of this book through intriguing discussions, a willingness to share ideas, and a humble approach to learning more about our centers.

Part I:
Benefits to Higher Education

Chapter 1

Communication Centers and Retention in Higher Education: Is There a Link?

Eunkyong L. Yook

There are few institutions of higher learning today that can boast of not being affected by the serious issue of student retention. The grave status of college graduation rates in a downward spiral has spurred President Obama to spend almost 2 percent of his State of the Union speech in 2011 on the topic of education, which included urging the nation to redress the college graduation rate to increase national competitiveness in global rankings ("Breaking Down," 2011). Statistics show that U.S. college attrition rates have increased from 32 percent to 40 percent in less than a decade, and that over 20,000 college students drop out after their first year (Cravatta, 1997; Deberard, Speilmans, & Julka, 2004). Student attrition before the sophomore year of college is one commonly accepted measure of retention. Given these startling statistics, colleges must find novel ways to address this urgent issue. The current study provides a summary of previous research on the link between communication, communication centers, and retention. Additionally, it tests a hypothesis, albeit with an unavoidably small sample size, that the existence of communication centers positively affects the average six year persistence rate of an institution, another measure of retention.

Retention in Higher Education

The common denominator of previous research on retention cites various factors that affect the retention of college students, all of which are linked to communi-

3

cation as the common denominator. Academic performance (Cone, 1991; McGrath & Braunstein, 1997; Payne, Pullen, & Padgett, 1996), socialization with other students (Cleave, 1996; McGrath & Braunstein, 1997), interaction with faculty (Perrine, 1998), mentoring and peer support (Johnson & Romonoff, 1999), and involvement in campus activities (Graunke & Woosley, 2005), all hinge upon competent communication, to a larger or lesser degree. Though one could argue that the first variable, academic performance, can be linked less closely with communication than the other four variables, academic performance not only involves doing readings and assignments alone, but often also involves participation in class discussions and class activities, and public speaking skills, as well as small group communication competence. In fact, research supports the link between communication and retention, stating that communication competence reduces the frustration that is often the reason for dropping out, and that, inversely, students with problems such as communication apprehension are more likely to have a lower grade point average and are significantly more likely to drop out (Hawken, Duran, & Kelly, 1991; McCroskey, Booth-Butterfield, & Payne, 1989; Rubin, Graham, & Mignerey, 1990). Communication skills are vital to student retention.

Communication has become salient in academia as it is not only important for academic success during college, but also for careers after graduation. Fortune 500 companies cite communication skills as one of the most important skills in the corporate world (Morreale, 1996). Almost all job advertisements state that employers seek applicants with good communication skills, indicating their importance in the workplace today. Additionally, participation in civic life in general depends on competent communication skills, from interpersonal conversations to public policy debates (Morreale & Pearson, 2008; NCA, 2001). Finally, to its credit, some within academia are acknowledging the importance of communication, not only as the channel through which we interact, but also as a field in its own right, enabling and promoting students' critical thinking abilities (Coppola & Daniels, 1996; Palmerton, 1992; Silberman, 1996).

In response to the rising salience of the need to focus on the communication skills, institutions of higher learning are placing an increased importance on the teaching of competent communication skills. As a result, communication across the curriculum programs have been created on many campuses, and communication centers have been established across the nation as sites that promote communication competence (Clayton, 1999; Morello, 1995; Morreale, Shockley-Zalabak, & Whitney, 1993; Palmerton, 1990; Von Till, 2002; Weiss, 1988). While many centers predominantly support communication courses, others equally support across-the-curriculum courses or any other course that places an increased importance on such communication activities such as presentations, reports, debates, or role plays (Anderson, 2001; Nilsson, 2001; Picou, Cantrell, & Barr, 1998; Shaftel & Shaftel, 1967).

A study by Yook (2006) investigated the relationship between communication centers and retention, and found that all of the variables commonly agreed upon by scholars of the retention issue such as academic performance, social interaction with students and faculty, mentoring and peer support, and involvement in campus activities, are ones that are affected by the work of communication centers. The literature reviewed in the study researched the link between academic performance and communication centers, citing students and faculty who believed that communication centers helped student speeches become more coherent and cogent, thereby increasing the quality of academic performance (Kangas-Dwyer, 2006; Neher, 2003; Yook, 2006). A survey of over two thousand students over a span of five years at a small liberal arts college found that students believed that working with the communication center was helpful to their academic goals (Yook, 2010). The same study found that students felt that their confidence was boosted after having a consultation session at the communication center. Inversely, Kangas-Dwyer (2006) found that communication training at communication centers and communication education resulted in the lowering of communication apprehension among students. Moreover, the increase in confidence was experienced not only by the students visiting the communication center, but also by the staff trained to help them (Paxton, personal communication, January 17, 2006; Roberts, 2006).

Student interactions with faculty were also found to be linked to the work of communication centers, albeit on a theoretical level. The logic is that communication center staff members are peers whose status is somewhere between that of a student and a faculty member, and that when students interact with communication staff members, they are "rehearsing" and becoming more comfortable with interacting with those in a position of relative power in the instructional process (Bandura, 1977; Bandura & Locke, 2003; Perrine, 1998). More directly, mentoring and peer support, which is exactly aligned with the *raison d'être* of communication centers, has been found to increase academic success and retention (Johnson & Romanoff, 1999; Tinto, Goodsell Love, & Russo, 1993).

As for the last variable found to affect retention, involvement in campus activities, communication centers can also provide opportunities for student participation in a more relaxed extracurricular setting. Events such as workshops, speaking and writing contests, and other activities sponsored by communication centers, many of which are organized and staffed by communication center staff who are near-peers, can provide another venue for participation and a feeling of identity with the campus community. The more the student can be empowered to achieve academically by being guided on communication skills and the more opportunities are provided to reinforce a sense of belonging to the campus, the more students are likely to persist in their academic endeavors and resist the temptation to take the path of least resistance by dropping out (Dewitz, Woolsey, & Walsh, 2009).

A Pilot Study of Peer Institutions

An additional investigation was conducted into the effect of communication centers on persistence rate. As mentioned earlier, there are a number of main variables found to affect student retention, including communication competence (McCroskey, Booth-Butterfield, & Payne 1989), academic performance (Cone, 1991; Graunke & Woosley, 2005; McGrath & Braunstein, 1997; Payne, Pullen, & Padgett, 1996), interaction with students and faculty (Cleave, 1996; Perrine, 1998), peer support (Johnson & Romanoff, 1999), and involvement in campus activities (Graunke & Woosley, 2005). One indice of retention is persistence rate.

The labels retention, retention rate, persistence, and persistence rate are related, yet distinct. Retention is the umbrella term signifying the percentage of students retained in an educational institution. Retention rate is the percentage of students continuing their second year of college education after their freshmen year. Persistence refers to a student's motivation to continue to work towards graduation. Persistence rate is the rate of graduation within six years (American Council on Education, 2003).

For the purposes of this study, persistence rate was selected, rather than retention rate. The main reason is that in investigating the effects of communication centers on retention, these effects would be most successfully gauged by looking at the effects of communication center usage during the range of all the years that the student was enrolled, not only during the first year. To put it another way, looking at the effects of communication centers on retention rate, or the rate of a freshman student continuing to the sophomore year, would be too restrictive as it assumes that the student would have visited the communication center during the first year, which would not be the case for all students. In fact, some students might not visit the communication center until their last year in college, as students who are not mandated to visit the center by their instructor will most likely not go to the center (Butler Ellis & Clark-Hitt, 2010).

The most recent statistics on persistence rates find that the overall persistence rate of all students in all institutions of higher learning (two-year and four-year) combined, looking at students 2004-2009 who obtained their degree within six years, is 49.4 percent (National Center for Education Statistics, 2010). In other words, less than one half of all students enrolled in institutions of higher education in the U.S. graduate within six years. This is a dismal situation indeed. The current study investigated whether the presence or absence of communication centers on campus, all other things equal, would have an effect on persistence rates of institutions of higher learning. Therefore the research question is:

> *Et ceteris paribus*, or all other things equal, institutions of higher learning with a communication center on campus will have higher retention rates compared to retention rates of peer institutions without a communication center.

Method

Independent and Dependent Variables

A current list of communication centers was obtained from the National Association of Communication Centers website (National Association of Communication Centers, 2010). Previous research on retention rates showed that retention rates for institutions of higher learning that were doctoral granting institutions versus those that were not, and public institutions versus those that were not were very different in nature (American Council on Education, 2003). This classification was used as a template for this study so as not to bias the results. Peer institutions for the institutions of higher learning with communication centers on campus were identified using the Carnegie classification template. If several peers were listed, the first three were researched for the presence or absence of a communication center. An Internet search was conducted for these peer institutions for words such as "communication center" or "speaking center" and follow up phone calls were made to confirm the presence or absence of a communication center to identify the peer institution that matched the institution with a communication center listed on the National Association of Communication Centers website.

Of the total 67 communication centers listed on the website, 30 were matched with their pairs in peer institutions. These pairs met the criteria of 1) both institutions (those with and without communication centers) listing their six-year persistence rates in the *2011 College Handbook* (College Board, 2011) and 2) communication centers existing before 2004. The *College Handbook* was selected for persistence rates as other college reference books either did not list six-year persistence rates or only listed four-year persistence rates. Using the 6-year persistence rate would allow students more opportunities to have potentially benefited from visiting the communication center during their span of up to six undergraduate years. An Internet search for individual institutional persistence rates resulted in websites reporting six-year persistence rates that either did not report the date of the report or did not have comprehensive lists. Existence of the communication center before 2004 was further ascertained by checking the National Association of Communication Centers convention participant lists for 2001-2004.

Analysis

A paired t-test between the institution of higher learning with a communication center and its peer institution without one was conducted with a significance level of .10. The relatively lenient significance level was selected as there are already a number of variables that have been found to affect retention; nevertheless, the investigation sought to determine if there was an effect of communication centers above and beyond the effect of the other variables. Therefore, a high level of significance of the effect of this sole variable was deemed unlikely. Of course being able to measure other variables such as communication competence, academic performance, interaction with students and faculty, peer support, and involvement in campus activities would be ideal. However, measuring those variables consistently across all institutions would be a gargantuan, if not impossible, task. So even though a high level of significance would not be highly likely, it would be interesting to note the findings even while using a low level of significance to test the hypothesis.

Results
A scattergram indicated the presence of an outlier, the University of Alaska. Perhaps the extreme weather conditions and distance from students' states of origins, as well as the relative isolation of the campus from urban influences may be a factor for the extremely low level of persistence, regardless of the presence of a communication center. To increase the integrity of the analysis the outlier was discarded. A preliminary test for the equality of variances indicated that the variances of the data for the two levels of the independent variable were not statistically unequal ($F = .76, p = .24$). A paired t-test was performed. The mean persistence rate for the group of institutions with communication centers was larger ($M=67.9, SD= 15.34, N=29$) than the mean score for the matched group of peer institutions without communication centers ($M=62.9, SD= 17.57, N=29$). Using the matched pair t-test for equal variances resulted in $t(28) = 1.89, p<=0.03$ (see table 1.1).

Table 1.1: t-Test: Paired Two Sample for Means

	Variable 1	Variable 2
Mean	67.86207	62.89655
Variance	235.1946	308.8818
Observations	29	29
Pearson Correlation	0.638619	
Hypothesized Mean Difference	0	
df	28	
t Stat	1.891663*	

Note. Variable 1 is institutions with communication centers in existence for over six years. Variable 2 is peer institutions without communication centers.
* $p<.05$.

Discussion

The results showed a statistically significant level of difference between the two groups; institutions with communication centers did have higher persistence rates (67.9 percent) than those with no communication centers (62.9 percent). In other words, there is statistically significant support for the hypothesis that communication centers affect retention positively, despite the relatively small sample size. Due to the small sample size, a more liberal significance level (.10) was used rather than the more conservative level (.05). However, the resulting significance level of .03 surpassed even the more conservative level despite the small sample size. These results support the hypothesis that, *et ceteris paribus*, institutions of higher education with communication centers will have higher retention rates than those without communication centers. However, future research with larger numbers will further strengthen the argument.

In the current study, the small sample size could not be avoided due to the small number of communication centers that were in existence prior to 2004, combined with the absence of credible sources of persistence rate data of some institutions of higher learning or their peer institutions, including two-year institutions. Of the college guidebooks, the *2011 College Handbook* was the only one with six-year persistence rates cited. While currently the numbers are relatively small, when more communication centers will have been in existence for the prerequisite six years or longer for the purposes of this study, future studies should be conducted using a larger sample to further inquire into the effects of communication centers on retention in higher education.

Conclusion

This chapter has presented an argument to consider the possible theoretical relationship between campus communication centers and college student retention. The literature on college student retention shows that there are many variables that affect it. Additionally, new theoretical, as well as empirical support has been provided to show the links between communication centers and student success and retention. Although a relatively new field of academia, this may become a fertile ground for future research, especially regarding the effects of communication centers on college student retention. With more empirical research and continued development of ways to assess the various facets of the communication center and what it can do for the college student, the argument presented in this chapter can be further clarified, sharpened, and developed.

We live in an era where the leaders of society need to be better educated to make wise decisions and where citizens can learn to practice their civic duties more effectively. Economic difficulties necessitate that students become more competitive in the hiring process, with college degree in hand. A more civil, articulate, and well prepared college graduate population is being called for by various stakeholders and leaders. As President Obama stated during his 2011 State of the Union address, we should seize the "Sputnik moment" to further our global competitiveness in the number of higher education degree-holders. The first step is to retain them in college.

References

American Council on Education. (2003). Student success: Understanding graduation and persistence rates. Washington, DC: American Council on Education. Retrieved from http://www.acenet.edu/AM/Template.cfm?Section=Home&TEMPLATE=/CM/Cont entDisplay.cfm&CONTENTID=33951

Anderson, R. (2001). Team disease presentation: A cooperative learning activity for large classrooms. *The American Biology Teacher, 63*(1), 40-44.

Bandura, A. (1977). Self-efficacy: Toward a unifying theory of behavioral change. *Psychological Review, 84*, 191–215.

Bandura, A., & Locke, E. A. (2003). Negative self-efficacy and goal effects revisited. *Journal of Applied Psychology, 38*(1), 87–99.

Breaking down the state of the union. (2011, January 26). *The Washington Post.* Retrieved from http://www.washingtonpost.com/wp-srv/special/politics/state-of-the-union-2011-breakdown/

Butler Ellis, J., & Clark-Hitt, R. (2010, November). *Student motivation and program improvement.* Paper presented at the annual conference of the National Communication Association, San Francisco, CA.

Clayton, M. (1999, September 7). Keep an eye out for innovative programs. *The Christian Science Monitor*, p. 14.

Cleave, S. (1996). Residence retention: Reasons students choose to return or not to return. *College Student Journal, 30*, 187-199.

College Board. (2011). *2011 College handbook.* New York: College Board.

Cone, A. (1991). Sophomore academic retention associated with a freshman study skills and college adjustment course. *Psychological Reports, 69*, 312-314.

Coppola, B., & Daniels, D. (1996). The role of written and verbal expression in improving communication skills for students in an undergraduate chemistry program. *Language and Learning Across the Disciplines, 1*(3), 67-86.

Cravatta, M. (1997). Hanging on to students: College student attrition rate after freshman year. *American Demographics, 19*(11), 41.

Deberard, M., Spielmans, G., & Julka, D. (2004). Predictors of academic achievement and retention among college freshmen: A longitudinal study. *College Student Journal, 38*(1), 66-81.

DeWitz, S., Woolsey, M., & Walsh, W. (2009). College student retention: An exploration of the relationship between self-efficacy beliefs and purpose in life among college students. *Journal of College Student Development, 50*(1), 19–34.

Garside, C. (2002). Seeing the forest through the trees: A challenge facing communication across the curriculum programs. *Communication Education, 52*, 51-64.

Graunke, S., & Woosley, S. (2005). An exploration of the factors that affect the academic success of college sophomores. *College Student Journal, 39*(2), 367-376.

Hawken, L., Duran, R., & Kelly, L. (1991). The relationship of interpersonal communication variables to academic success and persistence in college. *Communication Quarterly, 39*, 297-309.

Johnson, J., & Romanoff, S. (1999). Higher education residential learning communities: What are the implications for student success? *College Student Journal, 33*(3), 385-399.

Kangas-Dwyer, K. (2006, April). *Assessment, the basic course, university accreditation, and allied funding: The important connection with the Speech Center.* Paper presented at the annual conference of the National Association of Communication Centers, Omaha, NE.

McCroskey, J., Booth-Butterfield, S., & Payne, S. (1989). The impact of communication apprehension on college student retention and success. *Communication Quarterly, 37*(2), 100-108.

McGrath, M., & Braunstein, A. (1997). The prediction of freshmen attrition: An examination of the importance of certain demographic, academic, financial, and social factors. *College Student Journal, 31*, 396-408.

Morello, J. (1995, August). *The Speaking Intensive Program at Mary Washington College.* A Report Submitted to the Committee on General Education, Mary Washington College, Fredericksburg, VA.

Morreale, S. (1996). Mailbag. *Spectra*, p. 5.

Morreale, S., & Pearson, J. (2008). Why communication education is important: The centrality of the discipline in the 21st century. *Communication Education, 57*, 224-240

Morreale, S., Shockley-Zalabak, P., & Whitney, S. (1993). The Center for Excellence in Oral Communication: Integrating communication across the curriculum. *Communication Education, 42*, 10-21.

National Association of Communication Centers. (2010). *Directory of centers.* Retrieved from http://www.communicationcenters.org/

National Center for Educational Statistics. (2010). *Persistence and attainment of 2003–04 beginning postsecondary students: After 6 years.* Retrieved from http://nces.ed.gov/pubs2011/2011151.pdf

National Communication Association, Proceedings from the Communication Across the Curriculum Strand. (2001). Summer Conference: Engaging 21st Century Communication Students. Retrieved from
http://www.natcom.org/Instruction/summerconf/summerconf.htm

Neher, W. (2003, November). *Assessment of the Speakers Lab at a small private university.* Paper presented at the annual conference of the National Communication Association, Miami, FL.

Nilsson, M. (2001). Student-taught review sessions: Fostering communication skills and reinforcing concepts. *Journal of Chemical Education, 78*(5), 628.

Palmerton, P. (1990, March). *Speaking across the curriculum: The Hamline experience.* Paper presented at the Conference for College Composition and Communication, Louisville, KY.

Palmerton, P. (1992). Teaching skills or teaching thinking? *The Journal of Applied Communication Research, 20*(3), 335-341.

Payne, B., Pullen, R., & Padgett, J. (1996). An examination of student attrition at a medium-sized southern university. *Psychological Reports, 78*, 1035-1038.

Perrine, R. (1998). Students' views of the characteristics of instructors' approachability. *Psychological Reports, 82*, 519-525.

Picou, A., Cantrell, P., & Barr, J. (1998). Suggestions for producing teaching excellence. *Education, 119*(12), 322.

Roberts, S. (2006). *Speaking consultant journal.* Unpublished manuscript. The Speaking Center, University of Mary Washington, Fredericksburg, VA.

Rubin, R., Graham, E., & Mignerey, J. (1990). A longitudinal study of students' communication competence. *Communication Monographs, 39*, 1-13.

Shaftel, F., & Shaftel, G. (1967). *Roleplaying in the curriculum* (2nd ed.). Englewood Cliffs, NJ: Prentice Hall.

Silberman, M. (1996). *Active learning: 101 strategies to teach any subject.* Boston, MA: Allyn & Bacon.

Tinto, V., Goodsell Love, A., & P. Russo (1993). Building learning communities for new college students. *Liberal Education, 79*(4), 16-22.

Von Till, B. (2002, April). *Tutor handbook for the communication studies lab and resource center.* Paper presented at the National Association of Communication Centers Annual Conference, Indianapolis, IN.

Weiss, R. (1988). A program for speaking and listening across disciplines. *Bulletin for the Association of Communication Administration, 65*, 79-84.

Yook, E. (2006, April). Assessing communication centers: A round table discussion. In K. Dwyer (Chair), *Assessment, the basic course, university accreditation, and allied funding.* Panel session conducted at the National Association of Communication Centers Conference, Omaha, NE.

Yook, E. (2010). [Survey of students visiting the Speaking Center]. Unpublished raw data.

Chapter 2

Speaking Our Minds: Communication Centers and Critical Thinking

Wendy Atkins-Sayre

The phrase "speak your mind" generally conjures up images of individuals speaking passionately about subjects that are close to their hearts. When we think about passionate speaking, we rarely envision research, outlines, planning, and practice. Instead, we imagine a speaker who is moved by the moment and speaking "off the cuff." Oral communication is clearly improved, however, with thorough research and reflection on the topic, careful audience analysis, and a heavy dose of delivery preparation. The emphasis in the phrase "speak your mind" should be on the "mind." It would be a mistake, however, to lose the idea of "speaking." After all, the phrase encourages us to take the ideas that have been formed in our minds and to share them publicly. There is no need to change the phrase, but merely to change the way that we commonly think about speaking. The answer lies in the emphasis on the connection between speaking and critical thinking.

Kenneth Burke (1941), describing the development of ideas as a conversation, creates a powerful metaphor for communication's relationship to thought. "Imagine that you enter a parlor," Burke says. "You come late. When you arrive, others have long preceded you, and they are engaged in a heated discussion, a discussion too heated for them to pause and tell you exactly what it is about" (pp. 110 – 111). Upon encountering this conversation, Burke argues that the individual carefully listens, tentatively enters into the conversation, and begins participating in the construction of ideas through conversation. In order to

13

most effectively "speak your mind," a person must be comfortable with the subject, be aware of the ways in which we talk about the subject, enter into the conversation, and then be able to learn from successes and mistakes in the conversation. It is this concept of conversation that hints at the connection between speaking and critical thinking. Rather than being a "mere performance," quality speeches develop through critical conversations and invite audience members into a larger social discussion.

Communication centers, because they are focused on improving oral communication, serve a critical function on college campuses. Students faced with the task of "thinking critically" through their writing and speaking may find themselves lost in attempting to complete an assignment, or may take a stab at critical thinking only to find that the product is less than stellar. What communication centers routinely do is to guide speakers in the art of critical thinking. Training and practice in oral communication leads to a better ability to participate in the kinds of conversations that matter—conversations in class, with instructors, in debates, and in the community. Taking a rhetorical approach to discussing ideas means that we pay attention to the "resources available in language and in people to make ideas clear and cogent, to bring concepts to life, to make them salient for people" (Campbell & Huxman, 2009, p. 2). These are, of course, concepts that are central to both critical thinking and quality conversations.

This chapter argues that development of oral communication skills are linked to critical thinking and that communication centers are, consequently, an important part of the learning process. I will first discuss more fully the connection between critical thinking and oral communication before turning more specifically to the role of communication centers in the development of critical thinking skills. Finally, I will outline suggestions for improving critical thinking guidance in the communication center.

Critical Thinking Through Oral Communication

Critical thinking can be defined in a myriad of ways, but the most fundamental contribution to our understanding of the critical thinking process can be traced back to John Dewey. Dewey (1922) argued for the importance of students becoming engaged with the material (rather than merely receiving and memorizing information) by struggling with questions or problems. As Dewey wrote, "Only by wrestling with the conditions of the problem at first hand, seeking and finding his own way out, does he think" (p. 188). Critical thinking is focused on "the art of analyzing and evaluating thinking with a view to improving it" (Paul & Elder, 2009). At its most basic, critical thinking is problem-solving, yet problem-solving can be approached in a variety of ways. As Chet Meyers (1987) points out, critical thinking processes can be discipline-specific, but generally center on logic. Consequently, students are able to learn general critical thinking skills that cross disciplinary boundaries.

Working from some of Dewey's ideas, communication scholars have argued for the connection between communication and critical thinking. Allen, Berkowitz, Hunt, and Louden (1999), for example, conducted a meta-analysis on research related to the effect that training in debate has on critical thinking skills and concluded that, "The impact of public communication training on the critical thinking ability of the participants is demonstrably positive" (p. 28). Learning to create arguments and then defend those arguments leads to a deeper understanding of and engagement with the subject. Looking at broader types of public speaking, others have argued that evaluating sources and arguments, concepts central to any public speaking course, leads to critical thinking (Mazer, Hunt, & Kuznekoff, 2007). Morello (2000) explains that the "discovery mode of communication helps students use talk as a way to explore new ideas, to think creatively and critically, and to learn in collaboration with others" (p. 109). In fact, Katula and Martin (1984) argue that speaking is a more complex form of critical thinking because speakers not only compose messages, but then struggle with a continual adjustment of an argument to an audience.

Aside from obvious examples of critical thinking in speaking, however, it is also important to note that communication has an inherent effect on the way that we think. Pulling from a host of theorists, Patricia Palmerton (1992) concludes, "The way in which we use language shapes the knowledge we have about our experiences with the world, and influences how we modify our interpretive frameworks" (p. 336). Oral communication—whether formal or informal (think peer conversations)—not only influences the way the audience thinks about a subject, but also shapes the thoughts of the speaker. Thus, Palmerton concludes, when we teach speaking, we should be careful to focus "upon the processes that influence the evolution of their thought, as well as the implications of their structural choices" (p. 336). Critical thinking, then, should be seen as a central component of oral communication pedagogy.

In recent years, attention to the importance of oral communication has increased on college campuses, although the emphasis has been more on oral competence than on critical thinking. As Morreale and Pearson (2008) discovered, there is significant emphasis on the importance of communication education both in academia and in the business world. Moreover, the emphasis on communication skills by accrediting agencies such as the Southern Association of Colleges and Schools has provided the needed impetus for colleges and universities to incorporate communication courses into their general education classes, to support communication across the curriculum initiatives, and/or to open communication centers (Hobgood, 2000).

Despite this shift in higher education trends, there is still some bias against oral communication. This bias can be traced back as early as Plato and his distrust of rhetoric as mere "cookery" or Rationalism's de-emphasis of rhetoric because of its lack of "connection to science and truth" (Foss, Foss, & Trapp,

1991, pp. 4 – 8). Of course, the rhetorical turn to belletristic rhetoric (more concern with the artistic components than the content) and the elocutionary movement (emphasis on voice and gesture) in the mid- to late-1700s also had a negative effect on the discipline, with the move connoting that style was more
important than content (Foss et al., 1991, pp. 9 – 10). The development of a separate academic field in the form of communication studies (branching off from
the English discipline) did much to remedy some of the historical damage
wrought in previous years, however oral communication is still often seen as
secondary.

Today's bias is partially attributed to the belief that the "real thinking" happens through learning course content and writing, while oral communication is
"mere packaging." As John Bean (2001), discussing similar problems with writing, argues, "writing instruction goes sour whenever writing is conceived primarily as a 'communication skill' rather than as a process and product of critical
thought" (p. 3). Similarly, as long as oral communication is viewed as merely
sharing ideas—not struggling with concepts—it will never be fully embraced as
a vital part of higher education. In order for communication education to be
connected with the act of learning, its part in critical thinking must be understood and underscored. As Morello (2000) argues, if communication across the
curriculum programs are to be successful, they need to be clear about what
unique contributions such programs make to the curriculum (p. 100). It is for
this reason that communication centers should focus on understanding best practices for enhancing critical thinking through the use of the center.

Communication centers, however, face an additional challenge in attempting to make themselves central to the college and university curriculum. They
are recognized by most faculty as being supplemental to their disciplines in
helping speakers more clearly and effectively communicate their thoughts.
However, communication centers, and oral communication more broadly, face a
tougher sell in attempting to convince faculty that tutoring in oral communication—a process that takes place outside of the classroom—can enhance learning
of discipline-specific material and critical thinking. Because faculty are central
to the success of the communication center (see chapter 10), this is an important
argument to make.

Critical Thinking in Communication Centers

The question that emerges from this understanding of the connection between
communication and critical thinking is how communication centers can best
facilitate critical thinking. Bruffee (1995), discussing tutoring in writing, offers a
compelling description of the role of the tutoring process in critical thinking,
arguing that the best way to understand the process of writing is to think about it
in terms of a conversation. As Bruffee sees it, writing is like a conversation in
that you begin the writing process by thinking through your arguments—having

an internal conversation about the argument. Next, you externalize your internal conversation by attempting to put your words onto a page so that others can read your thoughts and respond to them. He writes, "If thought is internalized public and social talk, then writing is internalized talk made public and social again. If thought is internalized conversation, then writing is internalized conversation re-externalized" (pp. 90 – 91). Peer tutoring, then, becomes a central part of education and, indeed, thinking because the act of talking through an argument with a peer enhances the critical thinking process. The need to speak to a particular peer audience, to think about the best language to describe the argument, and to clarify points that were clear internally but not clear to the audience (the peer tutor), forces the individual to more carefully craft the conversation.

In other words, conversation is an essential part of reflective thinking, argumentation, and writing. As Bruffee (1995) writes, "The first steps to learning to think better are to learn to converse better and to learn to create and maintain the sort of social contexts, the sorts of community life, that foster the kinds of conversations we value" (p. 90). Bruffee's description is not unlike Burke's (1941) concept of the ongoing conversation. What communication centers do is present speakers with practice conversations so that they are ready for the "real conversations" that will present themselves.

Oral communication of ideas, in particular, provides an important point of entry into critical thinking for any discipline. This means that centers devoted to improving students' abilities in oral communication become a central part of the critical thinking learning process. In particular, center tutors should be trained to guide students through a process that leads to critical thinking. They should have quality peer conversations, pulling from Bruffee's (1995) ideas, which are "emotionally involved, intellectually and substantively focused, and personally disinterested" (p. 91). The importance of the *peer* component is that students have a reassuring sounding board for struggling with their entry into discipline-specific conversations.

Critical Conversations: Advice for Centers

Although critical thinking should occur at a number of junctures during the consultation process, there are steps that can be taken to make sure that communication centers are fully guiding students and faculty in this area. Some of the steps may come naturally to staff members, while others may need to be explained, discussed, modeled, and coached.

First, conversations in the center should focus on the concept of audience in the discovery and invention stages, well before "speech writing" begins. Although this may seem like an obvious concern, too many speakers do not take into account the differences between their own knowledge and beliefs and that of the audience. Consequently, a large part of any conversation with clients should focus on encouraging the speaker to approach the topic from a variety of standpoints that might reflect those of the imagined audience. Reflecting back on the definitions of critical thinking put forth earlier in the chapter, this process encourages the speaker to approach the speech through a series of problems (What does the audience know/think? How can I change their opinions? How can I connect with the audience?), to struggle with the topic, and to approach it from multiple perspectives. Although much of the critical thinking process dealing with audience can happen with the speaker alone reflecting on the topic and the audience, it is the conversations with tutors—vocalizing their thoughts, getting immediate feedback from a trained tutor, and then adapting their thoughts based on that feedback—that is a critical component of the process. Even if these types of questions do not make a marked impact on the content of the presentation, the process of critically analyzing where the audience stands on the issue and what their responses might be will strengthen the preparation process for the speaker.

Second, once the "speech writing" stage has begun, peer conversations should turn to targeted critical thinking questions in order to strengthen and develop the argument. Assuming that the student has now gathered evidence and started to sketch out an outline for the presentation, tutors should help guide them through a critical thinking process. Richard Paul and Linda Elder (2009), in their book, *The Miniature Guide to Critical Thinking: Concepts and Tools*, provide a useful set of starting questions for a conversation based on the elements of thought. First, speakers should walk through the concept of purpose and goal of the presentation. What is the speaker trying to achieve with the message? Second, the speaker should think about the questions at issue. In rhetorical terms, this might be thought of as the rhetorical problem, or obstacles that the speaker encounters in reaching the goal. For example, are there other approaches to the topic or arguments in opposition to the stated goal? Does the audience have a different set of information or assumptions? Third, what assumptions has the speaker potentially made and how might those assumptions lead to flawed reasoning? Fourth, what is the speaker's point of view and how might that point of view be different from other audience members' views? Fifth, what type of information is available to support the argument? What are the facts and opinions surrounding the question? Sixth, what theories and concepts would support these conclusions? Seventh, what conclusions and solutions can be assumed based on the available information? How did the speaker reach this conclusion? What conclusions are logical or flawed? Finally, what are the implications and consequences of this line of reasoning? How might it affect others? How might others receive this argument?

After walking through a conversation led by these questions, speakers would clearly be more prepared for the presentation by approaching the topic in multiple ways and taking audience factors into account. The process of the conversation, however, would also benefit the speaker in becoming more comfortable with the material and, in many ways, "owning" the topic more or investing more in the topic. As Paul and Elder (2009) conclude, "Critical thinking is, in short, self-directed, self-disciplined, self-monitored, and self-corrective thinking.

It requires rigorous standards of excellence and mindful command of their use. It entails effective communication and problem solving abilities and a commitment to overcome our native egocentrism and sociocentrism" (p. 2). As most faculty could attest, were our students to walk through this process for each assignment, the classroom environment would change dramatically. Consequently, communication centers and the guided conversations that they provide become a vital component of training students to think this way on their own.

Third, beyond the planning and writing stages, communication centers should also help speakers be more prepared for on-the-spot adaptation to the context. For example, when extemporizing, speakers might adapt the content of their speeches based upon immediate audience feedback, the occasion, or even a change in thinking while they are speaking. This is a difficult process that requires speakers to be able to quickly run through a set of questions (What do I know? What does the audience know? What does this feedback mean? What is the best way to adapt the message based on this new information?) while also continuing to communicate with the audience. The critical thinking questions that emerge in sessions in the communication center might help prepare speakers to make more informed and confident with on-the-spot speaking decisions that will enable them to reach the audience more effectively.

Fourth, beyond the oral communication task, centers should help create students who are comfortable being self-reflective. These are, in Paul and Elder's (2009) terms, more "practicing," "advanced," or "accomplished thinkers" (p. 20). Students, especially first and second year students, may come to a center as "unreflective thinkers" ("unaware of significant problems in our thinking") or "challenged thinkers" ("faced with significant problems in our thinking") (Paul & Elder, 2009, p. 20). The outcome of effective tutoring sessions in a communication center might initially lead to "beginning thinkers" ("try to improve but without regular practice") as we walk them through the suggested critical thinking questions (Paul & Elder, 2009, p. 20). In subsequent sessions, and once students are accustomed to regularly asking themselves critical questions, students might become "practicing thinkers" ("regularly practice and advance accordingly") (Paul & Elder, 2009, p. 20). Ultimately, conversations that begin in communication centers might create students who have developed a lifelong commitment to approaching learning from a critical perspective.

Finally, communication centers provide support for critical thinking on campus by working directly with faculty to create assignments that inspire this activity. Although peer conversations in the center can help improve any course assignment, it is the assignment itself that might be overly restrictive, thus preventing quality critical thinking. Center directors should work with faculty to help them construct the most effective oral assignments. The fundamentals of effective oral assignments (time limits, source requirements, outline requirements, etc.) might be clear to faculty, but directors must also be careful to provide feedback and guidance on assignments that will allow for more opportunities for critical thinking. For example, what is the purpose of the assignment?

What is the faculty member attempting to do by assigning this work? How is it tied into the discipline and/or the profession? The purpose of the assignment has to provide a compelling and meaningful reason for the student to engage the problem. Hosting faculty workshops on assignment design, providing materials that make suggestions for improving assignments, and/or working one-on-one with faculty may help change the environment on campus from one devoid of critical thinking challenges to one where students are encouraged to think critically in most assignments. The benefit of this shift might mean that students would see an emphasis on this skill across the disciplines and would begin to internalize the process.

Potential Problems

Although making critical thinking central to the mission of a communication center is possible, the process is not without potential problems. First, training tutors to be comfortable walking through the process may take time, additional reading, and practice. There is skill involved in guiding speakers through the process, but it may also involve creativity in opening speakers up to approaching the subject in a myriad of ways. Second, because the process is difficult, tutors may find that speakers are initially resistant to the process or truly incapable of processing the information in a different way. Of course, this obstacle emphasizes the importance of using the communication center as an intervention point in convincing students of the importance of first reflecting on the ways that they think about ideas and then communicating their ideas. Third, time is a factor that might pose a large obstacle to communication centers. It takes time to walk speakers through the process of critical thinking and centers may find that they see students at the last minute, and as a result only have a limited amount of time to work with each speaker. It is important to emphasize that even a few well-developed questions on the part of the tutor, however, can push the speaker along in the process of thinking critically. Additionally, the emphasis on what communication centers do to strengthen the substance of the presentation— specifically in the area of critical thinking—may motivate students to visit the center earlier in the speech-writing process, and more than once, and may motivate faculty to incorporate an early center visit into assignments. Consequently, although there are potential problems with a focus on critical thinking in the center, they are not insurmountable.

Conclusion

If communication centers begin to sell themselves as a vital component of the curriculum not only because of the contribution that they make to oral communication competence, but also because of their ability to enhance the critical thinking skills of our students, then faculty might begin to incorporate centers into the curriculum in a more significant way. What would an increased emphasis on critical thinking mean for communication centers? It might mean that centers need to rethink the types of training that tutors complete before beginning their work with the center. For example, readings on critical thinking would help develop a tutor's ability to ask the right questions in sessions and to guide speakers in the right direction. Role playing and even staff debates might push tutors to practice thinking through critical questions so that it becomes a natural part of their conversations with clients. Centers might consider borrowing from or creating their own critical thinking guides, with suggested questions and thought processes that would effectively guide tutors and clients through a critical thinking session. Given this change in emphasis, centers might also consider revising mission statements and publicity materials to highlight the importance of critical thinking in the tutoring process.

The possibilities for building critical thinking into communication centers are numerous, but centers should think of ways to make this critical work more apparent. Of course, many communication centers have already made critical thinking a central part of their missions and practice. What we are doing in centers is not only having critical conversations with students about their projects, modeling and motivating critical thinking through the exchange that happens in tutoring sessions, but also preparing speakers to publicly take part in the conversations about ideas that circulate all around us. These conversations are critical to the learning process and should be celebrated for the impact that they have on college and university campuses.

References

Allen, M., Berkowitz, S., Hunt, S., & Louden, A. (1999). A meta-analysis of the impact of forensics and communication education on critical thinking. *Communication Education*, *48*, 18 – 30.

Bean, J. C. (2001). *Engaging ideas: The professor's guide to integrating writing, critical thinking, and active learning in the classroom.* San Francisco: Jossey-Bass Publishers.

Bruffee, K. A. (1995). Peer tutoring and the "conversation of mankind." In C. Murphy & J. Law (Eds.), *Landmark essays on writing centers.* Davis, CA: Hermagoras Press.

Burke, K. (1941). *The philosophy of literary form: Studies in symbolic action.* Baton Rouge: Louisiana State University Press.

Campbell, K. K., & Huxman, S. S. (2009). *The rhetorical act: Thinking, speaking, and writing critically.* Belmont, CA: Wadsworth.

Dewey, J. (1922). *Democracy and education: An introduction to the philosophy of education.* New York: Macmillan Company.

Foss, S. A., Foss, K. A., & Trapp, R. (1991). *Contemporary perspectives on rhetoric* (2nd ed.). Prospect Heights, IL: Waveland.

Hobgood, L. B. (2000). The pursuit of speaking proficiency: A voluntary approach. *Communication Education, 49*, 339 – 351.

Katula, R. A., & Martin, C. A. (1984). Teaching critical thinking in the speech communication classroom. *Communication Education, 33*, 160 – 167.

Mazer, J. P., Hunt, S. K., & Kuznekoff, J. H. (2007). Revising general education: Assessing a critical thinking instructional model in the basic communication course. *The
Journal of General Education, 56*, 173 – 199.

Meyers, C. (1987). *Teaching students to think critically.* San Francisco: Jossey-Bass Publishers.

Morello, J. T. (2000). Comparing speaking across the curriculum and writing across the
curriculum programs. *Communication Education, 49*, 99 – 113.

Morreale, S. P., & Pearson, J. C. (2008). Why communication education is important:
The centrality of the discipline in the 21st century. *Communication Education, 57*,
224 – 240.

Palmerton, P. R. (1992). Teaching skills or teaching thinking? *Journal of Applied Communication Research, 20*, 335 – 341.

Paul, R., & Elder, L. (2009). *Critical thinking: Concepts and tools.* Tomales, CA: Foundation for Critical Thinking.

Chapter 3

Communication Centers and Liberal Arts Education: Problems and Possibilities Associated with Cross-disciplinary Engagements

Corey J. Liberman

Nearly sixty-five years ago, Wynn (1947) discussed a newly created communication center at the University of North Carolina which facilitated educational opportunities for those interested in the areas of radio, recording, motion pictures, still photography, and graphic art. Among the major goals of the center, according to Wynn, was "to provide training in the effective use of the tools of communication for educational and professional purposes" (p. 366). What is perhaps most interesting about the communication center at North Carolina, however, is that it focused on educating motivated parties not about communication per se, but rather about the media that helped communication become available to the masses. In essence, it was as though the center provided advice and tutoring about media outlets, rather than the communication processes (i.e., message construction) that require the interactive technologies about which Wynn was speaking.

Was the communication center at the University of North Carolina successful? Did it effectively achieve its major aims? Based on Hay's (1990) claim that assessment of such centers is likely to be plagued by logistical and data-driven issues, as well as the fact that the center at the University of North Carolina did not have publishable testimony regarding its effectiveness, the answer to the foregoing question is rife with ambiguity. To some, the mere fact that the center is no longer in existence might force one to question the success of the communication center. To others, however, the fact that there now exists more than 70 communication centers at institutions across the country (as per recent data from the National Association of Communication Centers) provides evidence that the center at North Carolina helped to create the initial impetus for increased attention paid to communication and the social processes that accompany it. As one grounded in the idea that a solid foundation is required before a village is created, I would favor the latter: that the communication center at the University of North Carolina primed scholars, educators, and practitioners to think about the importance of communication and to discover how to increase human communication competencies.

The purpose of this chapter is to explain the role of the communication center in an environment that has not yet gained much attention: the liberal arts institution. This is not to say that communication centers do not exist at liberal arts campuses, because such centers are currently thriving at such institutions as the University of Mary Washington, Agnes Scott College, Davidson College, Eckerd College, DePauw University, Coe College, Luther College, Curry College, Concordia College, Drury University, Hamilton College, Allegheny College, Carlow University, College of Charleston, Randolph Macon College, University of Richmond, Hampden-Sydney College, and Ripon College, just to name a few. This is to say, however, that currently not much literature exists on the success and effectiveness of communication centers at liberal arts institutions. Based on the very notion of what it means to be a liberal arts institution, it would seem, at least on the surface level, that a communication center on a liberal arts campus would not only be a welcome addition, but would also complement the mission statement on which most liberal arts colleges and universities rest. However, one must not overlook, nor underemphasize, the potential issues that evolve as talks about the creation of a communication center on a liberal arts campus ensue. As such, this chapter will discuss both the possibilities and potential problems of creating a communication center in a liberal arts environment. In so doing, a basic overview of communication centers is provided first. This is followed by the overarching rationale for creating a communication center on liberal arts campuses. Next is a section that highlights some of the potential problems and possibilities that accompany the creation of communication centers on the liberal arts campus. Finally, the chapter concludes with a section recommending ways to frame the importance of such communication centers on a liberal arts campus.

Communication Centers and Higher Education

When did the study of communication begin? This is a question that has always plagued both instructors and students of communication. Rogers (1994), taking a post-rhetorical, post-Aristotelian perspective, contends that the formal study of communication began in the mid-twentieth century, when Wilbur Schramm, whom many consider to be the father of human communication, began to study the use of communication for purposes of informing the mass public about national news. Where, when, and by whom the formal study of communication began is much more ambiguous in Peters' (1999) text, though he does claim at the start of his exposition that "my aim is not to explore the full variety of communication problems as reflected in the thought and culture of the twentieth century, but rather to tell the story of how communication became such trouble for us" (p. 3). Although the ways in which Rogers (1994) and Peters (1999) frame both the history of, and rationale for, the field of communication as an academic area of inquiry differ, one thing is certain: both scholars argue that communication is integral for every social experience one encounters, as well as potentially problematic for both the creators and recipients of messages. Based on even a cursory review of the communication literature, this is the case for the study of relational satisfaction (see, for example, Bochner, 1978), superior-subordinate communication in the organizational setting (see, for example, Redding, 1979), small group decision-making (see, for example, Gouran and Hirokawa, 1984), and persuasion in the area of health (see, for example, Ratzan, Payne, & Bishop, 1996). Each of these authors, similarly to Rogers (1994) and Peters (1999), framed communication as both problematic and remediable. There is no better way to espouse the importance of communication than by reading Bochner's contention that "it is one thing to claim that not very much has been achieved or that aspirations should be limited . . . it is quite another to chart a better map, to find a path out of the thick forest of despair" (p. 180). The communication center is emblematic of the path about which Bochner was speaking.

According to Hobgood et al. (2001), among the overarching purposes of any communication center are "tutoring for students' preparing oral presentations or for participation in group activities, interviews, discussions, or debates" (p. 3). The fact that oral communication is considered the skill most sought by employers, coupled with the fact that most employers find oral communication to be the skill most lacking by college graduates, forces faculty and staff members to question where there exists a curricular disconnect (see, for example, Morreale & Pearson, 2008). According to existing scholarship, there seem to be two overarching loopholes that help elucidate the poor oral communication skills demonstrated by college graduates or, as Schneider (1999) claims, the mass creation of "the age of the inarticulate" (p. A16). As Hobgood (2000) points out, one reason that college students might lack necessary oral communication skills is the mere fact that courses in oral communication are (even for students matriculated in the communication major at some institutions) considered electives. In fact, although most colleges have oral communication proficiency in their mission statements (at least loosely speaking), many institutions leave it to faculty members to incorporate these variables into their pedagogical approaches. One student enrolled at a small Northeastern liberal arts college (personal communication, March 9, 2011) was quite perturbed by this:

> I must say that most faculty members do require oral presentations dealing with class material. The problem, however, is that we are not taught how to give a public presentation, aside from how to dress and how much time we have to make our presentation. In the end, most professors say that we will not even be graded on our public presentation style, but rather on the information that we present. In the end, what is the purpose of giving a presentation if we are only going to be graded on the information? Why, then, won't a paper be suitable? More importantly, why would we spend our valuable time preparing such a presentation if we are not going to learn, nor will we be graded on, presentation techniques?

A second reason that students might lack necessary oral communication skills is that, for the most part, those who either teach courses dealing strictly with oral communication, or those who embed oral communication instruction into their courses (e.g. required public presentations), focus primarily on elocution. That is, rather than focusing on the prerequisites for effective oral communication, such as gathering data and conducting audience analyses, most instructors focus merely on the delivery of the presentation itself. In doing so, many neglect considering speech-making as a process, but rather focus solely on the presentation as an end in itself. Preston (2006) makes this claim when she asks whether and to what extent "[we] have overemphasized message construction and message delivery rather than focusing on all aspects of the communication process" (p. 58).

In the end, perhaps college graduates are not well-versed in oral communication because such courses are not mandated and, for those courses that do have oral communication requirements, students are only learning how to *give* a public presentation and not *how to* orally communicate. Morreale and Hackman (1994) support this claim when they argue that "developing students' oral competency goes beyond merely improving public speaking performance and oral skills" (p. 250). They continue by claiming that "a course in public speaking, grounded in speech and thought development, and a comprehensive model of oral competency, can improve a students' ability to think in an organized and logical manner" (Morreale & Hackman, 1994, p. 250). According to these scholars, the great majority of students are learning how to deliver a public speech (the behavioral domain), but are lacking knowledge in the cognitive (knowing), affective (feeling), and ethical (valuing) domains. In a similar vein, Wilde, Cuny, and Vizzier (2006) claim that most students who learn about oral communication are learning about how to perform a public speech, rather than such variables as empathetic listening, attentiveness, encouragement, and reflection. One would, therefore, be in a position to claim that, at best, oral communication courses are teaching performative, behavioral techniques, and, at worst, are requiring students to give public presentations without much guidance or feedback. Neither of these seems particularly fruitful.

Among the original rationales for the creation of communication centers was to teach students the rhetorical strategies needed to understand the process(es) associated with oral communication. According to Morreale, Osborn, and Pearson (2000), "humans are born with the ability to vocalize, but not with the knowledge, attitudes, and skills that define communication competence" (p. 2). They continue their argument when they state that "the ability to communicate effectively and appropriately is learned and, therefore, must be taught" (p. 2).

Have communication centers been effective to this end? According to a study conducted by Cronin and Glenn (1991), the answer to this query is in the affirmative. Based on their data of a communication across the curriculum (CAC) program (which, comparatively speaking, is similar to the mission of a communication center), Cronin and Glenn found that students enrolled in the CAC program at Central College, incidentally where the communication across the curriculum program began in 1976, reported both an increase in their oral communication skills and an increased desire for more oral communication training. In addition, Cronin and Glenn found a significant, positive correlation between participation in the CAC program and a subsequent increase in students' performance in their non-communication courses. Of paramount importance is Cronin and Glenn's contention that "oral communication across the curriculum programs help students . . . become more aware of the value and academic credibility of the speech communication discipline as they undergo direct training" (p. 365). That is, not only do such programs help students develop their oral communication skills, and the prerequisites that help create oral effectiveness, but students also begin to perceive communication departments more positively, forcing them to forego the stereotypical notion that communication and talking are synonymous with one another and motivating them to take more communication courses.

Communication Centers at Liberal Arts Institutions

The necessary prerequisite for a liberal arts education, proposed approximately 1,600 years ago, is a curriculum that values rational, critical thinking in the areas of rhetoric, grammar, logic, music, astrology, arithmetic, and geometry. Fleury (2005) provides a much more detailed definition when he explains that:

> The liberal artist cultivates a capacity, indeed a desire, to resist her or his comfort zone—the realm of specialization—and to travel many paths, to see the self, others, and the world from multiple perspectives. These paths lead to a certain model of citizenship, one committed to diversity, multiplicity, and participation. The end of liberal education is to produce good citizens. To the extent that we see citizenship as engaging diversity, multiplicity, and active participation, then it is necessarily bound with communication, for it is through

symbolic encounters that we perceive the world, establish value systems, construct relations, manage conflict, distribute resources, and more. (p. 74)

Although definitional variations for a liberal arts education are prevalent, all liberal arts institutions have one common goal: to educate students comprehensively, so that they become well-informed and intellectually capable inhabitants of a global environment. This is not to say that students enrolled at a liberal arts institution do not declare a major focus of study, because they do. However, students are also required to take a multitude of courses from several of the liberal arts disciplines, including the social sciences, the hard sciences, the humanities, fine arts, and performing arts. What becomes somewhat paradoxical, however, is the fact that one could escape an oral communication course and still graduate with a liberal arts degree. If, as Morreale et al. (2000) claim, "competence in oral communication—in speaking and listening—is prerequisite to students' academic, personal, and professional success in life" (p. 1), what is a liberal arts institution to do?

On the surface level, there seem to be two potential options for overcoming this issue. First, liberal arts institutions could mandate that students take a course in oral communication. However, mandating a course of this nature seems to contradict the very notion of a liberal arts education—one that values flexibility in the accruement of a general knowledge base. However, since rhetoric is embedded in the overarching mission of any liberal arts institution (in one form or another), and since most instructors require student presentations, perhaps requiring a "stand alone" course in oral communication becomes seemingly less important. A second option, however, is the creation of a communication center—something that is not required of, but rather afforded to, students. Although not speaking directly about liberal arts institutions, nor about communication centers in general (her focus was on the closely related area of communication across the curriculum programs), Friedland (2004) presents three goals of coaching students in oral communication: "improv[ing] communication and presentation skills, gain[ing] experience, techniques, and comfort in receiving criticism and feedback, [and] help[ing] students learn to recognize the biases and judgments they make based on peoples' presentation and communication styles" (p. 302). It seems as though Friedland's goals of a communication coaching center are quite in line with Zekeri's (2004) claim that "communication and interpersonal relationship skills, problem solving, and critical thinking are essential in the workforce as we begin the 21st century" (p. 419). A communication center, therefore, because of the importance that it places on such things as interpersonal and group communication (Wilde, Cuny, & Vizzier, 2006), listening (Preston, 2006), and oral communication skills (Yook, 2006), is extremely suitable for a liberal arts institution and the type of education that it fosters.

What, then, is the overarching rationale for creating a communication center on a liberal arts campus? Whether a student decides to focus his/her studies in philosophy, history, religious studies, biology, mathematics, English, political science, business administration, sociology, psychology, or the like, he/she will be afforded, as Fleury (2005) cogently contends, knowledge in the areas of exposition, persuasion, and expression. In so doing, Fleury takes what he calls a "Communication Against the Disciplines" perspective, insofar as he believes that these three areas should not be discipline-specific: students, regardless of their declared major, should learn (a) how to become interpretive and explanatory (exposition), (b) how to create rational, valid arguments (persuasion), and (c) how to become elocutionary (expression). This, in essence, is part of the mission of a liberal arts institution: that, regardless of one's major, all students should be provided with general knowledge and a yearning for intellectual growth and achievement. In fact, even the most cursory review of rhetorical theory will introduce the reader to the three necessary requisites of oral communication and persuasion: having a credible source (ethos), having a well-documented and well-framed argument (logos), and appealing to the audience's emotions (pathos). These requisites are necessary regardless of discipline. Although he writes about communication across the disciplines, rather than communication centers specifically, Fleury validates this idea quite well when he claims that "[such] programs are well positioned to facilitate such a liberal education—one that fosters and supports citizenship" (p. 78). He continues by claiming that "[such programs] provide the terrain for investigating the blends and clashes of many voices: citizen as arguer, citizen as storyteller, citizen as service learner, citizen as radical, citizen as bureaucrat, and more" (p. 78). Communication centers, because of their very nature, can do just this.

Potential Problems and Possibilities

There are always costs and rewards associated with any new endeavor; as the costs go up, so too do the potential rewards, and vice versa. As such, it seems suitable to first present the three potential problems associated with the creation of a communication center on a liberal arts campus. Although this list is neither exhaustive, nor necessarily mutually exclusive, it does present some of the issues that must be overcome in order for the fruits of a communication center to emerge. First, and perhaps most problematic, is the *"I am not a communication major so why should I have to learn about it"* argument. Although this might seem like a valid question to the student not well-versed in communication theory, this student would benefit from reading Morreale and Hackman's (1994) article, wherein they report that "research has consistently related oral competency and communication training and development to academic and professional success" (p. 250). That is, oral communication is important regardless of one's academic major and/or future career aspirations. One student enrolled at a small Northeastern liberal arts college (personal communication, March 9, 2011) illustrates this first potential problem quite well:

> In all honesty, when am I ever going to have to prepare a public presentation? I
> am not going out into the real world to lecture or to tell people how I feel. If
> people ask me questions, I will be able to answer them. To be quite honest, I
> know how to talk to people in a way that they understand me. Although I un-
> derstand why someone in the fields of marketing or business or sales would
> need to truly understand the theory behind public speaking, I really don't see
> myself needing this skill. I might be wrong, but this is just how I feel.

This testimony came from a third-year student, majoring in history, who wants
to become a librarian after graduation. In essence, this student is under the assumption that librarianship and communication competence are not correlated
with one another. Indeed, as Hobgood et al. (2001) indicate, communication
centers do provide coaching in the area of interpersonal communication, upon
which the dialogue between librarian and library patron is predicated. Although
librarians certainly use communication for multiple purposes (i.e., student orientations, instructional workshops, media presentations), much of the communication that occurs between librarian and library patron is based on confusion and
ambiguity: the patron needs help finding certain materials and the librarian is
trained to know how to help the patron in need. Any textbook, text chapter, or
journal article dealing with the area of interpersonal communication will dictate
that understanding one's role in a given relationship is a necessary prerequisite
for effective communication. Given the present example, the history student
would have to understand not only her role in this relationship (information pro-
vider), but also how to communicate in a way to foster comfort, satisfaction, and
reliability. By looking at just some of the most cited interpersonal communication theories in the field, understanding the relationship between self and other is
necessary for effective communication: in this case, the communication between
librarian and library patron.

Another interesting example surfaced when a student concentrating his studies in the area of mathematics (personal communication, March 9, 2011) questioned the importance and utility of communication theory when he said:

> On the one hand, it is funny that most of my friends laugh when I tell them that
> I am a math major, joking around that I will become a lab rat after graduation.
> On the other hand, however, they are correct. I want to be an actuary after I
> graduate. It is a lucrative career that, for better or worse, has little to no direct
> contact with the public. Why do I need to know how to be a perfect public pre-
> senter and oral communicator?

It is this very idea that has both worried and encouraged those in academia for
quite a long time: how can those students matriculating in majors not so closely
tied to communication on the surface level understand the importance of oral
communication for their future career trajectories?

In fact, there was a surge of research conducted to determine the extent to
which type of and how oral communication was important for students majoring
in the field of engineering (e.g. Dannels, 2002; Dannels, Anson, Bullard, & Pe-

retti, 2003; Darling & Dannels, 2003), much of which corroborates the research dealing with communication centers and communication across the curriculum programs. Regardless of major, oral communication skills are important for career success. According to Dannels (2002), "many of the . . . technical disciplines, with long and strong curricular traditions focusing on technical knowledges, have also begun to recognize and explore the role of oral performance in their curricula [and] engineering is one such technical discipline experiencing a strong shift toward oral communication instruction" (p. 256). Additionally, Garside (2002) claims that "disciplines differentiate themselves from each other based on areas of study and expertise . . . yet, there are instances where an interdisciplinary approach to education is advantageous to the entire higher education community" (p. 62). Darling (2005) perhaps frames it most appropriately when she asks "how do we teach communication skills within a community that appears to have such antipathy to central tenets regarding the role of rhetorical work in the creation of knowledge and identity?" (p. 29). In other words, and given the foregoing examples, how can history and mathematics majors understand the role of communication in their future employment industries? Although this is no easy task, the communication center provides one tool for teaching such communication competence (Morreale & Hackman, 1994).

A second potential barrier for the communication center on a liberal arts campus is the "*I am not a communication major so why should I have to learn the same kinds of material that they learn*" argument. Stated differently, students might argue that communication instruction should be discipline-specific. Although there have been both advocates for (e.g., Dannels, 2002) and proponents against (e.g., Fleury, 2005) a communication in the disciplines (CID) approach to teaching oral communication, this argument seems unnecessary in a liberal arts institution, for its general mission deals, at least somewhat, with the acquisition of a general knowledge base. If one glances at the early rhetorical work that has truly been the framework for the entire academic field of communication, many of the claims were, in fact, discipline-specific; they dealt primarily with the study of persuasion in the areas of politics, law, and government. This is not to say, however, that rhetorical strategies have not been used by those in other fields or careers such as marketing, public relations, linguistics, music, and acting. They, too, have used rhetorical strategies, but they have just used them differently. A fourth-year student majoring in theatre arts (personal communication, March 9, 2011) provides a prime example of this:

> I remember a time that I was required to play the role of Puck in Shakespeare's *A Midsummer Night's Dream*. I loved playing the part because it was just so me. But I realized that I would have to portray this character to the audience, making them realize that Puck was both mysterious and wise, a trickster and a gentleman. Oral communication does not become more important than in a moment like that. In fact, I remember many of the things that I learned in my public speaking class and was able to apply them to this situation. I remember

things like ethos, pathos, logos, and audience analysis, and I have truly used
these in my acting ever since.

In fact, sociologist Erving Goffman (1959), who was instrumental in framing the
study of interpersonal communication and who has been regarded as one of the
most influential communication scholars of all time, used the metaphor of theatre to illustrate how and why social beings communicate. Social beings, he argues, are actors who perform different roles with different audiences about different themes at different times in different environments. The student in the
aforementioned example knew the link between communication and theatre all
too well and was able to benefit from such understanding. According to Fleury
(2005), liberal education "is designed to [have] students question received wis-
dom, practice an array of communication styles, and play with established
communication conventions" (p. 73). This, in essence, is exactly what the theatre major was claiming—that to emerge in a theatrical role requires taking communication theory and applying it. All too often, however, students not matriculated in a communication department overlook and underemphasize the role of
communication in their everyday lives; they see communication and talking as
synonymous. A very similar example is that of a second-year art major, who
explained the relationship between aesthetics and communication (personal
communication, March 9, 2011):

> As an aspiring artist, I often ask myself a fundamental question: is what I see as
> beauty what others see as beauty? In fact, I wrote a paper about this topic just
> last semester. What is important is not that people think that my art is beautiful
> or that it tells the right story, but rather whether I can convince them, through
> my artistry, that beauty is present and that a story is being told. Communica-
> tion theory has a lot to do with this. Convincing others is not an easy thing to
> do, but, even through art, it is possible.

This example, too, illustrates the link between communication and a field not
represented much in the communication literature: visual communication (see,
for example, Price, 2011). If a liberal arts institution abides by the very mission
of a liberal arts education (to provide a comprehensive wealth of knowledge so
that graduates will be informed citizens), it is quite important for students to
understand how communication theory is embedded in everything that we, as
parents, friends, teachers, educators, historians, biologists, thespians, or politi-
cians, do. A communication center is a vehicle for such an endeavor.

A third potential barrier for the communication center on a liberal arts campus is the *"Communication is too skills-based and has no place in the liberal
arts curriculum."* In fact, there have been recent dialogues through the National
Communication Association's listserv about the role of public speaking courses
in both humanities and social science divisions at colleges and universities
across the country. As one might imagine, communication scholars vehemently
protest the notion that public speaking should be eliminated from general education requirements, arguing that the process of oration is much more complicated,

convoluted, and theory-based below the surface. For example, Docan-Morgan (2009) highlights the role of audience analysis in the creation and performance of a public speech, arguing that message framing is dependent on communication recipients. However, audience analysis is a much more in-depth process than one might prematurely assume. It requires knowledge of audience demographics, audience emotion, audience knowledge, audience interest, audience comfort, and audience expectations. In fact, this idea surfaced in a dialogue with a student minoring in business management and interested in cosmetic marketing (personal communication, March 9, 2011):

> If I am going to create an effective cosmetic pitch, I had better know who my potential consumers are and what these potential consumers want. I have to know what they want in a product, what products they currently use, how much they are willing to pay for a cosmetic product, and so forth. This type of market research is one of the first things that we learn in our basic marketing course: that in order to be successful, analyzing the potential consumer base is a must. In the end, this is truly the difference between success and failure.

Docan-Morgan's (2009) assessment of public speaking projects clearly underscores the importance of such audience analysis and frames communication as more than merely skills-based. Similarly, Ahlfeldt (2009) discusses the role of oral communication in civic engagement, arguing that persuasive and informative speeches must be properly tailored to all potential stakeholders and this process is much more than merely skills based. The process, in the end, according to both Docan-Morgan (2009) and Ahlfeldt (2009), requires more than mere presentation skills. It requires knowledge of the five canons of rhetoric forwarded by Aristotle (invention, arrangement, style, memory, and delivery). A student majoring in accounting made this point quite clear (personal communication, March 9, 2011):

> Although I know that I am never going to be asked to give a press conference, I am going to have to explain to my fellow coworkers what all of the numbers mean. However, I am going to need to realize that marketers and HR folks and sales people are not going to understand my accounting lingo. I am going to have to frame my messages in a way that everyone can understand: from the 20-hour-a-week intern to the Chief Executive Officer. This certainly requires knowledge of the oral communication process.

Although these three potential problems are proposed (I am not a communication major so why should I have to learn about it, I am not a communication major so why should I have to learn what they learn, and communication is too skills-based and has no place in the liberal arts curriculum), it is important to highlight the possibilities associated with a communication center at a liberal arts institution. First and foremost, having a communication center at a liberal arts institution will be yet another way of achieving its mission of (a) developing a students' broad, general knowledge base, (b) developing intellectual capabilities and curiosities, and (c) preparing students to be well-educated, well-informed citizens of a global society. By having students learn and discuss not only oral communication as a product (elocution), but also oral communication as a process (all of the antecedents necessary for orality), they will be afforded the opportunity to demonstrate how communication is truly the tie that binds knowledge, intellectual curiosity, and model citizenship.

Is it possible that this can be taught in a stand-alone course, even one that is framed from an oral communication perspective? Absolutely. However, published scholarship in this area seems to paint a different picture. As Garside (2002) contends, "unfortunately, many students have little or no opportunity for structured practice in communication skills instruction outside of oral communication courses" (p. 52). In a similar vein, Darling and Dannels (2003) found that "one of the most common places communication instruction occurs in engineering curricula is the senior capstone course" (p. 3). The problem with embedding oral communication instruction in other courses, such as a capstone course, is that teaching effective oral communication skills will likely be overshadowed by other, seemingly more important issues, topics, theories, and the like. In addition, it becomes very problematic to have a student's only exposure to oral communication instruction in one class and, given Darling and Dannels' (2003) example of the engineering field, a class that students take in their final year of matriculation. The communication center can help resolve these problems by providing students with exposure to oral communication instruction early in their collegiate careers, as well as throughout them, incorporating Schneider's (1999) hope of better educating the ephemeral inarticulate.

A second rationale for creating a communication center at a liberal arts institution is that it can help students who are enrolled at institutions that do not require an oral communication course. In this case, and although this is in conflict with the claim that a communication center should complement, rather than replace, a basic communication course, such a center could overcome the obvious (or perhaps not-so-obvious) undesirable alternative of having no support at all for oral communication. Students can learn, for example, how to create a public presentation, how to deliver a public presentation, how to interpersonally connect to peers, how to effectively interview, how to engage in empathetic listening, how to manage relational conflict, how to be an important member of a decision-making group, how to be verbally assertive, how to be verbally questioning, how to design appropriate messages, how to alleviate communication apprehension, and the list goes on. Trained professionals employed by the communication center will be able to assist students, regardless of major, in these areas.

When attempting to determine both the practical and theoretical issues associated with teaching engineering students communication skills, Darling and Dannels (2003) pose three salient questions that must be entertained: what oral communication genres and skills are important in the engineering workplace; what are perceived audiences and consequences of oral communication in the engineering workplace; and what is the relative importance of oral communication as it relates to writing in the engineering workplace (p. 4)? Although engineering is not a discipline represented in the liberal arts curriculum, all that one would have to do is substitute such words as history, political science, mathematics, and philosophy for engineering, and this becomes a discussion relevant for liberal arts institutions. On the surface level, these questions might seem to be more aligned with the communication in the discipline (CID) paradigm instead of communication across the discipline (CAD). However, at the deeper level, a communication center would be extremely appropriate for answering the queries posed by Darling and Dannels (2003).

A third rationale for the creation of a communication center at a liberal arts institution is to increase oral communication instruction opportunities for those institutions that do, in fact, have a required oral communication course. That is, it is likely that once a student has finished his/her oral communication course (likely public speaking), there are no or few, opportunities for advanced-level courses in areas such as rhetoric, persuasion, and/or debate. This issue was raised by a student matriculating in communication arts (personal communication, March 9, 2011):

> I learned a lot about communication by taking the public speaking course. In fact, I learned that I am a much better communicator than I thought I was. My only complaint is that it was sort of basic and I wish that there were other courses at the upper level that I could take in the future. For most, public speaking is the course that they either want to avoid or want to just get through. For me, and probably some others, an additional course in public speaking would be beneficial.

The communication center and its staff can help fill this void, especially for students who either need additional oral communication instruction or those who wish to hone their skills. One of the routine questions that communication centers face, according to Hobgood et al. (2001), is "how does a center or lab avoid being seen as providing merely remedial services" (p. 8)? One of the answers to this query is that the center positions itself not only as a resource for students interested in *learning* oral communication skills, but also a resource for students interested in becoming *better* oral communicators. As such, a communication center at a liberal arts institution can provide the forum for such advanced interest in, and experience with, oral communication.

A fourth rationale for creation of a communication center at a liberal arts institution is to help students see how and, more importantly, why communication is not discipline-specific, but rather cross-disciplinary. Cronin and Glenn (1991) and Friedland (2004) advocate for communication across the curriculum (CAC), which frames oral communication as something that should be embedded in, and part and parcel of, the educational process, regardless of one's major. Perhaps, as Dannels (2002) warns, it is much easier for students majoring in areas such as marketing, political science, and management to see the link between communication and career success as compared to students majoring in areas such as biology, mathematics, and philosophy. That is, communication becomes a more obvious prerequisite for career success in the fields of marketing, political science, and management. However, this is not to say that the link is not there in fields such as biology, mathematics, and philosophy. It is there. Students just need to learn how communication functions in their respective majors, a task that would be quite apt for a communication center and its staff.

A final rationale for the creation of a communication center at a liberal arts institution is to prepare students for the future. Whether one graduates with a degree in accounting, history, chemistry, or sociology, one thing is certain: communication is of paramount importance. Scholars writing about the need to incorporate more oral communication instruction into educational curricula are not being critical. Rather, they are being constructive. They are merely acknowledging a gaping hole in the educational process and are calling for increased attention to the incorporation of oral communication into pedagogical practices. If, as Morreale and Pearson (2008) point out, communication instruction provides the opportunity for one to "[become] a responsible participant in the world, socially and culturally . . . [and to] succeed as an individual in one's career and in business" (p. 228), it becomes important to increase the attention paid to oral communication in the educational spectrum. The communication center is a great resource to begin this journey.

Conclusion

At a recent meeting of the New York State Communication Association, several scholars, educators, and practitioners participated in a panel discussion entitled *More than an instrument: Communication as a liberal art*. The panelists both answered and raised several questions about the link between communication and a liberal arts education, such as how does communication fit within contemporary liberal arts education? How might the field of communication be expanded by considering it in relation to other liberal arts? What are some of the ways that the study of communication can enrich undergraduate curricula in the liberal arts? Although no solid answers surfaced, these queries did provide a very rich dialogue. In fact, one of the panelists ended the session with an intriguing question: rather than framing communication as *a* liberal art, could one frame communication as *the* liberal art? Although the answer to this question is well beyond the scope of this chapter, it does make one realize how important the study of communication is at the liberal arts institution. If, as the great majority of mission statements dictate, students enrolled at liberal arts institutions graduate with a deeper understanding of, and appreciation for, such things as social issues, political issues, ethical issues, moral issues, historical issues, cultural issues, and intellectual curiosity, then communication is necessarily built into the very fabric of a liberal arts institution. In the end, communication both produces, and is produced by, a liberal arts education. The creation of communication centers at liberal arts institutions is yet another way of both educating and showcasing the importance of communication instruction.

References

Ahlfeldt, S. L. (2009). Serving our communities with public speaking skills. *Communication Teacher, 23,* 158 – 161.

Bochner, A. (1978). On taking ourselves seriously: An analysis of some persistent problems and promising directions in interpersonal research. *Human Communication Research, 4,* 179 – 191.

Cronin, M., & Glenn, P. (1991). Oral communication across the curriculum in higher education: The state of the art. *Communication Education, 40,* 356 – 367.

Dannels, D. P. (2002). Communication across the curriculum and in the disciplines: Speaking in engineering. *Communication Education, 51,* 254 – 268.

Dannels, D. P., Anson, C. M., Bullard, L., & Peretti, S. (2003). Challenges in learning communication skills in chemical engineering. *Communication Education, 52,* 50 – 56.

Darling, A. L. (2005). Public presentations in mechanical engineering and the discourse of technology. *Communication Education, 54,* 20 – 33.

Darling, A. L., & Dannels, D. P. (2003). Practicing engineers talk about the importance of talk: A report on the role of oral communication in the workplace. *Communication Education, 52,* 1 – 16.

Docan-Morgan, T. (2009). I now see how I can use these skills: An applied project for the public speaking course. *Communication Teacher, 23,* 110 – 116.

Fleury, A. (2005). Liberal education and communication against the disciplines. *Communication Education, 54,* 72 – 79.

Friedland, E. (2004). Oral communication across the curriculum: What's a small college to do? Report of a collaborative pilot by theatre and education faculty. *The Journal of General Education, 53,* 288 – 310.

Garside, C. (2002). Seeing the forest through the trees: A challenge facing communication across the curriculum programs. *Communication Education, 51,* 51 – 64.

Goffman, E. (1959). *The presentation of self in everyday life.* New York, NY: Doubleday.

Gouran, D. S., & Hirokawa, R. Y. (1984). The role of communication in decision making groups: A functional perspective. In M. S. Mander (Ed.), *Communications in transition* (pp. 168 – 185). New York, NY: Praeger.

Hay, E. A. (1990). Nontraditional approaches to assessment. *Association for Communication Administration Bulletin, 72,* 73 – 75.

Hobgood, L. B. (2000). The pursuit of speaking proficiency: A voluntary approach. *Communication Education, 49,* 339 – 351.

Hobgood, L. B., Sandin, P., Von Till, B., Preston, M., Burk, T. L., Neher, W., & Wanca-Thibault, M. A. (2001). NCA 2001 summer conference: Engaging 21st century communication students. *Proceedings from the Communication Labs Strand,* 143.

Morreale, S. P., & Hackman, M. Z. (1994). A communication competency approach to public speaking instruction. *Journal of Instructional Psychology, 21,* 250 – 258.

Morreale, S. P., Osborn, M. M., & Pearson, J. C. (2000). Why communication is important: A rationale for the centrality of the study of communication. *Journal of the Association for Communication Administration, 29,* 1 – 25.

Morreale, S. P., & Pearson, J. C. (2008). Why communication education is important: The centrality of the discipline in the 21st century. *Communication Education, 57,* 224 – 240.

Peters, J. D. (1999). *Speaking into the air: A history of the idea of communication.* Chicago, IL: The University of Chicago Press.

Preston, M. M. (2006). Communication centers and scholarship possibilities. *International Journal of Listening, 20,* 56 – 61.

Price, C. J. (2011). Using visual theories to analyze advertising. *Visual Communication Quarterly, 18,* 18 – 30.

Ratzan, S. C., Payne, J. G., & Bishop, C. (1996). The status and scope of health communication. *Journal of Health Communication, 1,* 25 – 41.

Redding, C. W. (1979). Organizational communication theory and ideology: An overview. In D. Nimmo (Ed.), *Communication Yearbook 3* (pp. 309 – 341). New Brunswick, NJ: Transaction Books.

Rogers, E. M. (1994). *A history of communication study: A biographical approach.* New York, NY: The Free Press.

Schneider, A. (1999). Taking aim at student incoherence. *The Chronicle of Higher Education, 45,* A16 -- A18.

Wilde, S. M., Cuny, K. M., & Vizzier, A. L. (2006). Peer-to-peer tutoring: A model for utilizing empathetic listening to build client relationships in the communication center. *International Journal of Listening, 20,* 70 – 75.

Wynn, E. (1947). A communication center. *The Quarterly Journal of Speech, 33,* 366 – 369.

Yook, E. L. (2006). Assessment as meta-listening at the communication center. *International Journal of Listening,* 20, 66 – 68.

Zekeri, A. A. (2004). College curriculum competencies and skills former students found essential to their careers. *College Student Journal, 38,* 412 – 422.

Chapter 4

The Communication Center: A Critical Site of Intervention for Student Empowerment

Sandra L. Pensoneau-Conway and Nick J. Romerhausen

The concrete benefits that communication centers on campuses can provide for students are numerous. It is in this space that students can receive the necessary resources to advance in core communication courses, upper-level communication courses, and in communication-related assignments in other departments within the college or university. The communication center provides a site of assistance for students to improve their ability to effectively connect outcomes of speaking and listening to a particular task, thereby gaining tangible success in the form of graded assessments or praise from an instructor. Additionally, such centers can help students reduce public speaking anxiety and build confidence (Ellis, 1995).

Beyond the material successes however, the communication center that operates as an extension of the university classroom holds unique possibilities by both assisting students in the more traditional aspects of the learning process, while also circumventing many of the traditional barriers posed by the nature of the "classroom." In this chapter, we intend to explore how communication centers hold the unique possibility of enhancing student empowerment. By providing access to a site wherein students can better meet the educational outcomes of communication while avoiding conventional assessment, such a communication center can effectively avoid the traditional hindrances of power that are inherent to a conventional classroom setting.

The unique feature of a communication center's individualized instructional meetings also provides increased possibilities for the site's facilitators to focus upon specific improvement strategies that mediate the outcomes of communication curricula and the distinct needs of each student who asks for assistance. In the case of one center's experience, those individualized needs have emanated from students who are not native speakers of English and student athletes who wished to work on interviewing techniques (Hobgood, 2000). Our intention is not to argue that the communication center is necessarily better than traditional classroom interactions in assisting students in meeting educational outcomes, but rather to explore its inherent possibilities as a site of intervention that mediates between desired educational results and the institutionalized barriers of the classroom.

In this chapter, we do several things. First, we place communication centers alongside traditional classrooms in an effort to portray the learning contexts of each. We address the ways communication centers and traditional classrooms differ from one another in terms of the learning environment and outline what communication centers can do that traditional classrooms cannot. This leads to our explication of the theoretical framework of empowerment. Here, we expand on the concept of empowerment and situate it as a facet of engaged pedagogy. After, we outline four barriers to empowerment that traditional classrooms hold and address how communication centers respond to each barrier. Finally, we end by constructing the communication center as a potential source of student empowerment.

Communication Centers and the Traditional Classroom

In recent decades more discussion has emerged concerning the inherent institutionalized barriers which make classroom experiences for students more challenging than other educational forms (see, for example, Fassett & Warren, 2007; Hendrickson, Gable, & Manning, 1999; hooks, 1994a; Kohn, 2010; Mayo, 2009; Steele, 2003). Large class sizes, addressing students with multiple learning strategies, following a linear schedule that addresses different course content, mediating relational development between performing authority and laxity, and having an obligation to produce a material form of assessment are only some of the many inescapable factors that are architectonic to most undergraduate curricula in higher education. Although a faculty member may take multiple measures to make the educational experiences in the class setting most liberating, she or he is still faced with the historical, social, and structural obstacles that are unavoidably foundational to the higher education exchange. These influences are not necessarily unscrupulous, as each serves a purpose to familiarize students with the structural influences of the "real-world." Nonetheless, such practices can hinder a student's ability to reach her or his potential.

Because communication centers are designed to give students assistance in their educational endeavors in classrooms, these sites hold unique possibilities as they do not have the same structural limitations imposed upon traditional classrooms to help students achieve educational goals. The original intent of the communication center was to give students assistance in public speaking, but the intent has now evolved into having many more goals as higher education continually values assessment of student learning (McCracken, 2006). As universities continue to see an evolving purpose of the ways communication centers assist students, there are well-documented successes in these changing endeavors: interpersonal interaction between clients and consultants can build trust (Ward & Schwartzman, 2009); these interactions can help reduce public speaking anxiety (Ellis, 1995); and data from communication centers can be used to conduct assessments to benefit students, departments, and campuses (Helsel & Hogg, 2006; Preston, 2006). In the context of the relationship between the classroom and communication center however, we turn to Ellis, Shockley-Zalabak, and Hackman (2000) who state,

> The communication laboratory can provide a supportive environment where students can grow and develop in ways not possible in the regular classroom. They also provide a place where innovative learning strategies can be developed, implemented, and tested, and where assessment, accountability, and research opportunities flourish. The demonstrated strengths of communication laboratories make them an important pedagogical strategy for the 21st century. (p. 161)

To further understand how communication centers uniquely provide student development outside the traditional classroom, we turn to the possibilities that a lens of empowerment contributes to the importance of the communication center in colleges and universities. In order to understand empowerment within the context of the communication center, it might help to juxtapose the center's instructional strategies against conventional classroom instructional strategies. The portrait we paint here is not representative of all classrooms; indeed, as more and more educators embrace alternative pedagogies, they are realizing that space matters. However, we argue that our portrait is all too common. In traditional classrooms, students are generally one of many students in an institutionalized setting full of desks—which may or may not be mobile—facing the same direction towards the teacher, who is located at the "front"[1] of the room. This configuration ultimately symbolizes whose voice matters, as we merely need to examine where the space directs attention. And in a classroom of knowledge generation, the point at which attention is directed—the teacher—is the symbolic font of knowledge. Students in this physical space understand that they learn from the teacher, not from one another.

Behaviorally, similar constructions of important voices and knowledge sources are present when students come to understand that in order to speak, they must raise their hands. While one act of many in the classroom, this simple norm of hand-raising speaks volumes, and communicates that the teacher ultimately decides who has permission to engage her or his voice—whose voice matters. The teacher, however, never has to raise her or his hand—the teacher's voice *always* matters.

These are just two of the countless classroom traditions that put educational participants in their places; these performances of "student" and "teacher" are learned early on, and are rarely questioned. These are performances of power. Issues of power in the classroom have not gone unexamined. In the critical (communication) pedagogy literature, Shor's (1996) comprehensive account of power sharing in the classroom is perhaps the most detailed discussion of performances of power. Wood and Fassett (2003) highlight the contingency and fluidity of power in the classroom, drawing upon Foucault to demonstrate that power is never at once solely in the purview of the teacher *or* the student, but rather located in the relationship among educational participants. In instructional communication literature, scholars have examined constructs such as teacher and student perceptions of power (McCroskey & Richmond, 1983), behavior alteration techniques as enactments of power (Plax, Kearney, & Tucker, 1986), and the relationship among learner empowerment and teacher power (Schrodt, Witt, Myers, Turman, Barton, & Jernberg, 2008). However, communication centers, in a way, potentially deconstruct performances such as these and break with tradition in order to provide students with a uniquely empowering experience.

Empowerment as an Educational Construct

Empowerment as a construct can be found within educational research focusing on various areas. Most commonly, scholars who do research within what we call radical pedagogies discuss empowerment as a desired outcome of educational practices. Radical pedagogies are gaining attention, and at the risk of being reductive, the term functions for us as an umbrella for pedagogies such as, but not limited to, critical pedagogy, feminist pedagogy, and queer pedagogy. While radical pedagogies certainly have some distinguishing characteristics, we generally consider them to be "alternative" to traditional pedagogies, or what Freire (2000) terms the "banking system" of education. Banking education describes a system metaphorized by teachers as depositors of knowledge and students as depositories of knowledge. Students withdraw the knowledge when necessary (such as on a test day), and then move onto the next lesson. This passive process ignores important concepts such as voice, co-constructed knowledge, power, identity, oppression, history, etc. In contrast, radical pedagogies actively engage these concepts and understand the classroom to necessarily be a contested site of identity politics and reality. It is here where we situate our understanding of empowerment.

Defining empowerment is not an easy task, as it largely depends upon who is doing the defining and in what context. However, there are some characteristics of the term that tend to run across definers and contexts. McLaren (2003) explains that "empowerment means not only helping students understand and engage the world around them, but also enabling them to exercise the kind of courage needed to change the social order where necessary" (p. 85). So for McLaren, empowerment entails student engagement beyond the walls of the classroom and students having a sense of social agency. This seems like a large undertaking, as we don't generally associate communication centers with such seemingly ambiguous and lofty terms like *social order*. As we continue our discussion, however, the communication center will clearly be a site in which empowerment emerges, in a way similar to what McLaren describes.

While McLaren (2003) writes largely in the context of critical pedagogy, others situate empowerment within similar, yet different, pedagogical contexts, such as feminist pedagogy. Webb, Allen, and Walker (2002) identify empowerment as the primary goal of feminist pedagogy and name its function as that of constructing the classroom as a democratic space of shared power among the students and the teacher. Through the process of empowerment, the student-teacher relationship is redefined, and rather than a one-way process of knowledge exchange, educational participants become, in Freire's (2000) words, "teacher-students students-teacher" (p. 109). The relationship becomes mutually beneficial, with each learning from the other. Indeed, deMarrais and LeCompte (1995) explain that "lack of empowerment . . . is a consequence of unequal social relationships . . ." (p. 81). The redefinition of the teacher-student relationship, then, serves to *re*-construct the classroom as one which *does* valorize voice, co-constructed knowledge, shared power, identity, reducing and naming oppression, history, etc. In further defining empowerment, McLaren is worth citing at length:

> I am using the term *empowerment* to refer to the process through which students learn to critically appropriate knowledge existing outside their immediate experience in order to broaden their understanding of themselves, the world, and the possibilities for transforming the taken-for-granted assumptions about the way we live. Stanley Aronowitz has described one aspect of empowerment as "the process of appreciating and loving oneself." (p. 89)

The questions remain: do classrooms actually embody empowerment? Are classrooms such as these still few and far between? What can communication centers contribute to empowerment and education? In order to answer this latter question, we turn primarily to engaged pedagogy as articulated by bell hooks (1994) in her germinal essay, "Engaged Pedagogy."

Engaged Pedagogy and Student Empowerment

hooks (1994b) emphasizes that, in her own schooling history and still reflected in classrooms today, students and teachers alike are expected to conform to the banking system of education, "a rote, assembly-line approach to learning" (p. 13). The purpose of education, for hooks, should be liberatory, for students to be active participants in their own educational processes. This cannot happen if we fail to take into account that students and teachers both are "whole" people (p. 15). In other words, we aren't just ever student, and we aren't just ever teacher. We are always already multi-faceted. We are faced with competing interests and pressures and forces acting at once upon us and through us. Banking approaches to education assume a much more homogenous student and teacher identity, and therefore, limit the opportunities for students to seek out and participate in meaningful, purposeful educational experiences.

Empowerment is a fundamental part of the engaged pedagogical process, as well as a necessary outcome. "'Engaged pedagogy'. . . emphasizes well-being. That means that teachers must be actively committed to a process of self-actualization that promotes their own well-being if they are to teach in a manner that empowers students" (hooks, 1994b, p. 15). In further exploring engaged pedagogy, Rose (2005) identifies particular features such a pedagogy would demonstrate:

> students are subjects and an integral part of the learning process itself; validity claims are revealed through open discussion and connections to students' lived experiences rather than through the instructors' declarations; and questioning is encouraged, indeed required, as part of the classroom process (p. 343).

We can see, then, that in engaged pedagogy, students and teachers share a primary stake in the pedagogical and educational process. Their fluid and dynamic relationship with one another creates space where students actively participate in the critical—based on questions rather than answers—practice of learning, not by memorizing information, but by creating knowledge and reality together through engaging with one another and with the world around them. Such a pedagogy acknowledges and affirms students' and teachers' identities, experiences, and voices in an effort to create a community of learners that feels a sense of social agency and ownership of and responsibility for their own learning. This pedagogy naturally leads to student empowerment.

Barriers to Empowerment

Even if a classroom is embedded in a radical pedagogical approach—such as engaged pedagogy—certain barriers to student empowerment are ever-present. Specifically speaking to those courses most likely to be served by communication centers (though certainly likely present in *all* classrooms), those barriers include: (1) limits to the instructional and personal attention the teachers can give to each student; (2) requirements to assign a grade, even if only at the end of the semester; (3) requirements to "cover" certain elements of the course content (course standardization); and (4) institutional pressure felt by most instructors to *not* teach in a manner incongruent with the banking method. We will attend to each of these barriers briefly, before shifting our focus to how the communication center can both address each of these barriers, and at the same time, serve as a context for student empowerment.

First, many college classrooms, paralleling classrooms across the country, are overcrowded, particularly given the ever-increasing budget issues facing higher education. In our own university, the introductory public speaking course—a general education course presently serving nearly 2,300 students per academic year—will experience an increase in enrollment from 25 to 27 students per section beginning in the Fall 2012 academic year. This is a direct result of multi-billion dollar budget cuts to the university. The course includes four speeches. This means that approximately six out of 14 contact weeks in a semester are spent *only* on delivering and listening to speeches. This does not include instruction in the skills and theory of public speaking, introductory information about the course (i.e., first day "business"), etc. In such a situation, instructors likely find it challenging (though not impossible) to work within a philosophy and way of teaching that embraces social change, co-constructed reality and knowledge, critical approaches to public speaking, inclusion of all voices, attention to interests, experiences, and identities of students, and other factors that contribute to student empowerment.

Second, most institutions require students to receive a grade, even if that is only at the end of the semester. Both of the authors have experience in courses—at the graduate level—where the process involved heavy feedback but no grades throughout the semester. While this allowed students to fully focus on the process of the work in the course without worrying (in the traditional sense) about what grades were assigned to that work, they nonetheless were bound by a system where grades mattered at some point. But the reality is that grades do matter; while we may want students to focus on the process of learning, we've created a system where one is judged by the grades one has received, regardless of how much one has learned.

Third, instructors, particularly in undergraduate general education courses (or even introductory level courses), are in many ways obligated to include certain elements of a content area into their courses—they are standardized courses. While instructors may have some freedom in determining *how* they teach course content, the content itself is not optional. While radical pedagogies are arguably *not* about content—not simply "add-a-lecture," as Wear (2003) quips (p. 550)— elements of such pedagogy rely on understanding how to teach content in a way that questions that content and incorporates the theoretical foundation of such pedagogies. A primary critique of such pedagogies is their lack of practical direction; they are not methods that we can pin down, but that take experimentation and testing. Standardized curricula often don't include space and time for such experimentation. This is most often the case when introductory level courses feed into subsequent courses. For example, many courses across the university expect students to complete some sort of oral presentation. The logical expectation, then, is that the introductory level public speaking course will provide some kind of common knowledge base for students in how to research, construct, and deliver a public presentation. This becomes complicated when, for example, students learn invitational speaking rather than more traditional forms; their other courses, however, require more traditional forms of informative and persuasive speaking.

Finally, Browne (2005) identifies the challenges university-level instructors face when engaging in radical pedagogies. Institutional norms and constructs often create pressures on teachers to conform to standard, traditional—and disempowering—practices. Such pressures to adhere to traditional methods of teaching often detract instructors from engaging in any kind of radical pedagogy. This could be for fear of student resistance (though radical pedagogies often understand student resistance as student expression of frustration at a disempowering educational experience), fear of negative student evaluations (particularly at a time when student evaluations are given more and more weight in retention of part-time and non-tenure track faculty), institutional ramifications for not teaching within traditional methods, or simply fear of the unknown. How does the communication center respond to barriers to empowerment, and potentially act as a site of student empowerment? We turn our attention now to these important questions.

The Communication Center as a Site of Student Empowerment

Barriers to Empowerment

The first barrier we identified involves the lack of time instructors have to attend to the individual needs and identities of students in classrooms most likely to be served by communication centers. When students seek out assistance—or even if they are required to visit a center for assistance—they are likely to receive one-on-one attention for the duration of their appointment. Even if that appointment is only 30 minutes, it is highly unlikely that, except for under unique circumstances, instructors are able to spend 30 consecutive minutes of time with an individual student. While this, in itself, does not lead to empowerment, this individualized attention creates conditions in which students are able to focus on getting their needs met.

Using a communication center can also provide instructors with more opportunity to attend to individual student needs. Hunt and Simonds (2002) argue that communication centers can teach skills to students that would otherwise be taught in the classroom. This means that in-class instructors may have more opportunity to attend to students on a more individual level. Even if communication center staff is comprised of undergraduates, they are presumably staffing the center because they have an advanced command of the introductory level content taught in the courses the centers complement. Despite the potential differences in levels of instruction between an instructor and an advanced undergraduate student, classroom instructors should still be able to count on some commonality of instruction that takes place in the communication center, so that the instruction wouldn't need to be repeated (though perhaps would need expansion) during classroom time.

Additionally, the communication center's services might actually make a critical, engaged, empowering classroom *more* likely, in that if students receive one-on-one attention in the communication center, they may feel more confident to approach instructors either during class, after class, or during office hours. Self-confidence and empowerment enjoy a mutually constitutive relationship, and so if students can experience increased self-confidence as a result of their one-on-one attention in the communication center, they may feel more empowered to be active participants in the classroom.

The second barrier we identified regards the requirement that teachers assign grades to students. Generally, the only time a grade will be assigned to a student using a center would come from that student's teacher—not the center staff—if the teacher required her/his students to use a center. Otherwise, whatever a student does in the center is done in an environment devoid of the political, complicated, and traditional practice of grading. This allows students to focus on their learning process, creates a safer environment wherein students can take risks with their ideas and practices, and fosters continued relationships (between center staff and students) that aren't constricted by the dynamics of grading. It better equalizes the relationship between the person seeking help, and the person helping (particularly if the person helping—the communication center staffperson—is an undergraduate). Again, this in itself does not guarantee a context of empowerment, but recall that deMarrais and LeCompte (1995) acknowledge that a context of unequal relationships is a context lacking empowerment.

The third barrier we identified was the challenges of a standardized course, and the necessity of "covering" (as opposed to creating) certain aspects of the course content, leaving little time for examining that content within the dynamics of social relationships, voice, identity, etc. Ellis et al. (2000) explain that such courses (i.e., standardized courses) are the most likely to be served by communication centers. In a standardized curriculum, students have little-to-no opportunity to foreground their own interests, questions, ideas, etc. within the curriculum, and in particular, in constructing the curriculum. Even though communication centers exist to assist students in particular content areas (e.g., students aren't likely to go to a communication center for help with organic chemistry), the pedagogical moment is student-driven in that the students' needs are foregrounded, rather than the needs of the material that must be "covered." Similarly, communication centers are necessarily student-centered in that center facilitators work to develop the most effective methods to assist *individual* students, rather than a large group or a majority of students.

There is not much room for standardization when it comes down to the actual assistive practices of a communication center because students have varying reasons for voluntarily coming to a center to gain assistance for a particular purpose. Each meeting is directed by an individual's needs and consultants work to respond accordingly. Some students may come to the communication center to practice a presentation for a course, refine interviewing skills for a future job search, discuss how to overcome some form of communication apprehension, or for other reasons that may or may not have direct relevance to the curriculum of a particular course. The center's staff members, who act as peers, respond to these needs accordingly and begin to work with students to assist them in achieving their own desired goals and outcomes.

This is true even when the center staff assist small groups of students rather than individual students. In these situations, the individualized attention still tends to be more frequent than in classrooms where one teacher may have upwards of five or six small groups of students to assist—the scenario remains that one teacher assists all of the students in a classroom to meet the outcomes of a course. In a communication center, a small group of individuals meets a consultant to also ask for assistance that will directly benefit each of them. The center's staff again responds to what students need by working with group members to achieve a desired goal. Whether in the case of individual or group consultations, communication centers appreciate student voice because the education is not directed by the educator. Any barriers posed by standardized curricula of traditional classrooms are not present in the communication center because facilitators respond to the questions posed by students rather than the questions posed by a test or course. Because communication centers involve educators responding to students, the social dynamics of meetings and consultations are directed by the learner who takes control of his or her education by asking for assistance rather than direction.

Finally, barrier four sought to name the institutional pressures faculty often feel to avoid teaching methods and methodologies that would undergird radical pedagogies and student empowerment. Understanding the dynamics of these pressures, we find that the communication center provides a space where both the center's facilitators and the students who use the center can have these sorts of "alternative" pedagogical experiences and not be bound by the institutional power dynamics. In Ward and Schwartzman's (2009) study, facilitators often used a storytelling approach, relating to the students through the use of stories in order to build common ground and shared experience. This sort of vulnerability on the part of the facilitators is akin to hooks' (1994b) call for teacher vulnerability as fundamental to engaged pedagogy. Additionally, Hobgood's (2000) portrait of one communication center highlighted the voluntary nature of faculty focusing on communication in non-communication courses. Such faculty would also likely promote the use of the communication center in such courses. This demonstrates a willingness on the part of faculty to embrace new ways of teaching and learning. With this embrace comes an acknowledgment that nontraditional ways of teaching and learning can have merit, and perhaps shouldn't be so quickly dismissed.

Communication Centers as Sources of Empowerment

Even beyond these four barriers, communication centers on their own can be an effective source of student empowerment. Hunt and Simonds (2002) highlight the ways in which communication centers can greatly reduce communication apprehension. This is of utmost importance for encouraging student voice. If, as Gawelek, Mulqueen, and Tarule (1994) argue, "Voice is the 'currency' of the academy," (p. 181) then we cannot take lightly the fact that some—indeed, many—students have communication apprehension. If students are afraid to speak—to use their physical voice—then it will be extremely challenging for them to critically engage the world around them—to use their philosophical and theoretical voice. Empowerment is inherently tied to issues of voice, and communication centers are uniquely positioned to directly impact students' conceptions and use of voice. Whereas Freire's (2000) concept of banking argues traditional classrooms may use a system where "the teacher teaches and the students are taught" (p.73), in the communication center the student asks for assistance and the staff assist. For example, the only paper a student will likely fill out which even resembles a test is a survey concerning how to make future consultations more helpful. While students may circle letters and write short statements on this sheet, the paper they will fill out has no wrong answers. Their choices, however, will be used to make their education more valuable and empowering for future students who will attend the center.

   In addition to voice, communication center facilitators must attend to the whole person. Ward and Schwartzman (2009) identify emotional intelligence as one theme that characterizes the communicative relationship between communication center facilitators and students (or in their words, "consultants" and "clients"). In their study, students felt as though the facilitators exhibited emotional intelligence, working to understand the feelings of the students. The students drew upon this emotional intelligence, and as a result, a relationship of trust began to emerge between the two. Traditional classrooms are interested in students feelings generally in the context of the three dimensions of learning (knowledge—cognitive; skills—behavioral; and emotion—affective). However, because it is difficult to measure the affective dimension of learning, the first two dimensions are given much more attention. (Take, for example, the process of creating learning objectives. The literature has a much better grasp of cognitive and behavioral learning objectives because they are more easily measured. In an age where learning must be measured for purposes of funding and so forth, the affective dimension often gets left unattended.) The classroom, therefore, still has a long way to go in terms of valorizing students' and teachers' feelings as a component of the teaching and learning process, yet this very component is important for a successful communication center (as demonstrated by successful facilitator-student relationships). Because communication centers don't have to attend to learning objectives and outcomes in the same way classrooms do, there is more room for attention to the affective domain of learning. In a similar way, the facilitators' use of empathy at this communication center helped students gain confidence in their communicative abilities.

Finally, in their study, Hunt and Simonds (2002) applaud the communication center for the ability to provide students with immediate feedback. When students are presented with immediate feedback, the potential for a dialogic encounter between the student and the one providing the feedback is more likely to occur. Students can come to understand the feedback in a much more substantial way when it can be part of a meaningful exchange, rather than just written or typed comments that are fleetingly given and fleetingly forgotten. Engaged pedagogy—and empowerment—relies upon dialogue as an epistemological practice (Freire, 2000). At the very surface level, when facilitators and students engage in feedback as dialogue, two important things happen: (1) the facilitators learn about their communication (in the sense that they learn how effective they are at providing feedback) and (2) students learn more about their performance within the particular skill set that brought them to the communication center in the first place.

Conclusion

Our analysis of understanding the communication center and its possibilities of providing certain aspects of student empowerment which traditional (and non-traditional) classrooms cannot is faced with several limitations. First, not every communication center functions in the same way. Some communication centers may serve a wide variety of purposes for all communication needs across a university while others may primarily work to serve the interests of students who are enrolled in departmental courses, such as the introductory course. Additionally, the configuration of the communication center may inform the potential the center has for fostering student empowerment. Second, in the case where a center sees many students but has few staff, students might have to stand in line for a significant time to meet with a consultant, or be asked to make an appointment which meets the needs of the center's staff. This is in addition to other administrative barriers, such as limited funding and material resources for the center. Third, our discussion is limited to describing the ideal center which is well-funded, open often, adequately staffed, institutionally valued, and available to all students on campus. However, as communication centers must serve a unique purpose for each department and campus to legitimize their presence, we know that few—if any—centers embody this ideal portrait. Fourth, we argue that the communication center can extend classroom learning, and provide a different type of learning than what students can encounter in a traditional classroom. While we believe that this different type of learning is not necessarily a limitation, we do understand that each learning context comes with its own disadvantages. Outlining each of them is not within the scope of our project, but we do acknowledge that the communication center should not (and, indeed, cannot) replicate or substitute for the positive learning experiences students can find in the classroom. Finally, we recognize that the empowerment that communication centers can provide is not necessarily inherent, but rather is "possible."

There are certain barriers in traditional classrooms for which radical pedagogies provide solutions. Different activities can be implemented to make learning more active, students can help write classroom policies to increase their personal investment in the structure of a course, and teachers can work to build relationships with individual students to make them feel that the educator has an interest in their individual needs. However, the pedagogies cannot be fully applied in the lecture halls which hold large numbers of students, in classrooms where the desks are bolted into the ground, and in the faculty member's office where students want to discuss how to earn a certain grade at the end of a semester. These structural and institutionalized barriers are realistic barriers to learning and are certainly not changing significantly anytime in the near future. However, because the communication center functions in an environment where these structural barriers are absent (or at least less present), there are multiple possibilities for students to control the destiny of their educational journeys. While there are numerous concrete outcomes provided by communication centers (which we earlier articulated) through understanding these places as sites of empowerment, we know that one more major contribution of the communication center is that it is inherently student-centered.

While increasing numbers of research studies address the technicalities of forming, managing, facilitating, and assessing communication centers, research has failed to address how communication centers complement the limitations of the traditional classroom and fit within radical pedagogies. In this chapter, we identified the potential for communication centers to serve as sites of student empowerment. Situated within the context of radical pedagogies—and particularly, engaged pedagogy (hooks, 1994)—the communication center both responds to barriers to empowerment in traditional classrooms and utilizes pedagogical methods that promote student empowerment. We argue that while none of these elements individually necessarily results in student empowerment, they create, when taken together in some theoretically informed combination, the conditions for the possibility of student empowerment in a way more likely to be actualized than in a traditional classroom.

Notes

1. We set this off with quotation marks to highlight the phenomenon of the physical location of the teacher in the classroom as serving as the existential center of power and attention. The common vision is of the teacher and a large desk being in front of a chalkboard and the students facing that direction. This is the traditional "front" of the classroom. However, when the teacher physically moves to another location in the room, the existential center also tends to move, as students tend to direct their attention to wherever the teacher is, regardless of whether or not that is the traditional "front."

References

Browne, K. (2005). Placing the personal in pedagogy: Engaged pedagogy in "feminist" geographical teaching. *Journal of Geography in Higher Education, 29*(3), 339–354.

DeMarrais, K. B., & LeCompte, M. D. (1995). *The way schools work: A sociological analysis of education* (2nd ed.). White Plains, NY: Longman.

Ellis, K. (1995). Apprehension, self-perceived competency, and teacher immediacy in the laboratory-supported public speaking course: Trends and relationships. *Communication Education, 44*, 64-78.

Ellis, K., Shockley-Zalabak, P., & Hackman, M. Z. (2000). Communication laboratories: Genesis, assessment, challenges. *Journal of the Association for Communication Administration, 29*(1), 155-162.

Fassett, D. L., & Warren, J. T. (2007). *Critical communication pedagogy.* Thousand Oaks, CA: Sage.

Freire, P. (2000). *Pedagogy of the oppressed* (30th anniversary ed.). New York, NY: Continuum.

Gawelek, M. A, Mulqueen, M., & Tarule, J. M. (1994). Woman to women: Understanding the needs of our female students. In S. M. Deats & L. T. Lenker (Eds.), *Gender and academe: Feminist pedagogy and politics* (pp. 179-198). Lanham, MD: Rowman & Littlefield.

Helsel, C. R., & Hogg, M. C. (2006). Assessing communication proficiency in higher education: Speaking labs offer possibilities. *International Journal of Listening, 20*, 29-54.

Hendrickson, J. M., Gable, R. A., & Manning, M. L. (1999). Can everyone make the grade? Some thoughts on student grading and contemporary classrooms. *The High School Journal, 82*(4), 248-254.

Hobgood, L. B. (2000). Toward speaking proficiency: A voluntary approach. *Communication Education, 49*, 339-351.

hooks, b. (1994a). Confronting class in the classroom. In *Teaching to transgress: Education as the practice of freedom* (pp. 177-190). New York, NY: Routledge.

hooks, b. (1994b). Engaged pedagogy. In *Teaching to transgress: Education as the practice of freedom* (pp. 13-22). New York, NY: Routledge.

Hunt, S. K., & Simonds, C. J. (2002). Extending learning opportunities in the basic communication course: Exploring the pedagogical benefits of speech laboratories. *Basic Communication Course Annual, 14*, 60-86.

Kohn, A. (2010). Grading: The issue is not how but why? In A. S. Canestrari & B. A. Marlowe (Eds.), *Education foundations: An anthology of critical readings* (2nd ed., pp. 174-182). Los Angeles, CA: Sage.

Mayo, C. (2009). The tolerance that dare not speak its name. In A. Darder, M. P. Baltodano, & R. D. Torres (Eds.), *The critical pedagogy reader* (2nd ed., pp. 262-273). New York, NY: Routledge.

McCracken, S. R. (2006). Listening and new approaches to the creation of communication centers. *International Journal of Listening, 20*, 60-61.

McCroskey, J. C., & Richmond, V. P. (1983). Power in the classroom I: Teacher and student perceptions. *Communication Education, 34*, 214-226.

McLaren, P. (2003). Critical pedagogy: A look at the major concepts. In A. Darder, M. Baltodano, & R. D. Torres (Eds.), *The critical pedagogy reader* (1st ed., pp. 69-96). New York, NY: Routledge Falmer.

Plax, T. G., Kearney, P., & Tucker, L. K. (1986). Prospective teachers' use of behavior alteration techniques on common student misbehaviors. *Communication Education, 35*, 32-42.

Preston, M. M. (2006). Communication centers and scholarship possibilities. *International Journal of Listening, 20*, 56-59.

Rose, N. E. (2005). Engaged pedagogy and political economy. *Review of Radical Political Economics, 37*(3), 341–345.

Schrodt, P., Witt, P. L., Myers, S. A., Turman, P. D., Barton, M. H., & Jernberg, K. A. (2008). Learner empowerment and teacher evaluations as a function of teacher power er use in the college classroom. *Communication Education, 57*, 180-200.

Shor, I. (1996). *When students have power: Negotiating authority in a critical pedagogy*. Chicago, IL: University of Chicago Press.

Steele, C. (2003). Stereotype threat and African-American student achievement. In T. Perry, C. Steele, & A. Hilliard III (Eds.), *Young, gifted, and black: Promoting high achievement among African-American students* (pp. 109-131). Boston, MA: Beacon Press.

Ward, K., & Schwartzman, R. (2009). Building interpersonal relationships as a key to effective speaking center consultations. *Journal of Instructional Psychology, 36*(4), 363-372.

Wear, D. (2003). Insurgent multiculturalism: Rethinking how and why we teach culture in medical education. *Academic Medicine, 78*(6), 549-554.

Webb, L., Allen, M., & Walker, K. (2002). Feminist pedagogy: Identifying basic principles. *Academic Exchange Quarterly, 6*(1), 67–72.

Wood, A. F., & Fassett, D. L. (2003). Remote control: Identity, power, and technology in the communication classroom. *Communication Education, 52*, 286-296.

Chapter 5

The Role Becomes Them: Examining Communication Center Alumni Experiences

Susan Wilson

Peer tutoring programs began to thrive at colleges and universities nationwide in the late 1980s and in turn, those initiatives spawned research on the effects of peer tutoring. For example, Rittschof and Griffin (2001) in reviewing peer tutoring literature, note that while both the tutee and the tutor derived advantages from the tutoring interaction, tutors often benefit more because of the preparation the tutor role requires. According to Roscoe and Chi (2007) tutors gain the most benefit when they use a knowledge-building or collaborative style, rather than a knowledge-telling style that relies on delivering information to the client. Elsewhere Chi (1996) describes effective tutoring as an "interactive portion of instruction" composed of "a continuous stream of exchanges between a tutor and a tutee" (p. 1). This "continuous stream," or engaging in "the conversation of mankind" (Bruffee, 1984), proves all the more salient when the consulting exchange centers on oral discourse rather a math problem.

Directors of peer tutoring centers nationwide would not be surprised by these research findings; they are well-aware of the benefits that tutoring provides, not only for the clients, but for the consultants/tutors as well. They have witnessed these effects first-hand. At our university, as the directors of The Writing Center, The Quantitative Reasoning Center, and The Speaking/Listening Center, we sought to look beyond anecdotal evidence, and decided to formally survey tutor/consultant alumni about their experiences. We wanted to be able to collect and analyze information in a wider and more comprehensive fashion about how being a tutor/consultant affected alumni. Early in the research process, we discovered The Peer Writing Tutor Alumni Research Project created by Kail, Gillespie, and Hughes (2002) and were by struck by how their project results mirrored our experiences and observations: "What interests us, and we hope what will interest you, is how significant the experience of collaborative learning is for peer tutors even after they graduate from college, leave the Writing Center or Writing Fellows Program behind, and plunge into their postgraduate lives" (Intro, para. 1).

Drawing on data collected from his institution, Harvey Kail (2006) argues that while we assess the benefits that clients garner from peer tutoring, we are less likely to "look systematically at what peer writing tutors take with them into their lives and their work from the training and experience in this unique 'center space' of higher education" (Kail, 2006, para. 2). In their most recent and joint publication, Hughes, Gillespie, and Kail (2010) argue that when "undergraduate writing tutors and fellows participate in challenging and sustained staff education, and when they interact closely with other student writers and with other peer tutors through our writing centers and writing fellows programs, they develop in profound ways both intellectually and academically" (p. 2). In this award-winning article they reiterate their invitation for other institutions to adapt the survey to an institution's particular focus. Thus, our survey includes more questions, including ones focusing on listening. Additionally, our survey was administered to speaking/listening consultants and quantitative reasoning tutors in addition to writing tutors. For the purpose of the present chapter, however, the author will focus on the speaking/listening consultant alumni's responses. Thus, the term "consultant" will be used in the following pages to connote speaking/listening consultants.

It is the author's contention that the accumulation of consultations over time with multiple clients on multiple communication projects helps the consultant become more competent. The multiple clients bring with them unique personalities, communication styles, and communication skills. By enacting "the role of consultant" over time, the consultant also "rehearses" for future contexts that will require similar skills, attitudes, and/or knowledge. Thus, consulting provides undergraduate students with the opportunity to refine their own skills, attitudes, and knowledge while developing skills, attitudes, and knowledge that they will use in post-graduation roles and contexts. This chapter will first provide a description of the method of data collection and analysis before discussing the results.

Method

At the beginning of spring term 2011, a survey was administered to students who had completed a consultant training course in the last ten years at DePauw

University, a small, liberal arts institution in central Indiana with well-established peer tutoring programs.[1] Among them, 167 Speaking/Listening Center consultant alumni were emailed. Fifty-six surveys were completed for a 35 percent return rate. In addition to completing the survey, some alumni emailed each of us personally.

The survey consisted of ten demographic and general questions. Respondents were then presented with a series of questions asking them to reflect on their consultant experience. Some questions asked them to rate an item, while others were open-ended. The majority of the questions applied to all consultants from the Speaking/Listening Center, the Writing Center, and the Quantitative Reasoning Center, while one segment of the survey asked questions developed particularly for the center where they tutored. Once survey collection was complete, the author used a qualitative approach "aimed at discovering the meaning events have for the individuals who experience them" (Hoepfle, 1997, p. 51). Reading through the comments to the general questions numerous times, I first listened to the voices within the responses. Next, the author noted and then clustered themes that occurred both under individual survey questions as well as across questions. The following clustered themes emerged: enhancing communication acumen; crafting constructive criticism; improving listening; developing flexibility; and identity and self-confidence. The quantitative data provides a broader description that underscores the alumni's experiences.

Results and Discussion

When students become consultants, their relationship to their peers necessarily changes. As one alumni reported "I can certainly say that this was one of my first experiences working in sort of an 'expert' role with my peers, and it gave me confidence in serving as a source of information and aid to others." Using Erving Goffman's terminology (1959), they are no longer solely part of what could be labeled as a social team of "students." Instead, consultants are cast in a different, more formal or professional, role. They occupy a liminal space being both students and "teachers."

Even the "teacher" aspect of their role is unusual. Gillespie and Lerner (2008) conclude that consultants fill a unique role since they can question and guide their peers' work without having to assign a grade as professors do. As one survey reported "As a tutor/consultant, I felt I developed into more of a professional peer for my university peers. When students came to the ARC [the Academic Resource Center that serves as the consulting space on campus], I could offer my assistance as both a classmate peer and trained tutor." In addition, consultants may view a change in their relationship with their institution: "I felt like I was giving back to the University by being an S-consultant.[2] Yes I was benefitting because it was a paid position, but I felt that I was making people better public speakers, which was hopefully seen in the classroom." Consultants saw themselves in a different and more professional relationship with their peers.

Not every student would be successful enacting this professional role. Consultant trainees are recruited on the basis of sound oral communication skills and interpersonal ability. Extending Goffman's metaphor, the consultant training course serves as a rehearsal for "playing" the role of consultant. As part of the training class requirements, students must observe, or "shadow," current consultants. In this way they have the opportunity to be an understudy for their future role. Consultants who are shadowed often comment that the training class student was so professional that they sometimes forgot that the student was just training. Once students successfully complete the training course, they perform in the role of consultant on average of between one and a half to two years. This span of time contributes to proficiency in the role. As one alumni respondent wrote "I think that I was already on my way to developing into a good communicator. That was one of the reasons I made a good tutor. My tutoring helped to enhance the abilities I already had (or was on the way to developing)." Thus, alumni reported that they refined or developed their knowledge and skills through their consultant role experiences

Alumni claim that enacting the consultant role has had a positive influence as they have enacted other roles, including personal and professional roles. One-hundred percent of respondents indicated that they had used the abilities, values, or skills they had developed as consultants in their occupations, while 77 percent of respondents indicated those skills, qualities, or values play a role in their social or family relationships. Among the roles that alumni associated with their work as a consultant were family roles (child, sibling, parent, partner, etc.) and career roles (educator, attorney, minister, non-profit personnel, human resources, etc.).

It is important to note that developing competence is individual-specific. Not all consultants experienced the same level of development or even development in the same abilities or skills. For example, a student's listening ability may have been highly developed even before becoming a consultant, while crafting constructive criticism may be a skill developed by enacting the consultant role. Some of the survey responses reflect movement from the stages Howell (1982) terms unconscious incompetence to conscious incompetence to conscious competence to unconscious competence. In the first stage a person is both incompetent and also oblivious to being incompetent. In the second stage the person tries to enact a behavior or skill, but is neither proficient nor consistent. The third stage is marked by proficiency and consistency. However, the person must remain aware and conscious of acting correctly. In the final stage a person enacts the behavior or skill well and consistently without effort.

Survey results reflect the fact that alumni feel very competent and accomplished in their speaking/listening ability. Their comments also indicate a high level of awareness about their competence and a desire to both develop and think about their own competence, what Baume (2004) labels as a fifth stage, reflective competence. Individuals who teach or train others often develop a propensity for reflective competence as seen in the alumni responses.

Enhancing Communication Acumen

Research suggests that consultants can experience improved success with the material that they tutor others in, particularly if the consultation was an interactional conversation aimed at knowledge-building (Roscoe & Chi, 2007). While a few consultants indicated feeling more comfortable with other academic subjects having worked with clients' projects, many alumni noted improvement in their own communication ability. In particular, responses from alumni indicated that they felt their presentational abilities and their rehearsal process improved because of their consultant training and experience. Alumni noted "Tutoring others challenged me to stay on top of my own speaking and listening skills"; "Working to tutor others, helped me identify areas on which to improve and be mindful"; and "Working in youth ministry I gave 20–30 minute sermons once a month so the ability to write, practice, and deliver effective talks was very important." They also commented on specific techniques that they still remember: "I am much more self-aware about how body language plays a role in a speech and also how fast I typically speak (and my need to slow down)"; "I especially learned the importance of practicing in front of others, videotaping my speaking to learn from it, and using PowerPoint in an engaging way"; "how important preparation is as well as knowing your material" and "even for minor meetings of no more than 10 minutes at work I jot down the major points I want to communicate and think about how to convey them." Alumni also drew a connection between their consultant work and their small group skills: "I use it as part of how I interact with the team I manage" and "As the child welfare intermediary, I often listened to others stories, but also had to offer reflection back to those individuals in order to make sure a message was being portrayed clearly to the group." Whether in the creation or delivery of a presentation or with small group work, alumni valued what they had learned as consultants.

Not surprisingly, alumni felt that their consultant experience proved valuable in the interviewing and hiring processes. Twenty-six percent felt that it was very important and 43.6 percent labeled it as important. According to one respondent, "Being a tutor or consultant is similar to being on a job interview. Random people would walk in and you had to be ready to help them and find out as much information as possible and also you had to keep the conversation going." Another reported: "My boss told me (after being at my current position for about a year) that I had great energy in my interview, which is what convinced her to hire me. I'm fully convinced that this happened because I felt comfortable in an interview environment due to my S Center training." In addition to increasing effective interview skills, alumni mentioned that interviewers frequently focused on their consultant background: "Yes, every job interview I have been on I have been asked about my experience in the S-Center. I have found that most employers are impressed by serving in such a role and find the skills learned as a result or the experience very applicable to the real world" and "I list the S-Center experience on my resume because it is one of the few examples that I can give of the recognition I have received being a skilled public speaker." Another alumnus notes "I had to conduct many 'faux' interviews in my work at the S Center and I found that this experience helped me do the same thing in my real workplace. Also, it helped me understand the difference between candidates that are nervous and candidates that aren't a good fit by giving me good questions to ask potential employees." Thus, alumni reported that working as a consultant improved their own interview skills, their credibility as interviewees, and their adeptness as interviewers.

Finally, consultants gained greater appreciation for learning and practicing oral communication: "It is not emphasized enough in school! We begin writing in kindergarten/first grade, and we usually write in every class and hear how important writing skills are. But speaking? We are lucky to give one or two presentations per school year." Working with clients, they also realized "How great the fear of speaking can be" and how to help people with communication apprehension.

Crafting Constructive Criticism for Diverse Situations

Among the things alumni repeatedly described as being a significant skill, value, or ability was the ability to give constructive criticism to others even in challenging situations. Important components of providing constructive criticism are the ability to listen critically, formulate appropriate feedback that is supported by evidence, and adapt to the client's attitude and style. As Topping (1998) suggests: "Learning how to give and accept criticism, justify one's position, and reject suggestion are all forms of social and assertion skills" (p. 256).

The opportunity to make assessments and provide constructive feedback is one factor that sets the consultant position apart from other types of typical undergraduate employment. One alumni respondent saw "communicating constructive criticism" as the most significant skill learned because "it was very reassuring when one particular student would always schedule her speeches with me. I felt like we developed a good relationship in that she could trust me to fairly evaluate her speaking and I felt comfortable offering her advice. I listened to her and she returned the favor by respecting my advice on how to improve her speeches." Another cited developing the ability "to build a vocabulary for criticism that I didn't have previously. It allowed me to articulate my issues or solutions to problems in a more concise and thoughtful way." One respondent indicated that "Being able to express criticism without being hurtful or demeaning is a definite life skill that I apply in every realm of my everyday life."

Giving constructive criticism in challenging situations helped refine the alumni's abilities even further. An area where alumni indicated that they felt effective giving feedback was in working with an increasing international student population. Like other schools, DePauw University made a decision to internationalize the campus. In 2005, the university's Office of Institutional Research reported that there were 48 international (non-resident alien) students. In 2010, the number of students in this category rose to 236. The increasing numbers of international students necessitated a more intentional connection between the students and the Speaking/Listening Center. Consultants who may have developed a level of competence working with domestic students found it necessary to expand their skills when working with international students. An alumnus commented that "generally the most difficult part of my job was when foreign exchange students would come into the center. Each time a student would come in and ask to practice their English, I would need to focus on my patience and listening abilities . . . so I could do my best to help them with their speaking skills. So while I was able to develop my skills of patience, leadership and listening with all students, I learned the most about myself and others when language was a barrier." Other alumni indicated that they changed their consultant style to accommodate "students who spoke English as a second language. I learned through those tutoring experiences to speak clearly and slowly, but not as if they were stupid." Working with international students helped alumni develop attitudes and skills that they may not have while working with domestic students.

For some consultants, working with second language clients was not problematic. Alumni indicated two additional areas that proved challenging. Developing an effective way to work with clients who were resentful about being required to come for consultation was viewed as a vital skill: "I learned the most from students who were in the S Center reluctantly or because of a requirement for class. These students were usually more difficult to work with initially and I loved when they walked away saying that they will make use of the S center in the future." Others found that consulting with the opposite gender clients influenced their criticism style. For example, one alumna wrote that for her "male students are less responsive or more defensive to criticism."

According to the survey responses, alumni utilize the constructive criticism skills developed as consultants to help family members and friends "prepare for presentations and interviews." In addition, constructive criticism skills are important in the workplace. One respondent mentioned that "Working as a tutor at the S-Center was my first experience in helping others learn techniques of oral presentations. This helped me immensely in my teaching career, where I coached the Jr. High Speech/Forensics team." Another said "Coaching skills are essential in my occupation . . . when working with peers with the same interest, there are specific approaches and methods that should be used to be successful." These comments corroborate Marcoulides and Simkin's (1991) argument that consulting provides "practice in peer review, and participation in what is likely to be a lifetime vocational task" (p. 84).

Improving Listening

An important set of questions we added to the Peer Writing Alumni Research Project survey centered on listening. Listening is a vital, and often undervalued, component of the communication process. One cannot be an effective communicator without being an effective listener. Moreover, one cannot articulate constructive criticism effectively unless one is adept at listening. Survey data indicates that alumni appreciate the critical link between speaking and listening. When asked "Did the tutor/consultant training improve your own listening skills?" Ninety-six percent of the alumni responded affirmatively. Some consultants started at what Howell terms "the unconscious incompetence stage." Indicative of this stage is this response: "Yes, I never really considered listening a key skill." Others began at the conscious incompetence stage characterized by statements like this: "The consultant training helped me learn how to listen as opposed to just hearing and interpreting what was being said. The training helped me to listen to more than just the words someone is saying and the importance of other nonverbal cues." After training and working as a consultant, respondents reported more conscious competence: "Taught me to listen first, think about what I'm going to say in response *before* saying it. Not all people follow this advice and many say things they regret later."

When asked to give an example of how they use their listening skills in their profession, alumni provided a wealth of responses. For some, they listened for what was unspoken and drew people out. An attorney responded that "A case can turn on one simple fact, and clients may omit facts or try to breeze by one when they are telling their side of a story. I have to listen closely and ask direct questions about those details because they can mean the difference between winning and losing a case." Another attorney mentioned that "Clients in the law firm come in and we must not only listen to their answers, but their body language, and what they are not saying just as much." Whether listening for minute details or examining nonverbal cues, listening is viewed as a critical skill.

For other alumni, listening requires "sifting" through communicative noise to find the key elements that a speaker is trying to get across. An alumnus whose work centers on customer services values the ability to listen to questions and "filter out redundant information to quickly get to the issue at heart." Another alumnus indicates a different reason to filter: "As a graduate student in an environment where English is generally a second language, listening has become more than just critically thinking about the content but also breaking through various accents." A respondent who was previously in youth ministry saw listening skills as "important for counseling students and trying to discern what they were expressing underneath all of the 'likes' and 'ums'." The ability to listen for the core message and avoid being distracted by communicative noise is particularly important in alumni's careers.

Alumni also use listening as a critical component in problem-solving situations as one respondent observed: "I conduct employee reviews and I use listening skills to hear employee concerns and construct responses and action plans as a result." Another respondent working in the business sector states, "I work with clients on a daily basis to better understand their needs for improving systems and business processes. If I didn't listen carefully, I'd miss out on a lot." Good listening skills were credited for helping with both in-house and external business communication.

An alumnus working in the medical field responded "I work with physicians and patients and there is a large body of research that indicates there are major communication barriers between the two parties. I have seen this first hand. My current role allows me to help train physicians, nurses and research staff how to communicate effectively with patients when discussing clinical research with them. Listening to patients and reading their nonverbal communication cues is vital in the dialogue between clinical care practitioners and patients." Another alumnus uses listening skills to be a more informed patient: "For me, it is very important to listen carefully to what my doctors are saying, to clarify what they mean if necessary, and to take away as much information from every appointment as I can."

Not only did alumni note the importance of listening in their career or graduate school endeavors, they also emphasized the importance of listening in their personal lives, interacting with friends and family. Listening was seen as an integral part of healthy marriages: "My relationships (especially my marriage) are deeply important to me. Being a good listener makes me a better wife and friend." Alumni indicated that listening is an important aspect of parenting. One respondent said "I'm currently the mom of four children—I listen all day long!" Listening to one's partner about how to parent was also identified as crucial: "As parents, my husband and I have to keep communication open about how we want to raise our daughter. He and I come from different parenting backgrounds, so we have to adapt. It's listening to what's really behind those ideas—what's driving him to want to do something one way and not another—that helps us find our common ground." Overall, 89 percent said that they use listening skills developed as a consultant in their family or life relationships.

In their professional life as well as in their personal life, alumni recognized the value of listening. Alumni indicated that they used their listening skills throughout their professional careers. One respondent noted that listening was helpful in playing the role of the newcomer: "My current position is still fairly new, so I use my listening skills all the time as I continue to learn and grow in this position." An established professional stated "Listening is a huge skill for a counselor and that [the S consultant training and experience] started me on the path of developing those skills." These kinds of comments were reiterated by many alumni who attribute the development or refinement of their listening ability to their work as consultants.

Developing Flexibility

Flexibility and adaptability are important skills for the adept communicator. As the surveyed alumni served as consultants between two and six semesters, they experienced multiple client consultations. Development, or refinement, of the ability to adapt or be flexible was seen as a valuable component of alumni experiences. Building on earlier work, Morreale, Rubin, and Jones (1998) argue that "Advanced skills are more than just knowing, doing, or feeling. They are blends of knowledge, skill, and attitude; they require greater levels of behavioral flexibility/adaptability" (p. 13) The following responses from the survey indicate that alumni developed flexibility by being able to adjust to diverse projects, different personalities, and by setting personal agendas aside. The responses also indicate that alumni feel that the flexibility they gained as consultants has had continuing effects, including the ability to adapt to different sizes of audiences, different personalities of audience members, as well as the goals of different audiences.

Alumni also valued helping students outside their own majors and in particular remembered presentations by psychology, biochemistry, and art students: "One thing that I always found interesting is you never knew what kind of project or assignment might walk through that door. It would be one person giving a personal/life story speech or it could be a group presenting on economic differences between two markets;" "I learned that everyone is different in the ways they speak and listen, and therefore to communicate most effectively, it's often necessary to change your style of communication based on your audience;" "I think my interpersonal communication improved more than my public speaking. Tutoring individuals in a private, professional setting helped me learn how to deal with many different personalities."

Flexibility was mentioned as playing a role in social and family relationships. One respondent describes how important flexibility is when working with another's ideas: "Some of my younger relatives were looking into colleges. I really want to just advocate for what I would have done and tell them exactly what to do: which colleges they should apply to, etc. However, I realized that our ideas of what is important during college were vastly different in many aspects. I realized I had to work with what they wanted and not just push what I felt best."

Identity and Self-confidence

The survey responses indicate that being a consultant contributed to consultants' identity in several ways. As educators, we always hope that what happens at the communication center finds its way into the academic and social community. One respondent reported that being a "consultant gave me confidence in myself that I was able to take out of the ARC. This transferred over to the classes I took and the presentations I gave. I thought of myself as a student leader, not just a student." Like many campuses, DePauw University is a very socially active campus. Students typically are involved in many clubs and organizations. Alumni reported that being a consultant improved their abilities in the social sphere: "Felt better established as a leader on campus;" "As Student Body President at DePauw, I was often required to speak in public. . . . Being an 'S' tutor helped instill me with the confidence and ability to be successful."

While serving as a consultant seems to be an important role for many students, for some students it seemed to provide a critical niche that reinforced or validated their personal identity: "As a self-described nerd, it gave me self-confidence that I was seen as an authority on public speaking and presentations. People respected my opinion" and "gave me the confidence to be the person I am and not just 'fit in' with others."

As a result of having sharpened their personal repertoire of speaking and listening skills, having refined their practice of providing constructive criticism, developing more flexibility, and gaining a sense of identity in the process, many alumni responses cited gaining confidence as an overwhelming benefit of having been a consultant. The term "confidence" was mentioned in responses throughout the survey. For example, one alumnus indicated "The S Center provided me with the confidence to actively participate in my law school class! If I had not been comfortable with public speaking, I do not believe I would have chosen law as a profession." In addition, respondents indicated that they developed confidence in communication abilities beyond public speaking, including conversational ability, interpersonal communication, and negotiation as described above. While these alumni mentioned confidence in their own skills, other alumni reported that they gained confidence from successfully helping others to develop communication ability. For example, one respondent indicated that the most significant aspects of the training/consulting experience were "confidence, ability to train and inspire others."

Kail (2006) argues "the most significant benefit that students take with them from their writing center experience is earned confidence in themselves" (para. 9). "Earned confidence" is an important term since it is markedly different than bravado or bluff. In analyzing our surveys, the author maintains that earned confidence is a result of effectively enacting the consultant role. Effectiveness in the consultant role is predicated on the rehearsal of key communication skills and the development of consultant-client relationships over time. The refinement of communication skills (presentational, interpersonal, small group, and interviewing), the ability to give constructive criticism to a variety of clients, the ability to be an effective listener, and development of flexibility, all contribute to feeling positive about the consultant role which in turn contributes to one's sense of identity. Alumni stress that much of what they enacted in the consultant role has transferred into their career roles, their graduate school roles, and their roles with friends and family.

Conclusion

The data discussed in this chapter provides a glimpse of the experiences of consultants at one institution. However, there are some limitations to this study. While the author worked to maintain a neutral perspective throughout my numerous readings of the survey data, a second coder could have helped to either verify the clusters identified or to introduce other clusters. Secondly, Kail et al. (2002) have used focus groups as part of their data collection. Discussion amongst alumni would certainly amplify the results. Finally, I would encourage others to modify or replicate the survey. Such efforts will add to what we know about the effects of playing the consultant role both as a student and in post-graduation life. In doing so, we can seek to answer such questions as, What are the commonalities between consultant perceptions of the effects of the experience of being a communication center consultant? What are the differences? Do the different theoretical underpinnings of different institutions' training classes result in different alumni attitudes, knowledge, or skills? How can training classes better prepare students for consultant role acquisition?

Learning how alumni extend the knowledge and skills acquired from their consultant roles into their post-graduation roles may ultimately be used to transform the ways we train our consultants. Additionally, the skills, values, and qualities that alumni identified as important would prove beneficial not only for consultants, but also for *all* students. Knowing what skills consultants take with them after graduation to apply to their post-graduation lives could prove useful in guiding curriculum and pedagogy in teaching effective communication skills.

Notes

1. Thanks to Dr. William Tobin for help in creating and consolidating the results from an electronic survey. Thanks to Drs. Kail, Gillespie, and Hughes for sharing The Peer Writing Tutor Alumni Research Project survey. Thanks to the S Consultants. Seeing your growth inspired me to begin this line of research.

2. Alumni respondents frequently refer to The Speaking/Listening Center as the S Center or the S/L Center. S Consultants refer to the communication peer tutors on our campus.

References

Baume, D. (2004, May). Leadership/Management: Conscious competence learning matrix. *Ethical work and life learning.* Retrieved from
http://www.businessballs.com/consciouscompetencelearningmodel.htm
Bruffee, K. A. (1984). Peer tutoring and the "conversation of mankind." In C. Murphy & J. Law, (Eds.), *Landmark essays on writing centers* (pp. 87-98). Davis, CA: Hermagoras Press.

Chi, M. T. H. (1996). Constructing self-explanations and scaffolded explanations in tutor-ing. *Applied Cognitive Psychology, 10,* S33 – S49.

Gillespie, P., & Lerner, N. (2008). *The Longman guide to peer tutoring.* (2nd ed.). New York: Pearson Longman.

Goffman, E. (1959). *Presentation of self in everyday life.* New York, NY: First Anchor Books Edition.

Hoepfl, M. C. (1997). Choosing qualitative research: A primer for technology education researchers. *Journal of Technology Education, 9*(1), 47 – 63.

Howell, W. S. (1982). *The empathic communicator.* Belmont, CA: Wadsworth Publish-ing Company.

Hughes, B., Gillespie, P., & Kail, H. (2010). What they take with them: Finding from the peer writing tutor alumni research project. *The Writing Center Journal, 30*(2), 12 – 35.

Kail, H. (2006, March). Situated in the center: The peer writing tutor alumni research project. Paper presented at the meeting of the Conference on College Composition and Communication, Chicago. Retrieved from http://www.writing.wisc.edu/pwtarp/?page_id=28

Kail, H., Gillespie, P., & Hughes, B. (2002). *The peer writing tutor alumni research project.* Retrieved from http://www.writing.wisc.edu/pwtarp/?page_id=286

Marcoulides, G., & Simkin, M. (1991). Evaluating student papers: The case for peer re-view. *Journal of Education for Business, 67,* 80 – 84.

Morreale, S., Rubin, R., & Jones, E. (1998). *Expectations for speaking and listening for college graduates advanced communication skills.* Retrieved from National Com-munication Association Reviewed Educational Resource website: http://www.natcom.org/uploadedFiles/Content/Education/Virtual_Faculty_Lounge/College Competencies.pdf

Rittschof, K., & Griffin, B. (2001). Reciprocal peer tutoring: Re-examining the value of co-operative learning techniques to college students and instructors. *Educational Psychology, 21,* 39 – 47.

Roscoe, R., & Chi, M. (2007). Understanding tutor learning: Knowledge-building and knowledge telling in peer tutors' explanations and questions. *Review of Educational Research, 77,* 534 – 574.

Topping, K. (1998). Peer assessment between students in colleges and universities. *Review of Educational Research, 68,* 249 – 276.

Part II:
Challenges to Today's Centers

Chapter 6

Ethics and the Communication Center: Chameleon or Tortoise?

Eunkyong L. Yook, P. Anand Rao, and Sarah M. Wilde

It is not surprising that surveys repeatedly find that business leaders, scholars, and higher education accrediting associations report that oral communication skills are among those skills college students most need to develop (Morreale, 2003). Employers have long stated that effective individual and group communication skills are needed to lead their businesses and that those skills are critical to economic success (Cronin & Glenn, 1991; Dannels, 2001; Schneider, 1999). In the academic world, those entities concerned with the philosophy of education such as the Boyer Commission and the Carnegie Foundation for the Advancement of Teaching have called for a closer link between communication skills and coursework (Dannels, 2001; Schneider, 1999). Additionally, scholars concerned with the learning process have called for employing oral communication skills to sharpen critical thinking and for viewing rhetoric as epistemic as a means of discovering and creating knowledge (Dannels, 2001; Morello, 2000; Palmerton, 1996; Scott, 1967). More recently, newspaper and journal articles have lamented over the problem of "mallspeak" and student incoherence and have called for institutions of higher education to take measures to remedy this societal problem (Schneider, 1999; Zernicke, 1999). As Morreale and Pearson (2008) state, "A pressing need exists for communication instruction at all levels of the U.S. education system" (p. 225).

In addition to strong concerns expressed by business leaders, scholars, and members of society in general, institutions of higher learning are also being pressured by concerns of a more practical nature—being accredited by regional and national accrediting agencies. Agencies such as the Southern Association of Colleges and Schools are raising their expectations for institutions of higher learning to find a solution to their students' communication deficiencies. In order to retain their accreditation status, colleges and universities need to find structured and accountable ways to improve oral communication skills, and to find feasible ways of documenting and assessing the validity of their programs (Morello, 2000; Morreale, Hugenberg, & Worley, 2006).

In response to such calls, institutions of higher learning have looked to their communication departments, and more specifically to the basic communication course, as a starting point in their search for a solution. According to a recent survey of United States institutions of higher learning, over half of all respondents report that the basic course is required in their general education requirements (Morreale et al., 2006). However, the basic communication course is just that—a beginning point for the process of improving students' communication skills, not a panacea for all communication ills (Roberts, 1983). The basic course alone is not the answer, as without continued practice and development competent levels of mastery cannot be maintained (Morello, 2000; Roberts, 1983). The problem is exacerbated by the fact that not all institutions of higher learning have communication departments, let alone a basic communication course.

Theoretical Approaches to Communication Education

CXC: Communication Across the Curriculum Programs

Given this situation, in response to society's call for improved communication skills, communication across the curriculum programs have appeared. Communication across the curriculum programs (CXC) provide structured curricular coordination across various disciplines with faculty pursuing the common goal of enhancing their students' oral communication skills. However, concerned communication scholars continue to strongly forewarn that CXC programs should be a supplement, and by no means a substitute, for basic communication instruction provided by the communication discipline (Cronin & Glenn, 1991; Dannels, 2001; Hobgood, 2000; Schneider, 1999). This statement can be seen as emanating, at least in part, from the fear of a dilution of communication education to nothing more than skills-based delivery, with little if any theoretical content (Dannels, 2001; Morello, 2000; Schneider, 1999), undermining the credibility of communication department missions nationwide.

Regardless of these fears, spurred by societal and practical pressures to improve college students' mastery of oral communication competence from many sources, CXC programs have been established in various formats and have been flourishing with many positive results (Dannels & Gaffney, 2009; Darling, 2005; Morreale & Pearson, 2008). Historically, one early example of institutional reaction to this call for improved communication skills is Central College, which received a National Endowment for the Humanities (NEH) grant in 1979 to fund faculty workshops on communication pedagogy (Roberts, 1983). Cronin and Glenn (1991) state that preliminary results from studies in programs at colleges such as Central College, Clarkson University, University of New Mexico, Saint Mary-of-the-Woods College, and Hamline University indicate that faculty and students alike react positively to communication intensive courses. Faculty and independent evaluators were also found to rate students with experience in communication intensive courses more favorably in communication competence levels than those without experience. Students also reported more mastery of course content and improvement in communication skills as a result of the communication intensive course. Earlier, Hay (1988) similarly reported positive assessments of communication intensive courses in CXC programs. Other scholars also support the positive effects of CXC programs on student learning (Dannels & Gaffney, 2009; Darling, 2005; Morreale & Pearson, 2008).

CID: Communication in the Disciplines

Since the inception of CXC programs, a new approach has been developing in the scholarship of communication education: communication in the disciplines, or CID. CID is based upon the philosophy that it is through oral genres that students learn how to communicate competently in their respective disciplines (Dannels, 2002). According to this approach, to teach effective communication within each discipline, disciplinary traditions, expectations, and priorities need to be investigated and taken into account. An ethnographic approach is encouraged to learn the cultural values and condoned behaviors in the various discipline-specific communities of learning (Dannels & Gaffney, 2009).

Disciplines such as biology, chemistry, engineering, and mathematics have begun to realize the increasing importance and role of good communication skills in the workplace. The Accreditation Board for Engineering and Technology has developed new standards to evaluate departments and colleges of engineering around the country (Darling & Dannels, 2003). Students should graduate with an ability to communicate effectively and work productively on teams. Businesses and industries nationwide are also recognizing the centrality of communication skills in professional engineering practices (Darling & Dannels, 2003).

Although evidence suggests that communication skills are critical to engineering practices, other studies report that these skills are being inadequately developed in engineering courses and curricula nationwide. Concurrent with the move toward discipline-specific instruction, numerous curricular changes are occurring in engineering education. Many of these communication intensive courses target technical communication as a critical skill to learn. Some of these communication courses for engineers and/or communication intensive courses focus on communication skills such as listening, visual aids, group creativity, and audience analysis. Also, senior-level courses include assignments that require brainstorming sessions or student team portfolios (Darling & Dannels, 2003).

Scholars have argued for the need to tailor communication education to the specific needs of various disciplines, in addition to promoting the skills we consider "basic" to our field (Dannels, 2001, 2002; Dannels & Gaffney, 2009; Darling & Dannels, 2003; Garside, 2002; Morello, 2000). Morello (2000) has called for scholars to "come forward with unique and innovative applications of rhetorical and communication theory in the context of oral communication activities conducted across the curriculum" (p. 11). Dannels (2001) argues that while the teaching of "basic" public speaking skills are the backbone of the communication across the curriculum programs, and serve as the *raison d'etre* of such programs on many campuses, the teaching of those "basic" skills is not enough. She rightly questions whether such instruction is only here to help universities rid their students of "mallspeak." In her research on the field of engineering, Dannels (2002) asks discipline-specific questions such as, "What oral communication genres and skills are important in the engineering workplace? What are perceived audiences and consequences of oral communication in the engineering workplace? and What is the relative importance of oral communication as related to writing in the engineering workplace?" (p. 4)

Another study of how instructors teach their students to communicate within their discipline was undertaken at DePauw University, an early adopter of CXC, with a requirement established in 1981. In this study, instructors from a variety of disciplines were interviewed about how they expect their students to speak about course content (Weiss, 1999). Weiss found that while it was not possible from the results to draw conclusions regarding the rhetoric of specific disciplines, it was clear that there were distinctions between disciplines in what they viewed as appropriate in students' use of terminology, what was viewed as acceptable evidence, uses of logic, and conceptions of truth. It was apparent, according to Weiss, that talk is not the same in every classroom. While this study was not centrally concerned or focused solely on communication practices within the disciplines, its investigation of how each discipline established its own value system of truth claims necessarily directs how those claims can be presented and represented. These differences are of vital concern to communication centers, established to serve the disciplines that diverge so widely on what they expect from their students.

CID may be a relatively new trend, but it is not a totally unexpected phenomenon, especially given the field of communication and the content of what we teach. Audience analysis and adaptation have always been an important part of competent communication, whether on an interpersonal or public level. As communication specialists are mandated with the task of overseeing CXC programs across campuses, it was inevitable that at some point they would be sensitized to the need to adapt to the various exigencies of the communication skills employed in different departments. The move to direct communication instruction toward the discipline creates a point of friction with CXC programs and that point of friction is most evident in the communication centers that are charged with working closely with those programs.

CAD: Communication Against the Disciplines

More recently, in his thought-provoking essay, Anthony Fleury (2005) advocates for yet another approach: communication against the disciplines. He criticizes the CID approach as being unnecessarily narrow, constraining liberal education of students in the otherwise varied ways of communication and negotiating meaning in the learning process. Acknowledging that disciplinarity is a powerful force in academia, he is wary of mimicking the bureaucratic structure of academia in pedagogy, arguing that it will impede the benefits of liberal education. Instead, he advocates focusing not only on communication in the disciplines, but also on placing CID in dialectical tension with the approach of teaching core communication principles to other disciplines. Although this new approach is refreshing and acknowledges the tension between core communication disciplinary pedagogy and catering to disciplinary preferences, Fleury's recommendation of using core communication styles of exposition, persuasion, and expression has been criticized as being too confining and not adequately reflective of all styles, including non-western communication (Palmerton, 2005).

The Communication Center: A Resource for CXC Programs

The communication center is an important component of the CXC program's pedagogical goals for colleges and students (Morreale & Pearson, 2008). Communication centers, under various appellations such as the Skills Center (Roberts, 1983), Speaking Lab (Hay, 1988), or the Speech Center (Hobgood, 2000) are places where students and faculty can receive individualized assistance on their CXC assignments and curricular planning. Individual faculty typically direct their students to visit the communication center by making such visits either mandatory or optional for their courses. Communication centers are significant resources for CXC programs because they provide the necessary resources to guide faculty who have not received graduate instruction in the field of communication. It is also a place where students can access resources and obtain feedback to construct, refine, and practice their speaking skills with the help of a skilled communication consultant (NCA, 2001). In some cases, the consultant is a faculty member from the communication department (Cronin & Grice, 1991; Hobgood, 2000). In other instances, consultants are trained undergraduates, selected and thoroughly prepared for their role of peer tutor based on innate abilities, previous oral communication experiences, and coursework in communication (Hobgood, 2000; Roberts, 1983). Scholars agree that communication centers are useful in enhancing students' communication competencies (Engleberg, Emanuel, Van Horn, & Bodary, 2008; Morreale & Pearson, 2008).

Given this philosophical trend towards adapting communication education to the oral tasks, expectations, and traditions of the various disciplines, the communication center at the University of Mary Washington initiated a project to find out what those discipline-specific expectations were. While some CXC programs are based in institutions where a department of communication is housed, not all CXC programs are, nor is there a uniform requirement of a required basic course in communication. Although repeatedly and strongly recommended by various scholars in the field, it is a sad reality that funding and administrative barriers prevent establishment of a basic course on some campuses. At the University of Mary Washington, speech faculty members are part of the English, linguistics, and communication department, and communication is not an independent major. However, given the importance of communication skills for a liberal arts education and for career preparation, communication is highly valued. Students are required to take at least two speaking intensive courses before graduation, and these courses may be in the field of speech communication, or another discipline. Currently there is no basic course requirement on campus, although there are several sections of public speaking and small group communication offered each semester. These sections are in such high demand, however, that they are routinely populated with students in their junior or senior year, with students trying to obtain overrides for enrollment.

The communication center is an important part of the Speaking Intensive Program at the University of Mary Washington, supporting students and faculty with their speaking intensive course assignments, as well as other students who need assistance with various communication projects. Like most communication centers, the center at the University of Mary Washington provides supplemental support for oral communication courses and assists faculty in incorporating communication components in their curriculum (NCA, 2001). As such, the director of the communication center, in line with the communication in the disciplines trend for CXC programs, initiated a project in 2002 to adapt more specifically to the needs, expectations, and requirements of various faculty with which the center works. Similar to the study conducted at DePauw University by Weiss (1999), University of Mary Washington consultants interviewed faculty to gather information about their courses and their specific needs and expectations for how their students should communicate orally.

Methodology

After compiling a list of all speaking intensive professors and their fields of study using a semester track book, the instructor whose students made the most use of the communication center during the semester was selected to be the representative of that discipline. Seven communication center consultants were each assigned a separate instructor with whom to meet. Professor assignments were made in a variety of ways. Some consultants selected a certain professor because he/she was a teacher in their major; others selected professors because they knew them from having a class with him/her. Finally, some instructors were selected because certain consultants had many consultations with professors in that field, and wanted to better understand the professors' criteria for evaluation. The seven disciplines that were targeted included biology, geography, mathematics, philosophy, linguistics, political science, and economics. Most majors at the University of Mary Washington have at least one SI class, but not all of the professors teaching these courses rely on the expertise of the communication center and its consultants.

The communication center consultation report form, used as the basis for critiquing all students visiting the communication center, was used for the faculty interviews. The form checks for competency in commonly accepted standards of speech: structure and delivery aspects such as elements of an introduction, body, and conclusion, and nonverbal aspects of eye contact, gesture, posture, vocalics, as well as visual aids. The majority of the professors interviewed used the basic form and then added additional communication components they deem important to their field of study to evaluate student performance. One professor, however, preferred to use his own grading rubric, rather than the consultation report form.

Discipline-Specific Expectations

The discipline-specific communication expectations, as reported to the consultants, were varied and generally supported the conclusions drawn by the studies outlined above. As Weiss (1999) found, talk was not the same in every classroom, and the values and expectations for each discipline were represented as unique to that field.

Some departments focus more on the delivery aspects, while others on the organizational structure of a speech. Political science, for example, focuses mainly on organization. Delivery of the material is not as imperative but proper dress is deemed as important. Attention getters are not required and are more seen as a matter of personal style. Most speeches in this department are based on adapted research papers. Visual aids such as posters or PowerPoint are not usually required; however, students should be careful not to use too many statistics and numbers in their presentations as those can be distracting.

Unlike political science, the math department views the use of visual aids as important. The math professor interviewed felt that her students need help making their visual aids more organized and less distracting. She found the basic consultation form to be very appropriate, but the sections on citing evidence were not applicable to her class assignments. One difference in the math department's assignments is that the majority of their presentations are done in groups. Transitions between group members were found to be concerns of the interviewed professor in the math department. The interviewee also wished that her students used more in-depth introductions.

The biology department, on the other hand, found that some of the characteristics the center uses in critiquing speeches were a bit too much. The professor interviewed felt that attention-getters, credibility statements, the use of audience relevance, and the signaling of the conclusion did not need to be directly stated. These characteristics should be used only if they would make the speech more enjoyable and understandable. A preview statement is not necessary and the need for a statement of purpose/thesis depends on the topic being discussed. Given the heavy focus on content, like with the political science presentations, technical slides with charts, graphs, and pictures are acceptable and customary. The biology department sees delivery as well as organizational components as important, specifically: eye contact, gestures, not using vocal fillers, transitions, and clear, organized main points.

The economics department also views both organization and delivery as important. The elements of delivery that this department specifically looks for include: the pace of the speech, eye contact, the use of a conversational tone, vocal inflections and the lack of nervous habits. The main points should be very clear and the body of the speech should contain transitions between main points as well as a transition to the conclusion. The conclusion also needs a summary statement.

The geography and philosophy departments both stress the importance of a strong organization. The geography department feels that introductory elements such as attention-getters, a thesis statement, audience relevance, a preview statement and a transition to the body of the speech are considered key characteristics of a good presentation. The philosophy department stresses a clear introduction with a thesis statement, an easy to follow presentation, and an appropriate conclusion.

Some of the interviewed professors went a step further and suggested other areas of importance that were not directly addressed on our basic consultation form. The linguistics, geography, and philosophy professors all found that their students need help with time management in their speeches. The geography professor finds that many students either do not keep within the time limit or do not speak for a long enough period of time. In addition to following the 20 – 25 minute time frame, the linguistics professor we interviewed suggested that her students need help in actively encouraging class participation during their presentations. The professor's suggestions of ways to do this include games or question and answer sessions. The philosophy professor also stressed the importance of handling questions well and meeting time restraints. The last two areas in which students struggle addressed during these interviews, include identifying an argument (philosophy department) and analyzing articles which are presented as oral critiques to the class (linguistics department).

While those who participated in the project learned much from the exercise of investigating disciplinary expectations, questions still remain. For example: How generalizable is this information across instructors? Is there a greater need for the more technical fields such as chemical engineering to improve their communication skills? Do students find it a problem to adapt to audiences consisting of members from various disciplines and to integrate multidisciplinary information?

There are two things to keep in mind when looking at the specific communication skills stressed by the various professors. A caveat to consider to these disciplinary preferences is that only one professor in each field was interviewed and grading criteria in one professor's class may differ slightly from another professor's criteria (Garside, 2002). This problem of not only having to consider disciplinary differences, but also needing to be cognizant of individual differences among professors in the same discipline is an issue that our colleagues in writing in the disciplines also address (Bazerman, 2005). For example, in one consultant's seminar class only delivery aspects of the presentation were graded. Content was not necessarily graded during the presentation because a separate research paper based on the presentation was also graded. After speaking with another biology seminar professor, the consultant discovered that the professor looks at both content and presentation delivery, and a separate research paper is not turned in by the students.

A second important consideration to keep in mind is that the grading criteria for an assignment where students are encouraged to attend the communication center may differ from the grading scale for another presentation in that class. For example, most economics majors who visit the communication center do so for their first presentation, but not for their lengthier debate that occurs later in the semester. The purpose of this shorter first assignment is to allow the students to feel more comfortable speaking in front of their classmates and to help them prepare for their debate. Although visual aids and an introduction were not found to be important characteristics for the shorter presentation in this field, they may play more of a role in the debate.

Because this is the first time consultants tackled the ethical question of where to draw the line in adapting to the expectations of various disciplines, there are some aspects to be changed in the future. For example, more faculty in each field would be interviewed and more fields such as computer science, chemistry, or business would be targeted. Professors would be encouraged to provide a more general list of specific communication aspects that could be evaluated in all types of speeches in that discipline. While these results may not be representative, they are not intended to necessarily describe the communication needs of each discipline. It was clear, however, that expectations for a successful presentation and student communication varied in some ways by discipline and instructor (Garside, 2002). It is this variance that presents the communication center with its greatest challenge.

A project was undertaken from the perspective of alumni of a Department of Mechanical Engineering at a large state university located in the West to discover what oral communication genres and skills are important in the engineering workplace. Five distinct categories of skills emerged from this analysis. The most important skills were found to be that of message construction—be concise, clear, logical, and specific. A second important skill was that of interaction—use teamwork, negotiation, and ask and respond to questions. The last three skill categories were delivery, listening, and using common sense in communication settings (Darling & Dannels, 2003).

Another study was done in the context of a National Science Foundation grant focused on developing instructional modules for teaming, writing and speaking in targeted chemical engineering courses (Dannels, Anson, Bullard, & Peretti, 2003). The project teams were comprised of students in six disciplines. Many of the students became frustrated by the varied expectations of different teachers and audiences.

The four emergent categories that summarized the learning challenge were: integrating multidisciplinary information, managing varied audiences and feedback, aligning content and communication tasks, and addressing interpersonal team issues (Dannels et al., 2003). In a reflection log, a student stated, "The type of information expected by each discipline is as different as oil and water, so making 'Italian dressing' out of it can be extremely difficult" (Dannels et al., 2003, p. 53).

Chameleon or Tortoise?

After information about specific expectations of the field were collected from various professors teaching speaking intensive courses, the reports were collected by the communication center director and collated in a folder at the center for the consultants' reference. However, rather than make our job of consulting with the students of these various professors easier, we found ourselves in a philosophical quandary: How far should we be willing to go to adapt to a specific discipline and instructor? For example, one professor mentioned that he did not see the need for a credibility statement in a chemistry seminar presentation. That led us to the important question: Just because that particular field (as represented by the professor and their experiences with the field) does not believe in some of the basic tenets of communication theory, does that mean that we automatically have to comply with their expectations as we guide their students? According to Palmerton (2005), "There is no question that believing there is only one valid way to communicate, and that being socialized to one discourse community without understanding that its code is just one symbolic system among many, can well contribute to negative outcomes" (p. 82). Given that our university currently does not have a basic communication course where students can be exposed to the basics of communication theory, are we giving the students the wrong impression about the field of communication—that communication education should change and adopt every discipline's expectations? Or, should we stay our ground, risking alienating the various departments and faculty, who are an important component of our speaking across the curriculum program? This question of power among disciplines in CXC programs is tackled by Garside (2001), though her advocacy for "seeing the forest," not only the tree, is a criticism of a communication department attempting to exert power over other disciplines in teaching the "correct" way to speak. There is no simple answer, of course, and what answers we are able to garner are informed by the unique ways in which the communication center is situated within both the college and the speaking across the curriculum program.

The communication center serves a broad constituency, and while most consultations are borne from assignments in speaking intensive courses, the center serves any student preparing for any number of in- or out-of-class presentations or communication situations. More than just preparing for a formal public speaking event, the communication center is used for consultations on group projects and other types of interactions. It is important to note that this charge necessarily complicates our answer to the questions listed above in that we cannot simply answer on behalf of in-class pedagogical concerns.

Practical Implications for Staff Training

In considering the role of the communication centers in adapting to specific needs/requests of a variety of disciplines and faculty, we outlined several scenarios in which it would be appropriate for center consultants to continue to work in this direction. First and foremost is that the center is a resource that all students may use to help them better perform on communicative assignments in class. By accumulating relevant adaptive information for different disciplines, courses, and faculty, our consultants can better help those students prepare for those presentations. This is akin to a consultant assisting a student prepare a speech for an instructor that a consultant has worked with (or has taken a class with) before. There is nothing wrong with sharing information on what they know that instructor prefers to see included in a speech, such as reminding a student in a public speaking class to provide a credibility statement. Additionally, this type of specific adaptive preparation can help make assignments more manageable for less-experienced students. Without a broad experience base, many students are left to fret over many details concerning their presentation. As is often the case with students in public speaking courses, students new to public speaking tend to prefer more structure in their assignments, which provides them with some level of predictability and control. While this is not ideal at all experience levels, by providing new students with clear guidelines concerning the expectations of their instructor and discipline, they can more easily prepare for what can be an overwhelming experience.

Finally, the use of more specific adaptive strategies can help both the consultant and the student better prepare for field-specific presentation styles. Time that would have normally been spent outlining a variety of approaches can be spent fine-tuning more than just the technical aspects of the presentation, including the construction of arguments, presentation strategies to maximize audience understanding, and strategies for greater feedback understanding. Within the narrowly defined mission of preparing students for discipline-specific communication genres, the continued development and application of this survey may not only be beneficial but necessary.

There are, however, natural and serious concerns related to the retooling of the communication center and its consultative work to this end. The first relates to the applicability of survey data to other courses. It is not clear from the information collected how much of the styles students would be adapting to are specific to the discipline, or are specific to the faculty. Regardless of the discipline, every instructor will have their own preferences for how students should adapt to their assignments. This is also true of faculty in communication, though they will likely be more experienced in not only adapting themselves to a variety of speaking situations, but also in instructing students on how to adapt to different audiences and speaking situations.

Similarly, it is not clear, from the data collected, how the discipline-specific communicative genres outlined in the comments made by faculty are reflective of the communicative genres students will be exposed to, and will be expected to adapt to, when out of the classroom. A student preparing for a presentation in a chemistry class, and adapting to a communication genre specific to the field of academic chemists, may find that if they do not enter academia but instead apply their knowledge of chemistry in the business world, they will be forced to adapt to a new, and very different, communication genre. This is a greater concern for students who change their majors, or enter new fields for graduate work, when their "speaking intensive" experience as an undergraduate expected them to adapt to a discipline-specific communication genre that is now not applicable. Finally, the immersion of a student in a discipline-specific communication genre is akin to only teaching a student in a public speaking course to give impromptu speeches. They will remain relatively inflexible communicators. This is why, in its endorsement of speaking across the curriculum programs, the National Communication Association was careful to state that it expected that speaking across the curriculum courses served only as a supplement to, and not in place of, the basic communication class (Schneider, 1999). It is important that students develop a variety of communication skills in a way that underscores the values associated with an engaged communication theory.

Implications for the Discipline—Across the Campus and Across the Country

As was noted earlier in this chapter, since the first debates in NCA over the proposal of a communication across the curriculum project, there has been a growing concern over the designation of courses as 'speaking intensive' that are not only not taught by communication faculty, but that do not teach communication theory (Schneider, 1999). Central to these criticisms is the fear that our discipline is not/will not be respected within academia. Hardly a new problem, the field of rhetoric and communication has long suffered from a lack of respect, as many of our colleagues view much of what we do as something between providing simple technical guidance to speakers to peddling modern sophistry (Condit, 1990; Schneider, 1999). What is notable about this survey, however, is that it suggests that even after the university's speaking intensive program has been in place for several years, little has been done to garner the respect and understanding across campus that we both need and deserve. There is broad support for the need that our students develop their communication skills; however, there is clearly little agreement on what that should entail. This is not only a concern for our campus, but it is also suggestive of how little credit communication and rhetoric is given throughout academe for doing much more than outlining technical aspects of presentation strategies. If the level of respectability of communication and rhetoric on a campus with both a speaking across the curriculum program and a communication center cannot be elevated, then there would appear to be little hope of garnering broader support for the discipline.

What this means for the further development of programs such as the University of Mary Washington Speaking Intensive Program and the assignments required for its courses is an important concern. Questions remain: Should all SI courses require a standard section on communication theory? How far should we allow those courses to be adapted to the specific needs of a discipline? Should we be concerned with the mix of SI courses a particular student takes? Of primary concern, both for this chapter and for the SI program, however, is how the communication center adapts to the use of discipline-specific communication genres. After all, in a university where a student's SI requirements can be (and are often encouraged to be) satisfied by taking courses outside of the communication program, the communication center is often our first, and sometimes only, level of direct contact with the student. Given this placement within the speaking across the curriculum program and the university, the communication center, and its consultants, are necessarily charged (and some may say burdened) with the need to represent the communication discipline and all it has to offer. It is possible that the center may fulfill the role outlined for the basic communication course by bridging the needs of the discipline-specific speaking intensive course with the rest of our discipline.

Informing this role is the work done by scholars in communication in the disciplines (CID) which notes the ways in which discipline specific oral genres can be both better developed and understood by students within this model, as these courses provide sites of knowledge production within the discipline (Dannels, 2002; Dannels & Gaffney, 2009). This approach is steeped in the notion that a broader rhetorical/communicative understanding of how we communicate about, reflect upon, and produce knowledge will direct speaking across the curriculum courses to a deeper appreciation for the discipline and how we communicate. This says that we do more in these courses than simply prevent "mallspeak" and superficially adapt to our audience, and we do not merely adopt a preordained speaking style specific to that discipline. In fact, speaking across the curriculum courses allow students and faculty to develop "complex, sophisticated meanings associated with speaking and the role of orality in their epistemologies and pedagogies" (Dannels, 2002; Dannels & Gaffney, 2009). In other words, adaptive strategies allow for a more detailed understanding of the discipline and the student's place within it.

The communication center is a natural site for this type of knowledge production to begin because it is complementary to the Speaking Across the Curriculum program. It is not only a resource for students registered in SI courses, it is also a resource for faculty and administrators interested in gauging the health of the speaking across the curriculum program and its students' communication skills. As an interface between the communication specialists that oversee the speaking across the curriculum program, the students enrolled in the courses, and potentially the faculty teaching those courses, the communication center can both reflect the development of the speaking across the curriculum project, and, more importantly, drive that development through the employment of sophisticated rhetorical techniques. This entails, necessarily, an affirmation within the communication center that, in the same way that the writing center does more than just check for grammatical mistakes, the communication center provides students with a framework for understanding and communicating that permeates not only every aspect of the speaking assignment (and not just its presentation), but also every aspect of the course. In other words, the communication center creates the site and begins to produce the knowledge our students need for a richer understanding of what it means to develop and use communication genres. Is this compatible with a project that collects and uses discipline-specific communication genres? Yes, if they are contextualized and employed with the student's and consultant's full knowledge and understanding that they are being employed. This may mean starting by outlining how a student can adapt to the requirements of a particular course/discipline, and how that differs from other disciplines, or discussing some of the reasons why these specific genres have developed. In all cases, an effort is made to add value to the consultation by providing the student with the information and guidance requested, while making clear what makes that information and guidance useful in this instance.

This is a tall order for the communication center, and it should not be assumed that the center is capable of alone doing all that we may wish discipline-specific SI courses do over the course of a semester. The broader changes will only occur if broader measures are taken, including the development of similar strategies throughout the speaking across the curriculum program. It may not be the only site, but the communication center is *a* site for this type of knowledge production. Furthermore, the communication center is also a site for the production of knowledge about the very nature of our discipline and how we may better meet the needs of our students within speaking across the curriculum and communication in the disciplines programs. There is much we should do to better inform our students and our colleagues about the importance and value of our discipline, and perhaps a necessary first step is to better inform ourselves about how our discipline is perceived and how it is placed within a speaking across the curriculum program.

References

Bazerman, C. (2005). A response to Anthony Fleury's "Liberal education and communication against the disciplines": A view from the world of writing. *Communication Education, 54*, 86 – 91.

Condit, C. M. (1990). The birth of understanding: Chaste science and the harlot of the arts. *Communication Monographs, 57*, 323 – 327.

Cronin, M., & Glenn, P. (1991). Oral communication across-the-curriculum in higher education: The state of the art. *Communication Education, 40*, 356 – 367.

Cronin, M., & Grice, G. (1991). Oral communication cross the curriculum: Implementation and accreditation issues. *The Carolinas Speech Communication Annual VII*, 34 – 45.

Dannels, D. (2001). Time to speak up: A theoretical framework of situated pedagogy and practice for communication across the curriculum. *Communication Education, 50*, 144 – 158.

Dannels, D. (2002). Communication across the curriculum and in the disciplines: Speaking in engineering. *Communication Education, 51*, 254 – 268.

Dannels, D., Anson, C., Bullard, L., & Peretti, S. (2003). Challenges in learning communication skills in chemical engineering. *Communication Education, 52*, 50 – 56.

Dannels, D., & Gaffney, A. (2009). Communication across the curriculum and in the disciplines: A call for scholarly cross-curricular advocacy. *Communication Education, 58*, 124 – 153.

Darling, A. (2005). Public presentations in mechanical engineering and the discourse of technology. *Communication Education, 54*, 20 – 33.

Darling, A. L., & Dannels, D. (2003). Practicing engineers talk about the importance of talk: A report on the role of oral communication in the workplace. *Communication Education, 52*, 1 – 16.

Engleberg, I., Emanuel, R., Van Horn, T. & Bodary. (2008). Communication Education in U.S. Community Colleges. *Communication Education, 57*, 241 – 265.

Fleury, A. (2005). Liberal education and communication against the curriculum. *Communication Education, 54*, 72 – 79.

Garside, C. (2002). Seeing the forest throught the trees: A challenge facing communication across the curriculum programs. *Communication Education, 51*, 51 – 64.

Hay, E. (1988). Communication across the curriculum. *Virginia Journal of Communication, 9*, 1 – 19.

Hobgood, L. (2000). The pursuit of speaking proficiency: A voluntary approach. *Communication Education, 49*, 339 – 351.

Morello, J. (2000). Comparing speaking across the curriculum and writing across the curriculum programs. *Communication Education, 49*, 99 – 113.

Morreale, S. (2003). Communication skills essential for scientists in today's job market. *Spectra 39*(2), Washington DC: National Communication Association.

Morreale, S., Hugenberg, L., & Worley, D. (2006). The basic communication course at U.S. colleges and universities in the 21st century: Study VII. *Communication Education, 55*, 415 – 437.

Morreale, S., & Pearson, J. (2008). Why communication education is important: The centrality of the discipline in the 21st century. *Communication Education, 57*, 224 – 240.

National Communication Association, Proceedings from the Communication Across the Curriculum Strand. (2001). Summer Conference: Engaging 21st Century Communication Students. Retrieved from http://www.natcom.org/Instruction/summerconf/summerconf.htm

Palmerton, P. (1996). *Talking, learning: Oral communication in the classroom.* Unpublished manuscript, Hamline University.

Palmerton, P. (2005). Liberal education and communication across the curriculum: A response to Anthony Fleury. *Communication Education, 54*, 80 – 85.

Roberts, C. (1983). Speaking and listening education across the curriculum. In R. B. Rubin (Ed.), *Improving speaking and listening skills. New directions for college learning assistance, no. 12.* (pp. 47 – 58). San Francisco: Jossey-Bass.

Schneider, A. (1999, March 26). Taking aim at incoherence: Spread of speech programs across the curriculum irks some communication professors. *Chronicle of Higher Education*, A16.

Scott, R. L. (1967). On viewing rhetoric as epistemic. *Central States Speech Journal, 18*, 9 – 17.

Weiss, R. O. (1999). Discourse fields across the curriculum. In *A Robert Orr Weiss Retrospective* (pp. 39 – 54). Depauw University: Greencastle, IN.

Zernicke, K. (1999, January 31). Talk is, like, you know, cheapened: Colleges introduce classes to clean up campus "mallspeak." *The Boston Globe*, A1.

Chapter 7

The Blind Leading the Blind? An Ethnographic Heuristic for Communication Centers

Deanna P. Dannels and Amy L. Housley Gaffney

"Fieldwork is one answer—some say the best—to the question of how the understanding of others, close or distant, is achieved."

John Van Maanen (1988), *Tales From the Field*

John Van Maanen, an organizational researcher known for his contributions to qualitative research methods, argues that one of the only ways to truly understand another culture is to submerse yourself in the life, norms, and activities of that culture. He is well known for the ways in which he does "fieldwork"—the act of going into the naturalistic setting of another culture and working to understand their daily activities. This process of going out into the field requires the researcher to leave his or her environment and walk into the environment of those being studied.

By contrast, the communication center is generally conceived of as a place students come *to*, not a place that goes *out* to students. Physically, many communication centers exist in central campus locations. Administratively, communication centers are often funded by central administrative units. Philosophically, communication centers support student communication activities and processes when those students come to them for help, not by going out to interact with students as they go through their daily classes and activities. Although some centers have initiatives where the director or tutors go out to classes to introduce themselves, demystify the center's purposes, and recruit students to participate, one of the main selling points of many communication centers is that students do not *have* to participate. The leap of faith, then, is that with a quality center, students will participate. The line from the film *Field of Dreams* comes to mind—communication centers work hard to make the mantra "if you build it, they will come" come true.

When students come to communication centers, though, they are coming for help on communication assignments that are often situated in unfamiliar content areas, contextualized within new classroom expectations, and localized within disciplines that feel foreign to them. Their challenge, therefore, is to be successful in a context that is often not their own. Even though they may be majors in the discipline in which they are being asked to perform, they usually are not yet experts in the communication expectations of that discipline. Moreover, even if they are being asked to perform within a general education course, it is likely still a specialized context in which they are new and unfamiliar. Given this, many students cannot bring the situated, contextual disciplinary expertise to the table when they arrive at the center. The tutors, as well, are typically not disciplinary experts in the situated expectations for particular oral communication assignments. Therefore, the perfect storm exists—the blind leading the blind towards hopeful success on communication assignments that carry with them the cultural weight of the discipline in which they exist.

What if, though, communication centers could gain insight into the often mysterious "other" discipline in which the student is participating through reframing from the "if we build it, they will come" mindset to a "we will come to you" mindset? Such a mindset—driven by an ethnographic heuristic—would suggest that communication centers philosophically and pedagogically go "into the field" of the disciplines in which their clients (students) live. We argue that a programmatic commitment to an ethnographic heuristic can reframe the traditional role of the communication center and hence begin to address the challenges brought to the fore when the blind are leading the blind.

Background: Communication Across the Curriculum and Communication in the Disciplines

At its core, communication across the curriculum (CXC) is a movement focused on improving students' learning and communication abilities through integrating communication into courses across the curriculum. For more than 35 years, communication faculty and administrators have infused curricula on their campuses with communication assignments, ranging from short speeches to discussion to debate. Much of the early discussion surrounding CXC was centered on describing how the movement could be established and providing justifications for why the movement was necessary (Dannels & Housley Gaffney, 2009). In the late 1990s, the movement was centered on reflecting critically on what had been accomplished while at the same time expanding the scope of CXC. In the past 10 years, the emphasis has been on exploring new realms (specifically, communication in the disciplines) and engaging in empirical investigations of CXC settings.

Throughout their history, though, communication-across-the-curriculum programs have usually been guided by two goals: "to increase the typical student's exposure to communication content and ways of thinking fostered by such content, and to increase learning of non-communication subject matter through the processes of message formation and delivery of that content in both written and oral forms" (Steinfatt, 1986, p. 465). These goals work to address the reality that many non-communication majors take no more than one course in communication—and sometimes none at all when the general education requirement is not in place (Cronin, Grice, & Palmerton, 2000). When CXC programs become students' only exposure to communication as a discipline, then, their success is important and often dependent on faculty training, program quality, balance in focus on communication versus course content, and developmental sequencing of communication activities (Hay, 1987).

Although CXC can take many different forms, there are several trends in programs that help explain the depth and breadth of the movement. Generally, CXC programs typically build on introductory communication courses (a trend which is advocated by professional organizations such as the National Communication Association) and provide extensions of communication into other disciplinary courses in various ways. Sometimes, CXC manifests itself as designated communication-intensive or speaking-intensive courses, of which students must complete a particular number in order to graduate (Cronin et al., 2000). These courses may also be tailored within specific disciplines so that a psychology major, for example, must take a particular upper-division psychology course that emphasizes communication. Instructors of these disciplinary courses are then supported through a central program on campus (or, in the case of some institutions, individual communication faculty who have the expertise and desire to help). Support can take the form of training, where faculty from other disciplines are trained in communication skills and content to the extent that they need to teach it to their students. Or, support may also be in the form of consulting, where communication scholars maintain an on-going relationship with specific faculty members and provide support to those faculty members and sometimes their students. Regardless of the above logistics of CXC, institutions implementing CXC typically support students in completing communication assignments outside of the introductory speech course. The nature of those assignments can vary greatly, and many institutions are now emphasizing a discipline-specific approach to CXC.

The discipline-specific approach to CXC has also emerged as a central part of CXC scholarship. Within the past decade, CXC scholars have highlighted the importance of recognizing the situated nature of communication within particular disciplines. The communication in the disciplines (CID) framework (Dannels, 2001) argues that because communication is—by its nature—contextual and localized, communication instruction should not be generic, but should be situated within the specific discipline's communication genres and understandings of competence. The move to situate communication instruction is further supported by accreditation boards in specific disciplines. For example, the Accreditation Board for Engineering and Technology articulates the importance of students' ability to communicate in the situated communication activities representative of that discipline (e.g., multidisciplinary teams).

The move to situated communication is also grounded in the philosophical belief that communication competence is locally defined and negotiated. For example, research from engineering suggests that effective communication means keeping information simple, focusing on results first, providing numerical support, and a focus on the object or visual, rather than on the speaker (Dannels, 2002; Darling, 2005). These criteria are different in important ways from the criteria for effective communication in design (e.g., architecture) critiques: effective critiques include a comprehensive explanation of visuals, transparent advocacy for design intent, a credible presentation style, and professional interaction management (Dannels, Housley Gaffney, & Norris Martin, 2008).

In contrast, within the field of medical education, Brown (2008) noted that attentive listening, varied question styles (both open and closed), clarification, summarizing, and both verbal and nonverbal rapport, were key to processing information from patients in order to make an effective diagnosis. Detailed explanations of communication skills required for breaking bad medical news include establishing an agenda for the interaction, tailoring information to the patient, providing information in ways that can be recalled and checking recall, responding empathically to emotion, and closing the interaction (Brown & Bylund, 2008).

In addition to differences in the definition of effective communication, disciplines also vary in the kinds of communication activities (or genres) relevant for their students. For example, both engineering and design students give presentations on a design they have developed, but design students are expected to demonstrate a personal interest in the design, while engineering students must distance themselves (e.g., Dannels, 2001, 2002; Dannels et al., 2008). On the other hand, students in medical fields need to learn how to share complex, possibly threatening information in one-on-one interactions with patients, rather than in formal presentations of projects (e.g, Brown, 2008; Brown & Bylund, 2008).

The diversity of communication just among these three disciplines is a microcosm of the broader complexities involved with teaching and learning communication in multiple contexts. For students, these complexities often emerge when they are facing an unknown communication assignment with discipline-specific requirements and standards for success. CXC practitioners do not have the luxury, usually, to provide students with the full support necessary to be successful in their communication assignments. Even though the assignment may be well written, thorough, and clear, it is possible that students are still struggling to understand what is expected of them (Straub, 1996). Therefore, communication centers provide excellent resources for students faced with communication assignments; at the same time, this movement to discipline-specific communication introduces new challenges for communication centers and their tutors.

Challenges of Disciplinarity

Although a discipline-specific communication across the curriculum framework allows for students to be entrenched and engaged in communication activities that will be relevant and timely for their future professional activities, a commitment to disciplinarity does generate several challenges for communication centers. Specifically, when students are involved in discipline-specific oral communication assignments, three challenges come to the fore: 1) understanding discipline-specific genres and communicative norms, 2) balancing communication expertise with disciplinary expertise, and 3) addressing perceived gaps between communicative form and content. The following section will illustrate these challenges and provide examples of how they might emerge in communication center activities.

Understanding Discipline-Specific Genres and Communicative Norms

It is likely that students who come to communication centers from a basic course or hybrid general education course will show up with fairly traditional communication assignments (e.g., an informative speech, a persuasive speech, a call-to-action speech). Yet students who are enrolled in disciplinary courses (in their major, for example) committed to situated, context-specific oral communication activities could very well show up at a communication center with assignments that are unfamiliar to the administration or tutors there. These assignments often reflect, in structure and content, the expectations for what it means to be a successful communicator in the particular discipline (Dannels, 2001, 2002). The challenge for communication centers then becomes one of deciphering the assignments to understand those expectations, as well as the broader communicative culture of the discipline.

For example, a software engineering student could be assigned a "scrum report" or a "sprint meeting." This oral assignment (often called by both names) occurs when a team has just finished a cycle of product development—called a "sprint"—and has produced a working version of the software. Typically, each developer on the team is required to spend five minutes or less detailing his/her task, time spent, work performed, estimate of percentage complete and problems encountered. This oral event usually becomes a breakpoint where audiences can measure progress in order to then share information with the customer, recognizing that the customer can change his/her mind, which would necessitate adjusting customer requirements for the next phase of software development.

A clearly outlined assignment description can provide students and center tutors with a basic understanding the purpose and function of the "sprint meeting" or the "scrum report." For example, there are usually particular assigned roles (e.g., scrum master, product owner, etc.) and generally these meetings are strictly timed. These disciplinary expectations might show up on the assignment sheet, providing tutors with a clear sense of some of the communicative expectations of the discipline. Yet the broader picture of the communicative culture of the "scrum" and its implementation might not appear in the assignment sheet. For example, often the scrum master or manager interrupts the speaker to ask questions or to pose suggestions. There is usually a whiteboard with task slips or project ideas that developers use as they discuss the day's work. In addition to these pragmatic issues, some of the additional disciplinary hues that color this genre add depth to the communication event. To explain: in agile product development teams such as those engaged in the "sprint meeting" or "scrum," there are those who are completely committed to the project and accountable for its outcomes. Additionally, there are those who are contributors to the project, but not necessarily fully accountable for its outcomes; they play more of a consultative role. In scrum vocabulary, there are chickens and pigs. The fable of the chickens and pigs goes something like this: the chicken and the pig get together to work on a breakfast of ham and eggs. In the quandary about whether to engage in this collaboration, the pig notes that for the chicken, only a contribution is expected; but the pig must give a total sacrifice. The chicken is involved, but the pig is committed.

While this might seem like a superficial fable to better understand team roles in software development, it plays out in important ways in communication activities such as the "scrum report" or the "sprint meeting." Students might need to understand why particular members are given more leeway to talk, while others are not. An understanding of who is fully accountable and who is a merely a contributor to the team is important to the overall success of the meeting and provides a communication framework for analyzing and planning communication behaviors. This kind of cultural understanding might or might not appear on an assignment sheet for a "scrum meeting" or a "sprint meeting" but it could possibly influence the ways in which team members communicate on a particular project.

This illustration is just one example of how a discipline-specific genre has particular forms, activities, norms, and cultural meanings associated with it. Broadening the example, in all disciplines, there are significant cultural ways of speaking (Philipsen, 1992), or rhetorical "argument fields" (Nelson, Megill, & McCloskey, 1990) that value particular forms of evidence, reasoning, and persuasion over others. The task, then, becomes understanding those fields and ways of speaking well enough (and in a very short time) to support students in learning them as well. These particularities of cultural ways of speaking and argument fields might not necessarily show up on an assignment sheet. Therefore the challenge arises for communication centers to understand enough depth about the disciplinary norms and culture in order to best support students' progress with the oral communication assignment.

Balancing Communication Expertise with Disciplinary Expertise

Communication centers are in a distinct position of being the recipients of the disciplinary seeds often planted by communication-across-the-curriculum advocates working from a situated perspective. If CID advocates are successful, then students will be engaging in communication assignments and activities that are born of the communicative needs, norms, genres, and competencies that are most valued within the discipline. Yet this centering of the disciplinary also brings with it a challenge of expertise: What if the norms and valued communication competencies of a particular discipline are not in direct alignment with that which is considered "good practice" from the communication perspective? Which expertise should be privileged?

For example, in disciplines of design (architecture, landscape architecture, graphic design, etc.) the primary oral communication activity is a "critique" (Dannels, 2005). The purpose of the critique is for the designer to showcase the progress on his or her design. Lower-stakes critiques happen literally at the desk—with one audience member (usually the teacher) listening to the student describe his or her design progress. In higher stakes critiques (often called "pin ups") students pin up their prototype on the wall (if possible) and present the progress on the design. Formal critiques happen at the end of a project and typically have both an internal and external audience. For all critiques, it is typical for the students to present for a short amount of time, after which the majority of the critique happens in the feedback session—where audience members ask questions about the design and students respond.

This feedback portion of the critique can be a high-pressure event. At times audience members ask extremely harsh questions and provide candid feedback on what does not work in the design (Anthony, 1991). There are moments, in fact, where the critic provides feedback that (to students) feels person-focused rather than focused on the design itself (Dannels, Housley Gaffney, & Norris Martin, 2011). This feedback is not necessarily in direct alignment with what some theories suggest about good feedback interventions which recommend a focus on the work, rather than on the personal, ego-involved aspects of the presentation (King & Behnke, 1999; Kluger & DeNisi, 1996). Yet in some design circles, this kind of feedback is valued; in fact, it is lauded as preparing students for the design workplace by mirroring some of the communicative behaviors that emerge outside of the classroom. In this case, the communication center is placed in a difficult position of having to support the students while potentially hearing of communicative behavior that is not in alignment with some of the core tenets of the communication discipline and the theories within it.

In another example, engineering students often have to give design presentations in which they speak to an audience (either a mock professional audience or an audience comprised of actual industry members) about their design product. In this disciplinary culture, members will often claim that the "object" (or the design product) should speak for itself, illustrating a broader cultural commitment to a discourse focused less on the person than the product. As Darling (2005) suggests: "in communities driven by the discourse of technology, speaking effectiveness occurs when the rhetor persuades without explicitly calling upon the ethos of the speaker" (p. 31). In this discipline, the focus on the object often elides the importance of the speaker—and yet the concept of ethos (and we would also suggest pathos and logos) is entirely wrapped around the speaker and is one of our core foci in public speaking pedagogy. Therefore, there is a potential that communication center staff and tutors are faced with students who are living in a communicative, disciplinary culture that contradicts some of the key pillars of communication pedagogy and practice.

Addressing Perceived Gaps Between Communication and Content

When students are involved with discipline-specific oral communication assignments and activities, there are often situated complexities that characterize those events. Those on the outside are not always privy to those complexities. Communication center tutors and staff, being structurally on the outside, can often be perceived by disciplinary members as peripheral to the actual work happening in the activity. Therefore, communication tutors—much as communication-across-the-curriculum advocates have experienced—could get relegated to helping students focus on form, presumably as distinct from disciplinary content. This persistent perceived gap between disciplinary form and content can present a real challenge to communication center tutors—tying their hands in a way that is not necessarily beneficial to the students.

For example, studies completed in engineering suggest that students often perceive communication as different than the "real work" of engineers (Dannels, 2002; Sullivan & Kedrowicz, in press). Some perceive the numbers as paramount to the communication event—distinct from the opinions and emotions that emerge when trying to communicate without numbers (Dannels, 2002). Communication is seen as a "soft" discipline, distinct from the "hard" numbers valued by engineering audiences (Sullivan & Kedrowicz, in press).

This perception that disciplinary content is distinct from the communication activities in which that content lives causes some hierarchical and practical challenges. Hierarchically, if communication is seen as separate from disciplinary content, and in some cases not the "real work" of the discipline, then it is relegated to a subordinate position. Even if there are situations where content is significantly more important than communication, the distinction between communication and content could translate into a distinction between content and delivery. Especially in cases where the oral genre is highly disciplinary (and hence it is unlikely that an outsider can understand the complexities of the content), it seems possible that students appear wanting support in polishing delivery, professionalizing a PowerPoint, or overcoming anxiety.

Although these are potentially important areas of support for students who come to communication centers, the perceived gap between communication and content could cause a challenge for a tutor or communication expert who is trying to support students in making content revisions. A student in computer science, for example, could come to a communication center looking for help on a poster presentation she is required to do for a mock scientific convention. If the tutor is unfamiliar with the content of the scientific design process, and the student is pressed for time, the tutor/student time will probably be spent on layout, color, talking points, and font choices (for example). Although these are important aspects of the poster presentation, treating them as separate from the disciplinary content reifies a perceptual gap that allows communication to be relegated as distinct from the "real work" of (fill in the blank discipline). Such distinction works against what we know can be true of communication and disciplinary knowledge construction—that by engaging in situated communication activities, students can bridge the gap between knowing the content and doing communication of that content (Bazerman, 1998; Housley Gaffney, 2010; Winsor, 1998).

Navigating Disciplinary Challenges: An Ethnographic Heuristic

It might seem that the aforementioned challenges that accompany discipline-specific communication assignments would leave communication centers in a seemingly impossible position. Certainly providing generic support for communication competencies cannot hurt. But when students appear with assignments that are highly discipline-specific, this generic support might not provide them with the tools for success. Therefore, it seems important that communication centers take on the responsibility for addressing disciplinary challenges so that they are prepared to offer faculty and students help that is relevant to their disciplinary work. In this section, we suggest that these challenges can be best navigated by a theoretical, pedagogical, and programmatic commitment to an ethnographic heuristic that—by reframing the traditional role of the communication center—builds an interdisciplinary foundation that can withstand emergent challenges.

To explain, an ethnographic heuristic suggests that the communication center becomes a space that works to bridge gaps between disciplinary boundaries by approaching the oral communication activity or assignment (and the students' enactment of it) from the inside looking out instead of from the outside looking in. Doing this allows tutors more insight into the important meanings associated with communication in the disciplines. In this way, tutors would not approach the oral communication assignment or activity from a "blind" perspective. Although the students might not be able to provide more than minimal information about the disciplinary activities, relationships, and communication styles; reframing the role of the center within an ethnographic heuristic makes the discovery of that information an important piece of the instructional process. By reframing the tasks of the communication center towards ethnographic discovery, as well, there is a potential to address many of the challenges emerging when students are asked to perform disciplinary genres that are foreign to the tutors. Although a commitment to discovery and understanding, by definition, places the center in a learning role, as opposed to a teaching role, this reframe does not necessarily mean that communication centers can or should not have a role in teaching—and in some cases changing the communicative cultural patterns, norms and behaviors of particular disciplines. Rather, an ethnographic heuristic presumes that if change is important and necessary, communication centers can best accomplish it if they have built an interdisciplinary relationship characterized by curiosity, empathy, trust, and identification. An ethnographic heuristic allows communication centers to engage in relational interactions that can build such a relationship.

In this section, we outline this ethnographic heuristic by discussing four ways of reframing the activities and participants within a communication center that can build a relationship of empathy, trust, and identification. Specifically, we suggest an ethnographic heuristic for communication centers would view: 1) the communication assignment as a window into disciplinary interactions, 2) the students as actors in dynamic activity systems, 3) the tutor as an engaged participant in disciplinary work, and 4) the instructional interaction as an exploration of parallel emics (the communicative norms, beliefs, and values that are particular to the discipline). These four components are represented in figure 7.1.

Figure 7.1. Ethnographic Heuristic for Communication Centers

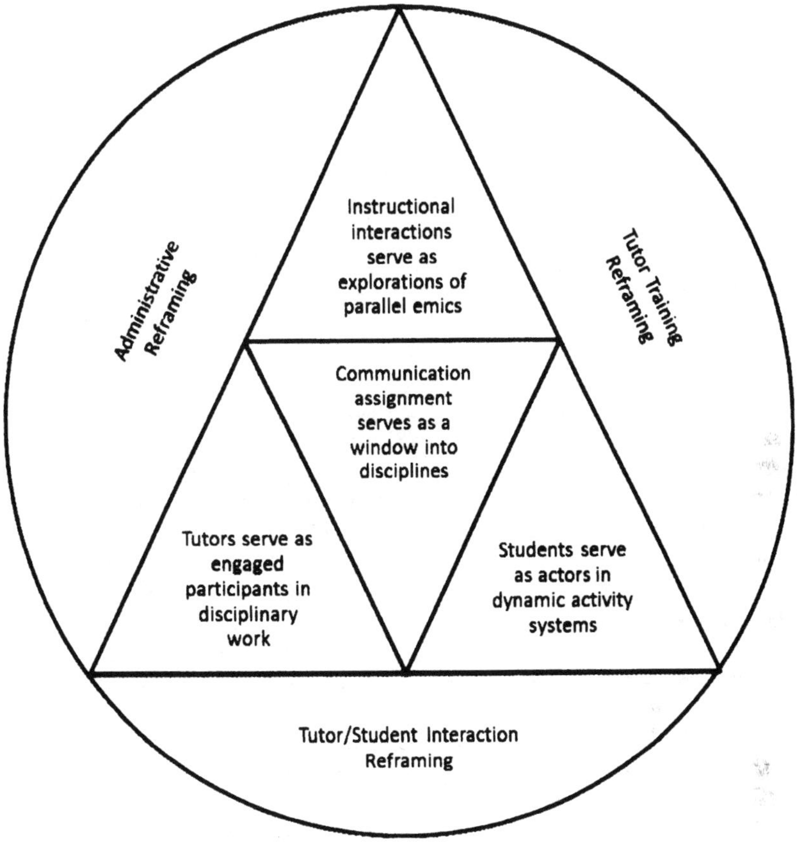
Instructional interactions serve as explorations of parallel emics
Administrative Reframing
Tutor Training Reframing
Communication assignment serves as a window into disciplines
Tutors serve as engaged participants in disciplinary work
Students serve as actors in dynamic activity systems
Tutor/Student Interaction Reframing

The Communication Assignment as a Window into Disciplinary Interactions

As illustrated, several theorists suggest that speaking is a cultural, disciplinary activity (Nelson et al., 1990; Philipsen, 1992). If you presume that each distinct culture has its own distinct speech code (Philipsen, 1992), then disciplines (as cultures) also have particular codes of speaking and communicating (referred to as disciplinary argument fields by Nelson et al., 1990). The oral communication assignment and other relevant materials that students bring to tutors in the communication center can hold clues to these cultural ways of speaking. Instead of viewing the assignment as functional, then, an ethnographic heuristic would suggest tutors should view the assignment as cultural. Such a perspective is grounded in ethnographic research practices, which assume cultures are not static, but rather composed of complex social actions, artifacts, and semiotic practices. Ethnographers rely on thick description of these actions, artifacts, and practices in order to understand relevant beliefs, practices, and values (Geertz, 1973).

Part of viewing the oral communication assignment as cultural not only involves looking at the assignment for insights into the expectations for speaking and the implicit or explicit norms for speaking in the discipline, but also understanding the assignment as it provides insight into particular disciplinary relationships and interactions. Specifically, the assignment has clues within it about the relational genre knowledge (Dannels, 2009) important for students' success. Relational genre knowledge suggests it is important not only to understand the structure or function of the oral communication activity but also the relevant relational interactions embedded within that activity. Specifically, relational genre knowledge calls attention to how students can and should "negotiate the relational and identity nuances . . . real and simulated, actual and idealized" (Dannels, 2009, p. 422) within the communication activity. An ethnographic heuristic would challenge centers to understand the oral communication assignment as a window into these culturally laden relational interactions.

Viewing the oral communication assignment as an ethnographic artifact could remind center tutors of these broader disciplinary meanings associated with the oral communication event. The tutor might not be able to discern the full complexities of the disciplinary culture from the assignment, but the tutor can become sensitized to important disciplinary values that could facilitate the tutorial process. If the challenge is in understanding the disciplinary culture and norms, navigating this challenge involves seeing the oral communication assignment as a product of some of those disciplinary norms and looking at the assignment with a lens that is focused on finding clues about the disciplinary relationships and ways of speaking culturally that are embedded in the assignment itself.

Working from this framework, communication centers could ask three central questions of the oral communication assignment: 1) What are the distinct disciplinary forms of speaking called for in this communication assignment? 2) What are the distinct disciplinary relational interactions (between speaker and audience) called for in this communication assignment, and 3) What are the distinct disciplinary expectations for performance called for in this communication assignment? Such questions, although they might not be able to be answered fully by simply looking at the assignment, can serve as a guide and reminder to tutors that the assignment can be a window into disciplinary interactions and norms that are important to the communicative activity.

The Students as Actors in Dynamic Activity Systems

Oral communication assignments in the classroom exist within complex activity systems that often bring together multiple audiences, expectations, and roles (Russell, 1997). Often assignments that are discipline-specific have a preprofessional element to them, which requires teachers and students to navigate academic and simulated contexts (e.g., an assignment that is supposed to simulate a workplace presentation existing within an academic setting). Such assignments prove difficult for students who are called upon to negotiate the actual (e.g., academic) identities and expectations with the simulated (e.g., future workplace) identities and expectations (Dannels, 2000; Freedman, Adam, & Smart, 1994). Often these systems are not static, either, and students are consistently working to interact with others who might not necessarily communicate in predictable ways. An ethnographic heuristic, then, reframes the students into actors within a larger communicative event, rather than isolated learners in need of support on one assignment.

Reframing the issue in this manner also means viewing students as dynamic agents of social and rhetorical action, rather than as static recipients of communication instruction. Recognizing the dynamic nature of the oral activity is about recognizing that the assignment or oral genre is not necessarily just about its form or function, but that it is about social and rhetorical process (Miller, 1984). Students, then, are participating in a recurrent system of social action, rather than a single presentation or speech. The tutor, then, could benefit the student by helping him or her recognize the multiple contexts within which the assignment occurs and the dynamic nature of the roles the students might need to play in those contexts.

For example, a design presentation assignment could necessitate that students translate technical information for a simulated lay audience, but at the same time students could be required to display their technical expertise for their actual audience. A team presentation assignment could ask students to showcase each member's speaking abilities within the academic context, even though workplace contexts would necessitate delegation of speaking responsibilities or use of technological support to streamline speaking for asynchronous viewing. Some of these potential conflicts might appear in the assignment itself. But if they do not, helping the student understand the dynamic nature of the speaking event could prove helpful. To this end, three key questions could help tutors better understand the dynamic activity systems within which the oral assignment lives: 1) What various communicative contexts are identified or implied as important for this communication assignment? 2) What potential role conflicts might students face in completing this oral assignment? 3) How might students rhetorically manage the varied expectations that emerge as a result of these multiple contexts or roles? Answers to these questions might not be fully fleshed out within the assignment itself, but asking the questions about the students' role as an actor within the larger system could allow the tutor to help reframe the role of the student from a passive one to a more active one within the disciplinary community.

The Tutor as an Engaged Participant

Traditionally, tutors in communication centers are in the role of being a consultant to students who need help (Wilde, Cuny, & Vizzier, 2006). As a consultant, by definition, the tutor does not participate in the communication assignment other than providing support for the student. Yet such a role further reifies the disciplinary boundaries between the student and the tutor and could perpetuate the perception that the tutor is only there to support the communication form or structure of the assignment, whereas the student is the sole owner of the communication and disciplinary content. If the tutor remains on the outside, they can only provide an "etic" (Pike, 1967) perspective—one that takes generalized communication constructs or pedagogies and overlays them on the disciplinary assignment or experience of the student. This perspective might not, though, provide students with what is necessary to be successful within a highly situated context.

Seeing the tutor through the lens of an engaged participant could help solve this problem. The concept of ethnographic engagement merges scholarship and practice in qualitative research methods and necessitates that the researcher make every attempt to move away from an etic perspective and become part of the culture he or she is studying through participation with those who are in that culture. It is difficult, of course, for the researcher to become fully native unless he or she spends a significant amount of time living as a participant observer in the culture (Patton, 2002). Such a stance, in research, places the researcher in the role of trying to live vicariously and gain understanding of the participants' world without judgment. The researcher is called upon to show "openness, sensitivity, respect, awareness, and responsiveness . . . it means being fully present (mindfulness)" (Patton, 2002, p. 40). This process allows researchers to gain an insider perspective—referred to as an emic perspective. Derived from the linguistic concepts phone*mic*s and phone*tic*s, an emic perspective in one that acknowledges the distinct and unique perspective of particular cultures (e.g., phonemics focuses on sounds used only in a single linguistic system) and an etic perspective focuses on universals shared across cultures (e.g., phonetics focuses on the universal aspects of languages). From a pure emic perspective, each culture has distinct cultures and no comparisons can be made across cultures, given their particular nature. Such a perspective can only be gained, in research, through informants who are native to that culture. Researchers, though, attempt to approximate an emic perspective by going into the field and understanding the culture through consistent interactions with them.

Tutors, as engaged participants, could acknowledge the conceptual schemes and categories that are regarded as meaningful, appropriate, and distinct to the members of the discipline in which the student is currently living. Essentially, as an engaged participant, the tutor could work towards gaining an emic perspective by placing validity in the interpretations of the insiders, given that the tutor best knows their distinct culture. Although tutors often work to apply generalizable communication concepts across disciplinary cultures, there could be problems associated with placing universals on a culture for which those universals might not hold meaning. In fact, in cross-cultural research, the process of assuming these universals or imposing them across cultures is considered an "imposed etic" (Berry, 1969) or a "pseudo etic" (Triandis, Malpass, & Davidson, 1971) because it does not recognize the distinct nature of the culture at hand. Tutors focused only on imposed communication universals could miss some of the distinct expectations of particular disciplinary assignments. An ethnographic heuristic would place the tutor in a more engaged, participatory role with the student, assignment, and representative disciplines, avoiding the problems that could emerge when imposing universals on particular communication events.

Admittedly, the tutoring context rarely presents the tutor with the opportunity to engage in the field—the naturalistic activities of the discipline (e.g., attending disciplinary classes, etc.)—but it is possible for the tutor to adopt the role of the engaged participant and to remain open and empathetic to the disciplinary activities that come to the table during the tutoring session. Being fully present in the tutoring space is not only about being present with the students' needs or questions or concerns, but it is being fully present with the disciplinary culture represented in the assignment that is brought to the center. Adopting this kind of mindset could break down the perceptual gap between form and content by placing the tutor in more of a collaborative role with the student as an engaged and emphatic participant in the tutoring session. Furthermore, this type of approach values working *with* students rather than *for* students.

Three questions might encourage the kind of engaged, empathetic participation discussed here: 1) How can the tutor become versed in the communicative content of the oral communication assignment and course (essentially, how can the tutor go into the field while remaining in the tutoring session)? 2) What strategies can tutors adopt to show openness and sensitivity to the disciplinary experiences of the students? 3) What strategies can tutors adopt to become more engaged with the communicative culture of their target disciplines? Questions such as these begin to reframe the role of the tutor into a collaborative partner in the disciplinary activities the students are experiencing.

The Instructional Interaction as an Exploration of Parallel Emics

At times, tutors are placed in the position of providing students with one of the only points of contact with the communication discipline. Additionally, some tutors may not even be communication majors, thereby unavoidably having more superficial knowledge of the expectations of the field. Moreover, often tutors have limited time in which to help students. Despite this reality, tutors are expected to make their best effort to provide solid recommendations grounded in the communication discipline. Therefore, there is a challenge for tutors. Students and teachers expect them to be the experts in communication, yet if tutors are engaged participants, they (by definition) need to rely on the situated expertise of students living within their respective disciplinary majors. Balancing this etic/emic perspective could prove to be difficult.

Berry (1969, 1989) suggests an alternative that could be useful in this situation. He suggests a "parallel emic" approach, which recognizes and assumes the distinct nature of particular cultures but does so while exploring many cultures in an attempt to identify constructs that emerge in multiple settings (and hence can be used more universally; called "derived etics") and to identify constructs that are distinct to particular settings (called "true emics"). The ethnographic heuristic could address challenges of disciplinary vs. communication expertise by seeing each instructional interaction as a process of exploring "parallel emics"—a process Berry suggests consists of exploring across disciplinary cultures to find patterns applicable to all as well as patterns distinct to particular contexts.

Tutors, by the nature of their job, have access to many disciplinary cultures. Therefore, part of the tutor's role could be to look for those communication constructs that are patterned across disciplines and those that are distinct to particular disciplines. In reframing the instructional space as one where participants negotiate parallel emics, the instructional task becomes less about what is privileged and more about what can be understood about several disciplinary cultures, including the communication discipline.

This negotiated interaction space would allow for tutors to talk with students about the varied universal and particular communication constructs across disciplines, in order to better understand how the assignment expectations fit. Clearly, this process partially depends on students' knowledge of and abilities to articulate their disciplinary perspective (which could be problematic for novice students) but the process of asking the questions could bring to the fore students' awareness in ways that allow for a productive instructional interaction. This process also brings to the fore a potential challenge: if tutors gain insight into both the "derived etics" and the "true emics" of disciplinary spaces, what if those constructs work against known best practices in communication? Perhaps the answer lies in the negotiation process where both parties learn more about why particular constructs are important in disciplinary contexts (communication or otherwise) even if those constructs might not be valued in the particular assignment at hand.

Three questions could be important to ask, when reframing the instructional space as exploration of parallel emics: 1) What constructs emerge in multiple disciplines that could be considered applicable across disciplinary cultures (derived etics)? 2) What constructs emerge within particular disciplines that are situated enough to be recognized as entirely disciplinary (true emics)? 3) How can tutors negotiate the points of tension between these derived etics/true emics and the communicative perspective on successful communication without devaluing either perspective? These questions serve to reframe the tutoring session as an instructional space where tutors acknowledge disciplinarity expertise without negating their role as an expert in communication.

Reframing the Role of the Communication Center

As illustrated, the pedagogical push towards disciplinarity in communication across the curriculum programs can cause significant instructional challenges for communication centers. Such challenges can best be addressed with a theoretical, pedagogical, and programmatic commitment to an ethnographic heuristic that reframes the traditional role of the communication center into one of ethnographic discovery. Reframing the role of the communication center through the lens of an ethnographic heuristic has the potential to dramatically increase the effectiveness of communication centers by engaging students in the complex conversations they need to have about their communication assignments. At the same time, the reframing may seem like a monstrous change to tutors' jobs. However, we believe that by implementing certain changes in a center, directors and staff can shift the culture of the communication center to embrace the disciplinary communication norms inherent in their institution, and that a shift in the culture will ultimately make the job of the tutor easier and more fruitful. In this next section, we provide practical recommendations for steps a center could take to embrace an ethnographic heuristic. The suggestions first focus on administrative components of the center before moving to practical changes at the level of tutors and students. These reframes are summarized in figure 7.2.

Administrative Reframing

A good starting point for reframing the interactions tutors have with students is with the structure in which the interactions occur. The administrative structure of the communication center will influence students' experiences with tutors in a variety of ways—from their comfort level sitting on a couch or in a chair for a conversation to the forms and content of feedback they receive. At an administrative level, the staff of a communication center can reframe those interactions by making changes that may be individually small, but are collectively substantial. Our three suggestions here are centered predominantly on the people involved in the center.

Figure 7.2. Reframing Communication Centers with an Ethnographic Heuristic

Administration	Tutor Training	Tutor/Student Interaction
• Collaborate with CXC initiatives • Help faculty clarify assignments before they are given to students • Hire students from multiple disciplines	• Train tutors to be curious ethnographers • Provide ongoing training that emphasizes developing understandings of disciplinarity • Train tutors to uncover emics	• Engage in conversation about the culture of the course • Let the student take the lead • Have students provide information on the course prior to tutoring

First, center directors and staff can *collaborate with communication-across-the-curriculum initiatives* on campus, if available. CXC programs can provide resources for tutors on the communication assignments used across disciplines and provide insight into the particular dynamics on your campus; for example, certain colleges or departments may be especially eager for communication assistance, while other administrators deem this type of work as unimportant for their disciplines. If such an initiative does not exist, compile a set of norms and expectations from different disciplines on your campus. A good starting point for this is to collect assignment descriptions from faculty and to add any available information on grading to highlight the key aspects of the communication required in the assignment.

Second, center staff can work with faculty (especially those who consistently direct their students to your center) to *clarify assignments before the details are given to students* to ensure that students can enter the center with a clear sense of the assignment. If a CXC program exists at your campus separate from the center, collaborate with that program to provide this resource. Third, the center administration can *hire students from multiple disciplines*. Although it is wise to use students from communication (for the disciplinary expertise they bring to the study of communication), a center will offer a richer understanding of communication with the inclusion of students from across campus. For example, having a student who has performed well in communication courses but is majoring in biology not only provides an excellent tutor for biology students, but also provides a resource for other tutors who are asked to help a biology student. Centers could even consider setting up targeted tutoring times for specific disciplines before major assignments are due (e.g., from 2 p.m. to 5 p.m. on Tuesday there is a specific session for engineering students, staffed by tutors with expertise in engineering).

These three suggestions all require some concerted effort initially, with the idea that changes will be ongoing and will evolve as the center evolves. By working in conjunction with an existing CXC program, communication centers avoid potentially duplicating work, as the faculty and staff of such a program likely already has familiarity with faculty and communication expectations across campus. Gathering resources such as previous assignments can be an ongoing process (for example, making copies of students' assignments when they come in for help) to build a pool of materials for tutors to examine.

The effort to gather resources can also be an excellent starting point for working with faculty. While faculty on campus may not be as aware of the center as administrators would like, there are likely to be faculty in every department or college on campus who have a special interest in pedagogy and learning. By identifying these faculty (perhaps in consultation with a center for faculty development or similar program), centers can reach out to faculty who have already self-selected as allies in improving education. These faculty can then be a resource for reaching out to other faculty in their disciplines, as well as helpful in identifying students from other majors who are good candidates to be tutors.

If a campus has introductory communication courses required of multiple majors, the instructors of those classes can also be helpful in identifying students who succeeded in the communication class but come from a different major. These students can then be recruited as tutors, and they can bring their disciplinary expertise to the center for other tutors. In addition to expanding the breadth of expertise of staff, the changes also communicate to the staff of the center and the administrators with oversight responsibility that the consideration of discipline-specific communication is valued in the center.

Tutor Training Reframing

Tutors are the front-line for the center; students seeking help work closely with a tutor, who has the potential to greatly help or painfully frustrate the student. Tutors' interactions with students will be influenced by what they are trained to do, but tutors' experiences as students will also affect their interactions. For example, if a tutor has always been taught a particular mantra about speech delivery, that tutor is likely to pass that thinking on to tutees without a second thought. Part of training tutors, then, is to help tutors to have those second thoughts and to raise their awareness of the need to be attuned to particular students, disciplines, and assignments. We offer three specific suggestions.

First, it is important to *train tutors to be curious ethnographers*. While this step may be easier said than done, the continual encouragement of students to be curious and to ask questions will reinforce the importance of this part of their job. Tutors can be trained in effective questioning. Resources such as those provided for qualitative research methods and interviewing such as Spradley's 1979 *Ethnographic Interview* are a good starting point for questioning, as are many introductory communication textbooks. Extending the training to developing specific questions that may come into play in the tutoring interactions will equip tutors to enter interactions with an ethnographic mindset. Another component of this training should be to help tutors recognize disciplinary boundaries; tutors should reframe those boundaries as opportunities. For example, tutor training may include examining multiple assignment descriptions for common themes and divergent understandings of communication. Additionally, presentations or a panel discussion of representatives from different disciplines will provide tutors with a deeper understanding of what it means to examine disciplinary differences. Tutors from other disciplines are also an excellent resource at this point because they have both the communication expertise and the disciplinary expertise.

Second, *train tutors to uncover emics.* Berry (1989) laid out a set of steps for conducting research on emics and etics. This process begins with initial examination of one's own culture (in this case, communicative understanding). Next, these concepts and understandings are compared to another culture as an imposed etic. But Berry does not stop there. In order to fully understand the other culture, there must be a close examination of the other culture in order for a comparison to be made. At the end of this examination, there may be overlapping understanding of communication; the overlapping points are a derived etic. In the case of tutor training, this process requires helping tutors understand their own perceptions of competent communication. Tutors, as they are then exposed to the communication from other disciplines, must understand where disciplines overlap and where they diverge. Tutors should be taught to ask questions about the different disciplines, such as: How does my understanding of what it means organize a speech work with this discipline's understanding? What aspects of communication are especially important to this discipline? What aspects of communication that I have been taught do not seem to be important to this discipline? Which communication constructs are patterned among disciplines? Which are not?

These components of training should also be carried through *ongoing training focused on disciplinarity.* As tutors work, it may be tempting to trust them to continually stay abreast of information gathered about different disciplines, but there is a much greater chance of that happening if tutors receive ongoing training that emphasizes these resources. For example, if an introductory biology class that teaches hundreds of students across multiple sections implements a new group speaking assignment, providing those resources to tutors—along with guidance on how to deal with the assignment—will help tutors be prepared for the numerous students who may appear seeking help with a biology presentation. Online repositories of information provide an easy way to share information about disciplinary norms and expectations. For example, we put together a website in conjunction with research we did on communication skills in the College of Design at North Carolina State University (2008). That website was designed to provide resources for students in design, but could also be used by tutors who wish to learn more about the communication expected of design students. Similarly, resources such as the Communication, Leadership, Ethics, and Research (CLEAR) program at the University of Utah's College of Engineering provides information for their students and consultants about communication expectations in engineering (University of Utah, n.d.)

We know that tutor training is often already packed with information to address and paperwork to complete. The changes suggested here can be integrated into existing training programs and can tap into resources that already exist. For example, if a center has a set of videos about tutoring (such as those hosted by the University of Richmond, n.d.), training can engage tutors in a discussion that not only deals with the interaction in the scenario, but also asks deeper questions about disciplinary influences on the interactions.

Tutor/Student Interaction Reframing

The tutor/student interaction is where the changes made to administration and training come to fruition. In order to ensure that students gain the maximum benefits of these changes, we propose a reframing of the tutor/student interaction that puts the emphasis on helping the student to identify and take advantage of communication in disciplinary ways. It is important to note at this point that these changes might seem to be time-intensive. While the time these interactions take is by no means negligible, gathering this information is too important to skip. Not every tutor/student interaction will require extensive questioning and as the materials and expertise in the center expand through administrative and training changes, the questioning will likely decrease. We see the reframe of tutor/student interactions as happening in three specific ways.

First, *students who enter the center should bring a copy of assignment details, as well as a course syllabus and previous related assignments.* These data points will help tutors establish (in consultation with the student) the communication expectations of the instructor. The previous assignments can provide a broader context for the overall course by explaining what students were asked to do in the past. If students are required to make appointments to come to your center, they can be asked to provide basic details about the assignment at that time to give the tutor advanced information about the assignment details in order to better prepare. During the interaction, the tutor can ask questions such as: Explain to me in your own words the assignment given by your instructor. How is this assignment going to be graded? What has the instructor indicated is especially important? Has the instructor shown or described any examples of this

108   Dannels and Gaffney

assignment? What did the instructor say about those examples? How does this assignment fit with other assignments in the course?

Tutors should *engage students in a conversation about the course and the interactions typical of that class.* For example, a design studio course maintains a highly interactive environment where students are continually dialoguing with faculty. This interactive environment then appears in the critique or pin-up, and having this background can help a tutor recognize the importance of interaction to this discipline. Students may be so focused on the specific assignment that they fail to see the broader picture of what they are being asked to do. Careful questioning on the part of the tutor can help illuminate the disciplinary components of the communication assignment. Questions that tutors may ask include: What types of activities or discussion do you engage in during this class? What communication is expected of people in [insert future career]? How does this assignment relate to those expectations? What interactions have you had with your instructor? What do you think he/she expects out of you when you talk with the instructor? Tutors can ask a variety of questions or only one or two based on the information they are receiving. Additionally, such information can be compiled in the center to be shared, or students can be asked to provide such information when they make an appointment or arrive that day.

Tutors also need to *let the student take the lead.* While it is tempting for tutors to exert their expertise or to jump to a premature understanding of disciplinary expectations, it is important that tutors let the student lead the conversation to highlight specific areas of concern. Students have the disciplinary experience that tutors may be lacking, even if the students are not cognizant of this information. The tutor can pull out key phrases and tangible behaviors that the student has identified and then encourage the student to apply that information to the assignment under discussion. Students may push back against this goal, particularly if they entered the center with the mindset that the tutor is there to tell the student what to do in order to get a good grade. However, the tutor can allow the student the room to lead and to uncover communicative expectations through careful questioning, such as: When you look at this assignment, what do you think is most important for you to do in order to do well on this assignment? What parts of the assignment do you think will be the easiest for you? What do you think will be your biggest challenge? Where do you see the starting point for the assignment?

The tutor/student interaction will be fluid, which is where tutors' training comes into play. While the tutors should not be made to feel as if they are following a rigid script, helping tutors to reframe the interactions they have with students will make that script an internalized part of tutors' schema for working with students. As these questions and this approach become more engrained in the culture of the center and in the minds of the tutors, the conversations will become more natural. Tutors will need to do less work to draw out information from students as they can draw on their own knowledge and skill in eliciting information. Furthermore, the tutor's questioning approach can reduce later concerns because they will be able to work with the student on appropriate tasks from the start. Thus, the seemingly overwhelming time commitment of asking these questions can actually result in a tutoring process as efficient as any other approach. Together, these suggestions push toward a shift in culture from encouraging tutors to see through the eyes of communication experts to helping them see the variety of ways they can help students, even if the communication feels new or different.

Conclusion

Barbara McClintock, a cytogeneticist, was awarded the Nobel Peace Prize in Physiology or Medicine for discovering transposition (DNA that can move or jump to new positions and hence create mutations that can transfer from one generation to the next). Her scientific discoveries, though, are more prominent because of the ways in which she came to them. She observed maize (corn) kernels over multiple generations to assess changes in patterns of coloration. She studied each kernel of corn, over and over, closely observing the patterns. She claims, "I start with the seedling, and I don't want to leave it. I don't feel I really know the story if I don't watch the plant all the way along. So I know every plant in the field. I know them intimately" (quoted in Keller, 1983, p. 198). Barbara McClintock is the scientific embodiment of the ethnographic heuristic. She, as Evelyn Fox Keller claims, "has the time to look, the patience to hear what the material has to say to you, the openness to let it come to you . . . and a feeling for the organism." (p. 198).

In many ways, McClintock offers a framework useful in multiple contexts, including communication centers. As communication centers become increasingly challenged by assignments that are disciplinarily complex and contextually mysterious, McClintock's frame of mind could provide one way to move through the challenges. Even if communication centers are unable to logistically take the time to observe each assignment kernel (if you will) as it changes and grows over time, the mindset of patience, listening, openness, and getting a "feeling for the organism" cannot hurt. And there is potential that such a mindset could actually help because it calls for attention to both *what* centers know and *how* they know it. Many communication assignments live in mutating disciplinary systems in which situated expectations are often hidden in complex genetic maps. If centers are unaware of these maps and systems, they are in a position of leading students (also unaware) through an endless maze—the blind leading the blind. The *how* question then becomes: how can communication centers begin to know the complex disciplinary organisms that generate the assignments they eventually see in the tutoring session? An ethnographic heuristic is a starting point. Perhaps instead of building the "field" and hoping students will come, the way through the maze is by going *into* the field—pedagogically and programmatically—to learn and teach from the inside looking out, rather than from the outside looking in.

References

Anthony, K. H. (1991). *Design juries on trial: The Renaissance of the design studio*. New York: Van Nostrand Reinhold.

Bazerman, C. (1998). *Shaping written knowledge: The genre and activity of the experimental article in science*. Madison, WI: University of Wisconsin Press.

Berry, J. W. (1969). On cross-cultural comparability. *International Journal of Psychology, 4,* 119–128.

Berry, J. W. (1989). Imposed etics-emics-derived etics: The operationalization of a compelling idea. *International Journal of Psychology, 24,* 721–735.

Brown, J. (2008). How clinical communication has become a core part of medical education in the UK. *Medical Education, 42,* 271–278.

Brown, R. F., & Bylund, C. L. (2008). Communication skills training: Describing a new conceptual model. *Academic Medicine, 83,* 37–44.

Cronin, M. W., Grice G., & Palmerton, P. (2000). Oral communication across the curriculum: The state of the art after twenty-five years of experience. *Journal of the Association for Communication Administration, 29,* 66–87.

Dannels, D. P. (2000). Learning to be professional: Technical classroom discourse, practice, and professional identity construction. *Journal of Business and Technical Communication, 14,* 5–37.

Dannels, D. P. (2001). Time to speak up: A theoretical framework of situated pedagogy and practice for communication across the curriculum. *Communication Education, 50,* 144–158.

Dannels, D. P. (2002). Communication across the curriculum and in the disciplines: Speaking in engineering. *Communication Education, 51,* 254–268.

Dannels, D. P. (2005). Performing tribal rituals: A genre analysis of "crits" in design studios. *Communication Education, 54,* 136–160.

Dannels, D. P. (2009). Features of success in engineering design presentations: A call for relational genre knowledge. *Journal of Business and Technical Communication, 23*(4), 399–427.

Dannels, D. P., & Housley Gaffney, A. L. (2009). Communication across the curriculum and in the disciplines: A call for scholarly cross-curricular advocacy. *Communication Education, 58,* 124–153.

Dannels, D. P., Housley Gaffney, A. L., & Norris Martin, K. (2008). Beyond content, deeper than delivery: What critique feedback reveals about communication expectations in design education. *International Journal for the Scholarship of Teaching and Learning, 2.* Retrieved from http://academics.georgiasouthern.edu/ijsotl/v2n2.html

Dannels, D. P., Housley Gaffney, A. L. & Norris Martin, K. (2011). Students' talk about the climate of feedback interventions in the critique. *Communication Education, 60,* 95–114.

Darling, A. L. (2005). Public presentations in mechanical engineering and the discourse of technology. *Communication Education 54,* 20–33.

Freedman, A., Adam, C., & Smart, G. (1994). Wearing suits to class: Simulating genres and simulations as genre. *Written Communication, 11,* 193–226.

Geertz, C. (1973). *The interpretation of cultures: Selected essays.* New York: Basic Books.

Hay, E. (1987, November). *Communication across the curriculum.* Paper presented at the meeting of the Speech Communication Association, Boston.

Housley Gaffney, A. L. (2010). *Communicating about, in, and through design: A study exploring communication instruction and design students' critique performance* (Doctoral dissertation). Retrieved from http://www.lib.ncsu.edu/resolver/1840.16/3314

Keller, E. F. (1983). *A feeling for the organism: The life and work of Barbara McClintock.* New York: Henry Holt and Company.

King, P. E., & Behnke, R. R. (1999). Technology-based instructional feedback intervention. *Educational Technology, 39,* 43–44.

Kluger, A. N., & DeNisi, A. (1996). The effects of feedback interventions on performance: A historical review, a meta-analysis, and a preliminary feedback intervention theory. *Psychological Bulletin, 119,* 254–284.

Miller, C. R. (1984). Genre as social action. *Quarterly Journal of Speech, 70,* 151–167.

Nelson, J. S., Megill, A., & McCloskey, D. N. (Eds.). (1990). *The rhetoric of the human sciences: Language and argument in scholarship and public affairs.* Madison: University of Wisconsin Press.

North Carolina State University. (2008). *Communication in design.* Retrieved from http://www.ncsu.edu/www/ncsu/design/sod5/communication/

Patton, M. Q. (2002). *Qualitative research and evaluation methods* (3rd ed.). Thousand Oaks, CA: Sage.

Philipsen, G. (1992). *Speaking culturally.* Albany, NY: SUNY Press.

Pike, K. (1967). *Language in relation to a unified theory of the structure of human behavior.* The Hague, Netherlands: Mouton.

Russell, D. (1997). Rethinking genre in school and society: An activity theory analysis. *Written Communication, 14,* 504–554.

Spradley, J. P. (1979). *The ethnographic interview.* New York: Holt, Rinehart and Winston.

Steinfatt, T. (1986). Communication across the curriculum. *Communication Quarterly, 34,* 460–470.

Straub, R. (1996). Teacher response as conversation: More than casual talk, an exploration. *Rhetoric Review, 14,* 374–399.

Sullivan, K., & Kedrowicz, A. A. (in press). (Re)situating communication in the disciplines: Taking gender into account. *Communication Education.*

Triandis, H. C., Malpass, R. S., & Davidson, A. (1971). Cross-cultural psychology. In B. C. Siegel (Ed.), *Biennial review of anthropology* (pp. 1–84). Stanford, CA: Stanford University Press.

University of Richmond. (n.d.). *Speech center: Consultant tutorials.* Retrieved from http://speech.richmond.edu/resources/tutorials.html

University of Utah (n.d.). *CLEAR Program: College of Engineering.* Retrieved from http://www.coe.utah.edu/clear/

Van Maanen, J. (1988). *Tales from the field: On writing ethnography.* Chicago, IL: University of Chicago Press.

Wilde, S. M., Cuny, K. M., & Vizzier, A. L. (2006). Peer-to-peer tutoring: A model for utilizing empathetic listening to build client relationships in the communication center. *International Journal of Listening, 20,* 70–75.

Winsor, D. (1998). Rhetorical practices in technical work. *Journal of Business and Technical Communication, 12,* 343–370.

Chapter 8

Learning to Tell What You Know: A Communication Intervention for Biology Students

Trudy Bayer and Karen A. Curto

Increasingly, scientists remark about the failure to prepare not only undergraduate students, but graduate students and postdoctoral fellows to communicate their science expertise with colleagues and the public. Emphasizing the importance of communication, noted scientist Stephen Jay Gould provides the following observation: "So many scientists think that once they figure it out, that's all they have to do, and writing it up is just a chore. I never saw it that way. Part of the art of any kind of total scholarship is to say it well" (American Association for the Advancement of Science, 2011). Despite the importance of acquiring competency not only in conducting science but also in communicating science, undergraduates, graduates and postdoctoral fellows often continue to have limited access to instruction and practical opportunities that facilitate the acquisition of oral communication competence (Bayer, Curto, & Kriley, 2005; Boyer Commission, 1998; Florence & Yore, 2004; Yore, 2000).

This was the case for senior biology majors enrolled in a required course on writing and speaking in the biological sciences. Although assumed to have a level of familiarity with biological terminology and the process of science, in general, these students struggled with preparing and delivering a six-minute talk on a current controversial biological topic. In an effort to improve these students' ability to demonstrate competency in scientific presentation, the biology instructor sought specific help by collaborating with the director of the university's communication lab, as well as participation in a semester-long bimonthly course, "Communication Across the Disciplines," that addressed the integration of writing and oral communication instruction into any course. The attendees included faculty from a variety of disciplines and addressed issues such as writing and speaking basics, nature of assignments, and assessment and revision. Attendees crafted a syllabus incorporating communication goals, learned about low stakes and high stakes speaking assignments, examined appropriate grading rubrics, and received assistance from instructional designers. Instructors also had access to the Communication Lab director who was available to work with them individually and also provide instruction to students. It was within this context that collaboration between the biology instructor and the Communication Lab director was initiated. This paper discusses the reported outcomes from this ongoing collaborative project between biology and communication faculty. Combining instruction in the general rhetorical principles of organization and delivery with instruction and feedback specific to the field of biology, this intervention illustrates a model for promoting general skills in both oral communication and speaking like a biologist. Unlike ethnographic or expert-driven approaches to disciplinary discourse and culture, the communication curriculum for this intervention was based on the students' self-reported oral communication deficits and instructional needs.

The decision to consult with students rather than experts in biology resulted from ongoing concerns by the biology instructor about the disappointing quality of the students' oral presentations. This situation persisted even though students had: conducted considerable research and were familiar with the science of their research questions; produced two written drafts on their topics; received disciplinary feedback on these written drafts from their biology instructors; and received basic information from the biology instructors on developing a presentation. Thus, in an effort to address this problem, we decided to survey the students required to complete this oral assignment to discover whether there were misconceptions or issues overlooked by the biology instructor.

Students' self-reports identified several general oral communication deficits as the primary obstacles to effectively completing their oral presentations and these results became the guide for instruction. Lowe (1994) describes this sort of student-driven approach as follows: "if a particular skill or way of thinking underlies the proper solution to a problem, we should try to find ways to let the student assess this skill beforehand, rather than letting him or her stumble up against it when trying to solve a larger problem."

Methodology

Research Questions

1. What, if any, oral communication knowledge would senior biology students perceive as necessary to successfully complete their scientific presentations?

2. How, if at all, would instruction in these self-identified areas of oral communication promote students' success in biological science communication?
3. How, if at all, would feedback from instructors and peers on their oral presentations be regarded by students?
4. How, if at all, would this instruction and presentation process affect students'
perceptions of their abilities to develop future scientific presentations?

This collaborative study by biology and communication faculty was conducted over a two-year period at the University of Pittsburgh. It included an
initial sample of 122 senior biological science majors enrolled in a required
course devoted to demonstrating competence in writing and speaking in their
discipline. Multiple sections of this course are offered each fall and spring semester with approximately 15–20 students in each section. Different biology faculty taught the course sections, however the requirements and format for this
course are standard across instructors.

The primary course assignment was a written persuasive paper that resolved
a controversial issue in biology. The paper contained sections on the science
background of the topic, the alternative viewpoints and the synthesis of a resolution supported by data from the primary research literature. After conducting
this research, students prepared their findings for oral presentation. Representative student research topics included: The Role of Autophagy in Inhibiting or
Accelerating Cancerous Cell Growth, The Use of Aquafarming as an Environ-
mentally Sound Solution to Overfishing, Evaluating the Credibility of Safety
Concerns Related to Chronic Cell Phone Use, or The Viability of Microalgae as
Fuel Sources. Topics were generated by the instructor and students selected their
research question from this pool. Topics were timely and changed each semester. As part of the topic assignment, the audience for each talk was defined,
typically as a community planning board or grant funding committee. These
audiences had some "basic biology" background, but specific tests, procedures
or the biochemical basis would have to be defined or clarified as part of the
background material in their talk.

Three written drafts, whose requirements were defined by checklists and
grade rubrics, provided several opportunities for students to revise, reformulate
and refocus their written argument. The first draft typically reflected attention to
background issues and alternatives to solve the controversy, but frequently
lacked a focus or well-supported resolution. This draft, peer previewed in class
to identify grammatical issues and flow of ideas, was returned to the student for
revision prior to being graded and discussed in individual conferences with the
instructor. The second draft underwent instructor grading and discussion only.
These two drafts, and their attendant peer and instructor feedback, provided the
disciplinary and conceptual framework for the conversion to the oral scientific
presentation.

Initial Survey

In preparation for the oral assignment, students were asked to complete a survey developed by the Communication Lab director. The purpose of this survey was to gather information about their previous instruction in oral communication, their self-perceived oral communication abilities and challenges, and what they thought was important for them to learn in order to successfully complete the oral scientific presentation required for this course. Student responses from this survey were used by the Communication Lab director as the basis for developing the oral communication instruction for these students. Table 8.1 lists the questions and results from the initial survey.

Table 8.1: Initial Survey Results

#	Question	Average Response
1	What communication courses or workshops have you taken?	67 reported none
2	Please indicate how often you participate in speaking situations such as meetings, presentations in class or other discussions (in class or outside organizations), teaching, sales, tours, etc. (1=Once a month, 2=2–3 times/month, 3=1–2 times/week, 4=3 or more times/week)	2.3
3	How well do you understand how to *organize* a presentation? (1=Not at all, 2=To a small degree, 3=To a moderate degree, 4=To a considerable degree, 5=To a high degree)	3.1
4	How comfortable do you feel when speaking before an audience? (1=Not at all, 2=somewhat comfortable, 3=moderately comfortable, 4=comfortable, 5=Very comfortable)	2.7
5	In general, how would you rate yourself as a speaker? (1=poor, 2=fair, 3=average, 4=above average, 5=excellent)	2.8

Note. N=122

Of the 122 students who completed the initial survey, 67 had never taken a course or workshop in public speaking or any type of communication, and 55 participated infrequently in speaking situations such as meetings, presentations, discussions, teaching, and so on. Mean responses for questions three through five about organization, level of comfort, or self-confidence in oral delivery skills tended to be in the middle range. These responses indicated that students had concerns about issues of organization and delivery. A clearer picture of the nature of these concerns was revealed from their responses to an open-ended question (table 8.2) on what they wanted to learn about giving a talk.

Table 8.2: Initial Survey Results for Question #6*

Category of Concern	Percent Response	Representative Comments
Organization	40	How to organize a presentation; how to support ideas; what key points to focus on; how in-depth to explain data; how to make smooth transitions
Aspects of Delivery	18	How formal does it need to be; eye contact during presentation; whether to talk with hands
Connecting & Adapting to Audience	17	How to engage audience; effective ways to get across to your audience; how to better address audience expectations; how to bring the listener into the presentation
Speaking Anxiety	13	How to not get stressed, nervous or uncomfortable; ways to not freak out; tips on how to be less nervous; how to feel more comfortable; how to deliver without my heart pounding
Using PowerPoint	8	

Note. N=122; *Question 6 read: "What specific issues or questions about giving a talk would you like to see discussed in next week's workshop?"

As seen in table 8.2, students overwhelmingly identified *general* questions about organization and delivery as their primary challenges. A more subtle, but persistent, concern about their connection to an audience was also evident. Nearly 20 percent of students' comments expressed concerns about relating and adapting to one's audience, reflecting considerable sensitivity about speaker/audience interdependence from a group with so little instruction in oral communication. To a lesser extent, table 2 also reflected tentativeness regarding the technical expression required by the presentation, mentioning concerns about using PowerPoint and visual aids—a topic addressed later in the semester with a separate PowerPoint workshop.

Communication Workshops

Two, two-hour oral communication workshops were developed by the Communication Lab director to address the specific challenges and concerns that students identified. Workshops were conducted by the Communication Lab director and attended by the biology instructor. Approximately 12–15 students attended each workshop session. The workshop's content, based on the students' survey results, was grouped into categories of concern focused on organization and delivery. The communication director began with a general oral competency theme, an axiom that good public speaking is audience-centered. To this end we explained that the initial survey was an example of our attempt to illustrate this axiom and discussed their concerns (as our audience) about organizing and delivering an oral presentation, speaking anxiety, and connecting to audiences as the dominant communication challenges they identified. We reported the data on their lack of instruction and practice in oral communication and expressed our belief that this lack of instruction and experience accounted for most of the discomfort and anxiety that they reported.

Even though students had completed two written drafts of their research and had been asked to bring a preliminary outline for an oral presentation of it to the workshop, many students struggled to articulate their specific research question and main findings. Olson (2009) reports that scientists generally focus on message accuracy rather than communication and thus presentations lack connectivity or continuity to a main message (p. 41). The workshop challenged students to identify and express their specific purpose, main findings, and best supporting evidence using an outline based on their second draft. The Communication Lab director began with an extended example about the general topic of baseball to clarify the notion of "a topic" versus "a specific purpose for a topic." The Lab instructor then explained the process of identifying the main points or findings from a large body of material, and then ways to synthesize this information for oral presentation to an audience.

Biology-specific examples extended the principles set up in the general example of baseball to demonstrate applicability of the same principles (topic, specific purpose, thesis, and supporting evidence) to several previous course topics regarding the impact of genetically modified foods on wild crops, or the safety of the MMR vaccines. Discussing the examples from previous classes and listening to other student's delineate their theses and evidence provided ample opportunity to apply the organizing principles and receive feedback as students took turns talking about their research.

For some students, this exercise was extremely challenging. If students were unable to recognize and identify their main findings, they were asked to continue thinking and trying to get to the core of their research conclusions. The Lab director would then later work with those students individually and those students would later discuss their research with the entire group.

For example, one student had selected the topic of evaluating the primary scientific literature on the origin of humans. He concluded that the "Out of Africa" theory provided the most compelling scientific data. However, when asked to articulate the main scientific reasons justifying that conclusion, he could only cite a general claim about "DNA" evidence. When asked to be more specific about why the DNA evidence led him to his conclusion, he was unable to articulate specific scientific evidence. However, by the end of the workshop, this student was able to articulate that "after evaluating the primary data on the origin of humans, the Out of Africa theory is most plausible because of the Y chromosome, mitochondrial chromosomal and general chromosomal DNA marker analyses."

At the beginning of the second workshop, students were asked to restate their revised thesis and supporting evidence. These statements differed from the rambling and unfocused attempts from the first workshop in both length and logical flow. Now that students had a clearer vision of what they might say, the Communication Lab director switched to the topic of delivery. The primary goals of the second workshop were to introduce students to the fundamentals of delivery, provide a practical method for improving delivery, and provide a speaking opportunity to both build confidence and to reinforce the organizational methods highlighted in the previous workshop. The model of topic, thesis and support evidence was applied in a simple exercise entitled "A Place We All Ought to Visit." In the exercise, each student identified a remarkable place, developed a thesis statement that explicitly identified two to three reasons for its desirability as a destination, and then presented these reasons in a clearly organized format that included support for each main point. The communication lab director gave students just several minutes to organize their presentations and then modeled the exercise by going first. This easy "low stakes" speaking exercise reinforced organizational principles and reduced anxiety, because as a template it established and strengthened a simple guide for oral presentations.

For most students, the communication workshops were their first explicit instruction in oral communication, and also the first time that they were called upon to talk about scientific data and their observations of it before their peers and biology professors. This instruction switched the focus from *what* they had learned to *how* to present this knowledge orally. We encouraged them to look at their material from a different perspective with the primary goal of *thinking communicatively* about it: getting to the core of what is most important, developing a sound scientific argument, and adapting it to their audience.

These workshops also provided ample opportunity for students to *practice* how one develops and presents material for oral presentation. Currently, due to increased enrollment, the communication workshops are being provided via DVDs recorded by the Communication Lab director. These recordings are played in class by the biology instructors with stopping points for the workshop exercises on organization and delivery, thus replicating the original workshop experience.

In the weeks following the workshops, students presented their research in their respective classes. Students received feedback from their peers immediately following their in-class presentations, as well as feedback from their biology instructor on a grading rubric. These presentations were also recorded for students' self-critiques. Thus they were provided with multiple and varied feedback used in a revision process to create a final presentation. In response to this feedback, students then revised their research for a final presentation.

Results

To evaluate the impact of this intervention, a follow-up survey was administered during the final class session. One hundred and twelve students completed the follow-up survey. As in the initial survey, we asked students to assess their self-perceived oral communication abilities. We asked for assessment of the general strengths and weaknesses of their final presentations, and then specifically to address the organization and delivery of their final presentations since these were their initial primary concerns. Finally, we also asked students to assess their confidence in being able to develop future scientific presentations (table 8.3).

In responding, students identified organizational strengths, confidence in their knowledge of the science, and greater comfort in orally presenting it as the primary accomplishments of their final presentations. These comments represented a clear change in students' perceptions from their initial abilities, replacing negative perceptions and statements with unambiguous statements of ability and confidence. "I was comfortable with the information I was presenting and the knowledge I had acquired" and "I became comfortable speaking in front of the class. I also was comfortable with arranging a coherent presentation" were representative of clear statements of students' self-perceived oral communication strengths.

Table 8.3: Post-course Survey Question # 1: Final Presentation Strengths

Categories of Strength	Number	Representative Comments
Organization	38	Ability to condense information; organization; it was much more organized; good information and structure; confidence, organization and clarity; eye contact, data and confidence; strong thesis/organization; made time limit
Confidence in Speaking	23	I felt more comfortable; I was much more relaxed; my ability to stay relaxed; I had a relaxed delivery and a focused presentation
Confidence in Knowledge	19	Comfortable with the information; knowledge of the subject and confidence in that knowledge; the knowledge I had acquired; comfortable with material; I realized it is easier to give a speech when you know the material very well; knowledge of topic; I was comfortably able to answer questions about the material
Delivery	8	Had more eye contact; didn't trail off at end of sentences; my delivery; I was *very happy* with how I spoke; looked up more; spoke clearly (not many ums)
Connecting to Audience	3	Successfully conveying my point to the audience; getting the audience's attention

Note. $N=112$

The follow-up survey results reflected clear changes in attitude toward the oral presentations as shown below in table 8.4. Students reported a positive change in their confidence and ability to organize their presentations from a mean of 3.1 on the initial survey to 4.2, as well as a positive change in their comfort levels, 2.7 on the initial survey to 3.6; and finally in their perception of themselves as speakers, 2.8 on the initial survey to 3.6. These results suggest a positive trend, however without a matched pair study design the results' interpretation are statistically limited.

Table 8.4: Follow-up Survey Responses

#	Question	Average Response Range (1–5)
4	How *organized* do you feel your FINAL presentation was?	4.2
5	How comfortable and confident did you feel in *delivering* your FINAL presentation?	3.6
6	How well prepared do you now feel to do *future scientific presentations* as a result of participating in the "oral component" (communication workshop videos, oral presentations) of this course?	3.6

Note. 1=None, 2=Some, 3=Moderate, 4=Comfortable/prepared, 5=Very well

We also asked students about the value of viewing their recorded talks. Seventy five percent rated this source of feedback as having impacted the final presentation from a rating of "somewhat important" to "very important." Several students voluntarily commented on the importance of feedback in follow-up surveys, identifying the chance to practice, view their recorded talk, or receive comments provided by the instructor or class peers as influential to the success of the final presentation. Table 8.5 lists some of these voluntary comments in response to the question: What was the most useful course component that helped prepare you for the final presentation?

An open-ended question in the follow-up survey identified presentation areas that remained problematic (table 8.5). Compared to the initial survey, there were fewer comments on areas that needed to be improved in the follow-up survey. Unlike the range of concerns initially expressed about developing and delivering an oral scientific presentation, the primary shortcoming students identified in the follow-up survey was speaking too quickly. Interestingly, of the 24 percent who commented on their delivery, one-third of those comments noted speaking too quickly as a problem. Speaking anxiety was mentioned only ten times in the final survey although the comments students made continued to describe it as a barrier.

Table 8.5: Follow-up Survey Question #2* Results

Categories of Areas Needing Improvement	Number	Representative Comments
No response to this question	58	
Delivery	24	Speak slower; speaking a little more clearly; too much reading from notes
Anxiety	9	Still sounded nervous; even with much practice, the nervousness that came from speaking in front of the class made me fumble a lot; I was very nervous
Organization	6	Transition from one topic to another; less information; length
Better content	6	More clarification of data; explaining things better; I think I could have explained some of the experiments more clearly
Better slides	3	Slide design

Note. N=112; *Question 2 read: "What areas of your FINAL presentation do you think could have been improved?"

The data on areas for improvement suggest future instructional goals, but the grade data for the course indicate that this intervention in general was successful. Grade assessment for the two-year (four-semester) period covered by the current research shows a consistent 30 percent of student's (33/112) scoring 90 percent or better in the course sections taught by the biology instructor and co-researcher of this project, regardless of semester. This represents an improvement over previous versions of the course, when little or no instruction was provided, in which 7 to 24 percent of students earned a 90 percent or better (Bayer, Curto, & Kriley, 2005). While these grades and percentages are derived from one of the author's sections, the surveys and intervention were administered by the other instructors for this course as well.

Discussion

Assessing Prior Knowledge

Educational approaches intended to improve students' competence in communicating in their disciplines tend to privilege the opinions of experts in identifying the norms and conventions particular to a specific discourse community. In contrast to this top-down approach, we were interested in what students perceived as necessary communication instruction and what impact, if any, responding to these needs would have on their oral competence. As senior biology majors about to embark on professional careers or graduate school, we considered the students in our study fledging experts in their field. Our primary concern was not the ethnography of speaking in biology, but rather in developing educational practices to improve their ability to talk about biology and the knowledge they had acquired.

Our initial research question addressed the issue of what oral communication knowledge senior biology students would perceive as necessary to successfully complete their oral scientific presentations. The initial survey allowed us to obtain this information by assessing students' prior knowledge and experience in oral communication and the instruction they wanted in order to develop an effective scientific presentation. As Zull (2002) emphasized in his work on the biology of learning, educators can be more effective in their teaching of any subject by first finding out what students already know about it, a premise that is also at the heart of our beliefs about one's audience in effective public speaking.

From our assessment of students' prior knowledge, we began the oral communication instruction based on their ideas and experience, rather than our own. Surprisingly, these students displayed a clear tacit understanding of the essentials of good oral presentations–relating to one's audience, good organization and evidence, and effective delivery. Exposed for many years through various social institutions to "speakers," these students seemed to know what constituted an effective presentation, even though they initially did not understand *how* to effectively negotiate or work through those elements. Assessing prior knowledge also revealed the *misconceptions* students had acquired about speaking in public. For example, many students initially reported a lack of comfort or fear about public speaking, because they believed that it was a natural ability, rather than a kind of knowledge that one acquires through instruction, practice, and feedback.

Challenging these misconceptions was a central component of our initial instruction. Our goal was to build a new set of connections about what constitutes competence in public speaking: that skill in public speaking is learned through study and practice, not something to be feared, or that one is "naturally good at or not" (Bransford, Brown, & Cocking, 2000; Halpern & Hakel, 2003; Zull, 2002).

Oral Communication Instruction

Our second research question was intended to assess whether oral communication instruction in the areas students identified would promote competence in using the language of their discipline. According to students' self-reports and grade data from multiple biology instructors, students demonstrated a significant improvement in speaking like a biologist, compared to no instruction in oral communication or just the chance to repeat a presentation in the previous versions of the course. This instruction was perceived as essential to the students in our study. However, in terms of accounting for improved student competencies in communicating the science of biology, specialized feedback from biology instructors and their biology peers was key.

The communication workshops provided students with the instruction they perceived as necessary to developing and delivering their scientific presentations. This instruction entailed examining fundamental rhetorical concepts of organization and delivery central to any oral genre. Although geared to biology students through examples and exercises, there was no explicit emphasis on the norms or conventions of speaking like a biologist.

The communication workshops were a crucial, effective feature of this intervention in promoting student competencies in speaking in their discipline when paired with the active, specialized feedback from their instructor and peers that provided guidance toward the correct expression of science communication in biology.

Feedback

The third research question addressed the significance of feedback, and whether it would be an element that students identified as important in developing a successful scientific presentation. Seventy-five percent of surveyed students ranked it as important, and their open-ended responses identified specific types of feedback that they valued as helpful. They mentioned all sources of feedback (instructor, peer, and self) as noted in table 8.6. This ongoing disciplinary feedback throughout the semester supported development of students' abilities in using the language of the discipline.

Table 8.6: Follow-up Survey Question on Feedback*

The feedback given to me on the first presentation and watching myself.

Watching myself helped a lot.

It was helpful watching myself so I could see what I did wrong.

Watching myself and having others watch my video helped me.

The practice of having to do it.

Feedback from the first presentation/video.

The professor's comments from the video.

Being critiqued, reviewed and doing it again.

Having already practiced it in a timed, graded presentation.

The feedback from the class, as well as the tape.

Talking together and the process of producing a paper.

Note. Question read: "What was the most useful course component that helped prepare you for the final presentation?"

The biology instructor's feedback was provided in individual conferences or as written comments on a grade rubric and was therefore specific to each student's science problem. Often this focused on issues of scientific background detail, data presentation, and interpretation. An example of discipline-specific feedback for a first presentation is illustrated in the following description regarding data discussion:

> Students seem content to mention that a particular treatment had an "increasing or decreasing" effect on some variable. Thus, for example, at this stage the statement "pesticide usage decreases tadpole survival" would be typical. While the statement may be true, it is only hearsay in the absence of the actual data, a level of significance and a proper citation. In a revision such statements are supported with the inclusion of the data and significance level, "tadpole survival was significantly ($p \leq 0.05$) decreased by 50% in the treatment group receiving the highest (50mg/L) dose (Bayer, Curto, & Kriley, 2005, p.13).

The biology instructor's feedback, while not explicitly focusing on the norms and conventions of speaking like a biologist, implicitly taught the student what those conventions were through correction, modeling, and example.

In addition to discipline-specific commentary from the instructor, students recognized peer feedback as significant. Written comments provided just after the first talk were provided to each presenter. These comments often revealed a consensus of concern regarding a particular problem. Students remarked that a consensus of opinion regarding a particular aspect of their scientific talk had considerable influence on helping them refine their presentation. Here was a chance for students to observe and learn the impact of their message on their audience who, with some level of expertise to appreciate the science content, could alert them to science issues specific to their topic.

Finally, self-review was recognized as important to these students. They cited the opportunity to re-think, revise, and re-present their research as a significant factor contributing to increased confidence in their knowledge of biology and the ability to communicate it.

These multiple forms of feedback were intended to encourage reflection and reconsideration as part of a knowledge cycle that included learning about biology, the organization and delivery of a scientific presentation, and the correct use of biology terminology. Our research, rooted in operative ideas of disciplinary culture, focused on educational practices to facilitate competence in using the language of biology. The process of receiving assessment, evaluating assessment, and revising/restructuring of the science and its expression, offered significant formative assessment opportunities. The specific nature of this feedback geared to each individual student was well received as reflected in post-course surveys. At a time when instructors are encouraged to create active and participatory types of pedagogy, this operative model is an effective method of promoting students' general and discipline-specific communication skills.

Impact on Future Scientific Presentations

In our fourth research question, we investigated whether a successful presentation would affect students' perceptions of their ability to develop future scientific presentations. At the conclusion of the semester, the majority of senior biology students in our study reported a significant change in their ability to speak about biology with added confidence in their skill to do *future* scientific presentations. They also reported a deeper understanding about the science of their topics. That so many of the students in our study left the course with considerable confidence to organize and deliver *future* scientific presentations speaks volumes about a change in their perception of their transition from novice to greater disciplinary competence. Eighty-one percent of students in the follow-up survey reported high levels of satisfaction with the science and the delivery of their final presentations. This change in self-perception and the ability to "speak biology" was a sharp departure from their reports of their initial self-perceptions that were dominated by comments expressing little comfort, confidence, and knowledge. This transformation in their self-evaluation of their abilities to develop and deliver future scientific presentations is perhaps the most compelling metacognitive dimension of this study. The many statements about increased knowledge and confidence, as well as *their perceptions* that they were able to *transfer* their ability to speak like biologists to future scientific presentations, are clear evidence of metacognitive growth.

Conclusion

Becoming more comfortable in using the language of one's discipline, being able to successfully engage with others within a specialized discourse community, feeling a sense of accomplishment and confidence in knowledge about a biological controversy, and knowing how to present material in an oral genre were common strengths that students reported in the follow-up survey. Many explicitly commented that talking about the science led to a deeper understanding of it and therefore to a greater ability to speak and write about it. In their own words, students acknowledged the critical thinking inherent in good oral communication: "The presentation helped me to better understand my subject matter"; "Having to explain things orally makes you understand it better overall"; or "I did feel that I understood the information better only because I had the chance to talk it out and verbally make sense of things."

Competency in biology is frequently assessed in an oral communication format ranging from formal research presentations, poster presentations, or an interview. The failure to communicate effectively masks students' knowledge, because they cannot express what they know. Our goal was to improve students' general ability to use the language of their discipline to more accurately reflect their scientific knowledge. The self-reported data from students, overall grade improvement, continued use over five years with hundreds of students, and adoption by all biology instructors of the course suggest that this intervention is successful in promoting general skills in both oral communication and speaking like a biologist.

Instructors hope that efforts to improve course modules match well with the course goals and contribute toward future real-world capabilities. This intervention seems to match well with improving students' oral presentation skills and competence in using the language of their discipline. Thus, the final oral presentation fulfilled the goal of being an authentic assessment, one well matched to our instructional goals and to learning skills useful in a science career beyond this course.

References

American Association for the Advancement of Science. (2011). *Communicating Science.* Retrieved from http://communicatingscience.aaas.org/Pages/newmain.asp

Bayer, T., Curto, K. A., & Kriley, C. (2005). Acquiring expertise in discipline-specific discourse: An interdisciplinary exercise in learning to *speak* biology. *Across the Dis-*

ciplines, 2, 1–25. Retrieved from
http://wac.colostate.edu/atd/articles/bayer_curto_kriley2005.cfm

Boyer Commission on Educating Undergraduates in the Research University. (1998). *Reinventing undergraduate education: A blueprint for America's research universities.* NY: State University of New York.

Bransford, J. D., Brown, A. L., & Cocking, R. R. (2000). (Eds.). *How people learn.* Washington, DC: National Academy Press.

Curto, K. A., & Bayer, T. (2005) Writing and speaking to learn biology: An intersection of critical thinking and communication skills. *Bioscene: Journal of College Biology Teaching, 31*, 11–19.

Florence, M. K., & Yore, L. D. (2004). Learning to write like a scientist: Coauthoring as an acculturation task. *Journal of Research in Science Teaching, 41*(6), 637–668.

Halpern, D. F., & Hakel, M. D. (Eds.). (2003). *Applying the science of learning to the university and beyond: Teaching for long-term retention and transfer.* San Franciso, CA: Jossey-Bass

Lowe, J. P. (1994). *Assessment that promotes learning.* Retrieved from Center for Excellence in Learning & Teaching website: http://www.psu.edu/celt/Lowe.html

Olson, R. (2009). *Don't be such a scientist: Talking substance in an age of style.* Washington, DC: Island Press.

Yore, L. D. (2000). Enhancing science literacy for all students with embedded reading instruction and writing to learn activities. *Journal of Deaf Studies and Deaf Education, 5*, 105–122.

Zull, J. E. (2002). *The art of changing the brain.* Sterling, VA: Stylus Publishing.

Chapter 9

Using Theory and Research to Increase Student Use of Communication Center Services

Jennifer Butler Ellis and Rose Clark-Hitt

Although assessment can seem like a daunting task, there is increasing pressure from a variety of internal and external audiences to define and measure success in our communication centers. For many, assessment of relevant metrics such as communication center usage is an ongoing process required by administrators to justify future funding. Ultimately, assessment is most useful when it can serve a variety of purposes and create feedback loops for continuous improvement efforts in the center. Thus, we argue that although initially there may be heavy start-up costs, using theory and research to develop assessment efforts and conduct formative research can pay large dividends down the road, as well as yield useful data for assessment and increase student utilization of communication center services.

Typically, student visits to the center are an important assessment outcome. However, despite availability, students may not make full use of communication center services. One route for increasing usage of center services is developing persuasive messages targeted at students. These persuasive messages would increase student awareness of communication center services and encourage them to use the services offered at the center.

Formative research is the process of learning about the target audience to determine the most effective routes for developing persuasive messages. Atkin and Freimuth (2001) described formative evaluation research for campaign development as answering "questions about target audiences for a program or

131

campaign, encompassing the collection of background information about audience orientations before initiating a campaign and assessment of the implementation and effectiveness during and after the campaign" (p. 125). Two phases of formative research, preproduction research and production testing, are critical for developing persuasive messages. In pre-production research, the goal is to learn about characteristics of the target audience (e.g., attitudes and beliefs) and the behaviors that are the desired outcome for the messages. In production testing, messages are evaluated on a small scale by audience members prior to mass dissemination of the messages.

The goal of this chapter is to provide suggestions for how to conduct formative research for the design and evaluation of messages persuading students to use communication center services. The use of persuasion theory is critical for pre-production research, providing a framework for evaluating audience characteristics as well as assessing persuasive message campaign efforts and outcomes. Thus, select persuasion theories will be briefly described (see sources cited for a more in-depth look at each theory) with examples for use in preproduction work. Various methods for conducting pre-production and production testing research will also be highlighted, including interviews, focus groups, and surveys, as well as practical tips for obtaining participation in each (e.g., electronic survey software, incentives). Finally, this chapter will discuss methods for evaluation of message campaign efforts.

Theoretical Approaches

Psychologist Kurt Lewin (1951) famously stated, "There is nothing so practical as a good theory" (p. 169). Theory can be a practical tool for identifying relevant audience characteristics and developing appropriate messages to persuade the target audience to use communication center services. With theory as our guide, findings gleaned from formative research may be used to customize persuasive messages in terms of content, structure, and source features. Specifically, by identifying student beliefs and attitudes about communication centers, we may increase student utilization of communication center services and ultimately improve communication center programs. This outcome would yield positive results with respect to assessment efforts as well as overall programmatic success. In this chapter we will provide a brief introduction to persuasion theories, with a brief overview of the theory of planned behavior (Azjen, 1991) (See chapter 10 for a complete description) and more detailed descriptions of the social norms approach (Berkowitz, 2005) and health belief model (Rosenstock, 1990). We also provide examples of how to use these theories to develop persuasive messages targeted at increasing student use of communication center services.

Theory of Planned Behavior

The theory of planned behavior (TPB) has been used as a guide for studying a wide range of behaviors including speaking to family members about organ donation (Park & Smith, 2007) and exercise (Azjen & Fishbein, 1980). The TPB is an expectancy-value theory, with behaviors influenced by the expectations individuals hold about the outcomes of the behavior, and the value they associate with the outcomes (Azjen, 1991). According to the TPB, attitudes, subjective norms, and perceived behavioral control together predict behavioral intention. Attitudes are positive or negative evaluations of some object and subjective norms are beliefs about whether individuals important to a person think he or she should engage in a behavior (Azjen & Fishbein, 1980). Perceived behavioral control involves "people's perception of the ease or difficulty of performing the behavior of interest" (Azjen, 1991, p. 183). In a meta-analysis of 189 studies using TPB, Armitage and Conner (2001) reported the three predictors account for 39 percent of the variation in intention and 27 percent of variation in behavior. Further, TPB suggests intention to perform a behavior will predict the actual behavior.

The TPB may be useful for communication centers message design. For example, by having students and/or faculty complete surveys reporting their beliefs (associated with the three types of predictors) about communication centers, we can learn what combination of the three predictors are significant and thus identify targets for persuasion efforts. Furthermore, if initial survey work guided by the TPB shows that a target audience has beliefs about visiting the communication center that are inaccurate (such as the belief that an appointment is too time consuming) it may be useful to target that belief with a message refuting that belief, showing that the center actually provides flexible timing, and that the consultation length can be customized to student wishes. For a more detailed overview of the TPB, please see chapter 10 in this book. While the TPB highlights expectations individuals may hold about various behavior outcomes, the social norms approach, another framework for studying target audiences and persuasive message design, provides guidance for identifying and addressing normative perceptions that may influence student use of the communication center.

Social Norms Approach and Communication Centers

It is possible that students have misperceptions about issues such as who uses the communication center (e.g., the belief that only poorly performing students use the communication center), or that most people have negative attitudes about usage of the communication center. Such misperceptions may inhibit students' willingness to use center services if they believe that the majority of students disapprove, or that the majority of students do not or would not use center services. The social norms approach is concerned with two types of norms: descriptive and injunctive. Descriptive norms are beliefs about what other people in one's social group are doing (Lapinski & Rimal, 2005), while injunctive norms are beliefs about "social approval of the act" (Park & Smith, 2007, p. 196).

The social norms approach revolves around providing accurate information to the target population to correct any misperceptions that may lead to negative or harmful behaviors. Moreover, the social norms approach is based in cognitive dissonance theory. When individuals are confronted with contradictory information such as accurate information about true norms when they hold misperceptions of norms, they are motivated to resolve the dissonance because it is uncomfortable (Berkowitz, 2005). Thus, perceptions of norms move closer to the true or actual norms. The social norms approach has been widely studied with regard to heavy drinking among college students, but it has also been applied in a variety of other contexts including environmental conservation attitudes (Primmer and Karpinnen, 2010), re-use of hotel linens (Goldstein, Griskevicius, & Cialdini, 2007), rumor spreading among students (Cross & Peisner, 2009), and tax compliance (Wenzel, 2004). To illustrate in the context of heavy college drinking, it has been documented that college students frequently over-estimate their peers' heavy drinking. Social norms messages provide accurate information about what the majority of students "think and do all on the basis of credible data drawn from the student population that is the target" to correct these misperceptions (Perkins, 2003, p. 11). These messages are positive, demonstrating that the actual norm is a more moderate level of behavior or attitude than the perceived norm.

To evaluate whether there is a misperception about communication center services, and thus the potential utility for a social norms intervention to correct any misperceptions, several steps are needed: identify perceived descriptive, injunctive, and actual norms, look for discrepancies between perceived and actual norms, and determine if messages may be used to correct misperceptions (Olin Health Center and Health and Risk Communication Center, 2008). First, survey data should be used to identify perceived descriptive and injunctive norms and actual norms about behaviors so that the actual norms and the perceived norms may be compared. If the results indicate that the majority of the population approve of visiting the communication center or would use it themselves, yet the majority believe that others do not approve or would not use the center, then it is appropriate to use a social norms approach in which messages undermine the misperceptions of the majority by providing correct information (Perkins, 2003). Providing such intervention messages is predicted to lead to less exaggerated perceptions about the attitudes and behaviors of others, and in turn influence behavior with lesser levels of the undesirable behavior (e.g., avoiding communication center services).[1] Another applicable theoretical guide is the health belief model which provides guidance concerning the value and cost students may place on using communication center services.

Health Belief Model and Communication Centers

Although the health belief model (HBM) may seem an unusual persuasion theory to apply to communication centers, the HBM describes factors that predict whether a person will engage in a personally beneficial behavior. When applied to the behavior of utilizing communication center services, the HBM guides us to consider the value and costs students may place on utilizing communication center services. Typically the HBM has been used to study whether or not people engage in various health behaviors, and has been traditionally applied to areas such as wearing bicycle safety helmets (Witte, Stokols, Ituarte, & Schneider, 1993), use of tanning booths (Greene & Brinn, 2003), and obtaining the tuberculosis vaccination (Rosenstock, 1990).

The HBM is an expectancy-value theory, meaning that behavior is determined by the value associated with the outcome of the behavior and the probability that the behavior will lead to a particular outcome (Rosenstock, 1990). Applied to health behavior, this translates into whether a person desires to avoid an illness, and the belief that performing a particular behavior will prevent the illness. According to the HBM, people are motivated to perform preventive health behaviors based on beliefs about perceived threat (severity and susceptibility), perceived benefits, self-efficacy, and perceived barriers. In addition, the HBM suggests that perceived threat is determined by 1) perceived susceptibility (the risk of contracting a disease) and 2) perceived severity (how serious or scary the outcome is, such as death, pain, or social consequences). Higher levels of perceived threat will be associated with greater likelihood of acting on recommended behaviors. Perceived benefits are beliefs that the action will be effective in diminishing the threat. The self-efficacy construct, the belief that one is capable of successfully performing the recommended action, was added to the HBM in the 1980s. Perceived barriers are any negative aspect of performing a certain action, such as high financial costs, or danger, such as side effects, unpleasantness, or inconvenience (Rosenstock, 1990).

The model also includes cues to action, which are "specific stimuli necessary to trigger appropriate health behavior" (Mattson, 1999, p. 243). Cues to action act as stimulants for self-protective behaviors. Cues to action may be internal or external. External cues include messages from media sources, advice from others, illness of someone close, whereas internal cues may be a symptom that alters perceived threat.

When applying HBM to the behavior of utilizing communication center services, the model leads us to consider student perceptions about the risk of utilizing communication services and the consequences of not using the services offered at the center. Furthermore, we argue that motivating students to voluntarily participate in efforts to improve communication skills is a natural extension of the HBM. Similar to health behaviors, having strong professional communication skills can have a substantial bearing on life outcomes such as whether one is hired for a job, whether one is able to maintain a job, or earn promotions. With regard to the health belief model, students must first perceive that there is some sort of threat (perceived severity of outcome and perceived susceptibility) associated with not having strong communication skills (e.g., poor job performance, lack of assignment potential at work, or lack of promotion potential). Second, students must perceive that there is an effective and reasonable action they can take to mitigate the risk and that the benefits of the action outweigh the perceived barriers (e.g., lack of time). Therefore, when using the HBM to guide formative research, one should answer the following questions to guide formative evaluation.

1. What are student perceptions of the advantages/disadvantages of visiting the communication center?
2. Do students perceive particular threats associated with not having strong professional communication skills (perceived threat)? If so, what threats do they perceive?
3. Do students perceive benefits for their future job performance associated with seeking professional communication skills assistance? If so, what benefits do they perceive?
4. Do students perceive barriers associated with visiting the communication center to improve their professional communication skills? If so, what barriers do they perceive?
5. Do students perceive barriers to improving their professional communication skills? If so, what barriers do they perceive?

Gaining answers to these questions is beneficial for developing persuasive messages targeting various student beliefs. For example, if formative research reveals that one reason students do not visit the communication center is because they fear criticism, messages designed to counter this perception can be targeted at students. Furthermore, training communication center staff to balance student critique with both positive messages and constructive criticism may also help communication centers develop a positive reputation and encourage more students to make appointments. Communication centers can also be a place for students to build confidence in their communication skills. By designing messages that highlight the potential threats associated with poor communication skills and the benefits of utilizing communication center services, students may be persuaded to schedule more appointments at the communication center.

Methodological Approaches for Data Collection and Message Dissemination

There are several methodological issues to consider for conducting formative research to develop and disseminate persuasive messages for your communication center. First, it is important to determine your goals, as these will dictate the theory, formative evaluation methods, and assessment procedures you use. Second, various research methods are useful for collecting information about your target audience, including interviews, focus groups, and survey instruments; the relative advantages of each are discussed. Third, there are several practical tips to consider for obtaining participation by your target audience members in your research efforts, including providing incentives and making participation convenient. Fourth, it is important to consider the role of partnerships with other stakeholders at your institution for collecting target audience data and for developing messages. Finally, recommendations for message dissemination are provided.

To maximize persuasive message campaign efforts it is important to also consider what methodologies would be most effective in communicating your message and when possible find ways to accomplish multiple purposes simultaneously (i.e., collect valuable assessment data and send important messages to various target audiences). This multi-tasking approach may help us better use our valuable and limited resources.

Establishing Desired Goals and Objectives

It is important to first determine the desired outcomes associated with your message intervention efforts. These goals will influence the theoretical foundation and message strategies chosen. There are several types of outcomes that you may be interested in for your message efforts, including improving student attitudes about the communication center, increasing awareness and knowledge of services provided, and increasing the number of people who would recommend communication center services to peers/friends. Likely, your most desired goal is to increase the number of student visits to the communication center. Once you select goals, the next step is to determine how to collect data to measure progress toward those goals.

Research Data Collection Methods

Interviews provide an opportunity for gathering information about student attitudes and pre-testing messages. The interactional process of interviewing involves asking and answering questions and may be used to give and get information (Stewart & Cash, 2008). Thus, one benefit of the interview methodology is the opportunity to not only get information from students about their attitudes, but to also share information about the communication center and services the interviewees might find useful. However, although in-person interviews provide rich qualitative data and generally generate a good response rate, they are one of the more expensive methods and typically require more time and paper (Hocking, Stacks, & McDermott, 2003).

Compared to in-person interviews, focus groups are a faster method for acquiring qualitative data. One of the major advantages of focus groups is that participants can respond to other participant answers and often arrive at different conclusions than the simple in-person interview (Hocking et al., 2003). Focus groups can be described as group interviews where a moderator guides the interview, while a small group discusses the topics raised by the interviewer (Morgan, 1998a). Krueger (1994) explains that focus groups involve "(a) people, . . . [who] (b) possess certain characteristics, and (c) provide data (d) of a qualitative nature (e) in a focused discussion" (p. 16).

Focus group projects involve four basic steps: planning, recruiting, moderating, and analysis and reporting (Morgan, 1998b). In the planning phase, the researcher determines the research questions that can be answered with qualitative data and identifies the target group or groups from which the participants will be recruited. The recruitment phase involves defining the target population, identifying the appropriate composition for each group, making initial recruitment contacts with potential participants, and determining the follow-up procedures that will ensure attendance (Morgan, 1998b). In the moderating phase, questions for the discussion guide are developed, arrangements for the focus group locations are clarified, and note-taking and recording issues are determined (Morgan, 1998b). The analysis and reporting phase of focus group interviews involves organizing, summarizing, and reporting the results of the focus group interviews (Morgan, 1998b).

Compared to interviews and focus groups, questionnaires are typically cheaper to administer and can provide participants with anonymity (Hocking, Stacks, & McDermott, 2003). This anonymity may encourage students to be more honest about their attitudes and beliefs, while focus groups and in-person interviews may place an unspoken pressure on participants to provide what they perceive as socially desirable answers. Another advantage of using questionnaires includes more flexibility for participants because they can complete questionnaires on their own time and in a location of their choice. There are also strong advantages to surveys from the data analysis point of view, such as the ability to obtain responses from a much larger sample of the population than with focus groups or interviews, and the ability to statistically assess relationships among variables that are important for the message design process. For example, when using survey data with the theory of planned behavior it is possible to perform multiple regression to determine the significant predictors of behavioral intention to use center services, therefore helping to focus message design efforts. Although questionnaires provide a relatively quick and easy way to assess student perceptions, attitudes, and behaviors, they do not allow the researcher to probe for more information or feedback (Hocking, Stacks, & McDermott, 2003). This reduced feedback loop may create problems if careful planning has not been done prior to mass distribution of the questionnaire. Furthermore, questionnaires do not provide rich qualitative data gleaned from in-person interviews or focus groups. Thus, researchers must determine the pros and cons for each methodology in relation to the questions being asked and the target population.

Maximizing Participation in Data Collection Efforts

There are several strategies for improving the likelihood that individuals will participate in formative research efforts. When using a survey methodology, it is important to consider how to make surveys as easy as possible for students to complete, and provide incentives for participation. To facilitate participation, there are several online survey software programs (e.g., Survey Monkey, Websurveyor) that may be used to create online survey links so that students can complete the survey electronically wherever and whenever it is convenient for them.

For incentives, items that have worked well for the authors in various projects have been providing extra credit for class in exchange for completing surveys, providing pizza and soda for focus group participants, and holding raffles for gift cards (e.g., raffle for four $25 gift cards) for those who agree to complete surveys or participate in an interview.

It is also important to consider how to reach large audiences to promote the completion of your survey instrument, especially if you are using an online survey. Seeking assistance of faculty members or instructors who support the communication center may be beneficial, as they may be willing to distribute a survey to their students. It is also beneficial to seek the help of a staff member or student with access to listservs with large numbers of student e-mail addresses to e-mail an electronic survey link. When contacting individuals requesting that they distribute your survey link, it is advisable to provide sample messages that they may use to paste into an e-mail, tweet, or Facebook post, for example, so that they do not have to do the work of creating a message. Other strategies may include contacting the administrator for your school's official Facebook Fan page to ask them if they could post your survey; this can be successful especially if you are offering an incentive such as a raffle for a gift card.

Sources and Stakeholder Buy-in

After collecting data about your target audience, the next step is designing persuasive messages for your campaign. One important consideration when developing persuasive messages is finding appropriate sources for some messages. Students or your target audience may find various messages more persuasive when coming from a variety of sources such as faculty, peers, alumni, and future employers. Thus, developing relationships with faculty who can provide quotes highlighting the benefits of using communication services may be a valuable resource when designing messages. In addition, asking faculty to write short messages about why they believe the communication center is important may generate a set of messages to choose from. Furthermore, acquiring student and alumni testimonials from individuals who have used the communication center regularly or for an important assignment may also be seen as persuasive by the target audience.

When conducting formative research it is important to consider a variety of people who can assist in your efforts. Program administrators of orientation programs, directors, and faculty may be useful contacts for assisting in data collection. Distributing a brief survey at the beginning of a class or orientation program may be a valuable opportunity to increase your sample size and collect data quickly. However, it is important when finding people who can help you that all efforts are made to minimize costs to the people who are assisting with data collection. If the survey cuts into too much class or program time, you may find these people less willing to help out the next time you want to survey students. Carefully estimate how much time you need before asking, so that you create allies. These allies can also be important communication center advocates and may persuade students to use the center when they are interacting with students. Thus, all efforts should be made to build relationships with important stakeholders.

Message Dissemination Suggestions (Communication Channels)

After collecting data about your target audience and designing appropriate persuasive messages, there are a number of communication channels available for disseminating messages designed to persuade students to utilize communication center services. Essentially this is the point where all your campaign efforts become highly visible (i.e., you have a message or messages that you want to communicate to your target audience). However, deciding what channel or channels will be most effective also requires an understanding of your target audience. Some channels may be largely ignored by a target audience while other channels may be viewed on a regular basis. Thus, to maximize the overall effectiveness of your message campaign and research efforts, a variety of communication channels should be considered. Traditional channels such as brochures and posters may be one way to communicate your message. In addition, sending messages via e-mail or posting messages on a website or on a Facebook group may also increase the number of students who see your messages as well as how often they see your message.

However, never underestimate the power of interpersonal persuasion. In a focus group conducted by the authors, we found that students felt we should send consultants to classrooms to give a brief plug for the communication center and encourage students to schedule appointments. Students claimed that this may help them feel more comfortable scheduling appointments because they can actually see friendly and approachable consultants who are willing to help them. Open houses held once or twice a year may also be an opportunity to disseminate messages encouraging students to use the services offered at the communication center. An open house provides an event where students can meet the communication center staff and learn more about how the center can help them. These interpersonal communication opportunities may be very persuasive to students and should not be neglected when designing a campaign seeking to motivate students to visit the communication center.

Message Campaign Assessment

Ongoing assessment of campaign messages, efforts, and overall communication programs and services is an important activity communication centers must prioritize. Thus, communication center personnel should consider conducting follow-up interviews or distributing surveys to determine how students have responded to the message campaign and if these messages are yielding the desired outcomes. Assessment provides valuable feedback that may be used to design effective messages that motivate students to use communication center services. Furthermore, this feedback may also be useful in better understanding the needs of your target audience so that you can better serve students when they come to the communication center.

Specifically, it is important to evaluate the effectiveness of your campaign efforts in terms of desired outcomes, as discussed earlier in the chapter, as well as the effectiveness of the message campaign process. The outcomes you measure should reflect the goals of the campaign (e.g., improving student attitudes about the communication center, increasing awareness and knowledge of services provided, and increasing the number of people who would recommend communication center services to peers/friends). Without assessment we cannot be sure our campaign efforts are making a difference. Assessment may also provide unexpected information such as positive or negative unintended consequences of the message campaign. Gleaning this information is vital for further adapting messages to the target audience and improving overall usage of communication center services.

To measure changes in student attitudes or beliefs, statistics such as *t*-tests may be used to statistically analyze quantitative data and test for differences in means scores for attitudes or beliefs measured before and after campaign or message exposure. To qualitatively assess changes in attitudes or beliefs, focus groups or interviews should be conducted before and after campaign or message exposure to assess student attitudes, beliefs, and behavioral intention.

To measure behavior change, outcome evaluation measures such as counting the number of visits students make to the communication center, the length of appointments, and workshop attendance may provide evidence of how persuasive the campaign has been. In addition to evaluating the overall effectiveness of your campaign efforts, this data may be useful to share with various stakeholders and administrators about the overall importance and success of your communication center.

Another important consideration goes back to the theoretical framing for your campaign. By using the data collected to assess the theoretical model, you can explore how significantly the message intervention contributes to student attitudes, beliefs, or behaviors as predicted by your model. This analysis may be helpful in identifying important predictors of attitudes, beliefs, and behaviors and may provide guidance for adjusting future message content or campaign efforts.

Finally, evaluating the message campaign process includes examining factors such as exposure to the messages (Atkin & Freimuth, 2001). Before a message can be persuasive, it needs to reach the target audience, thus it is useful to track various aspects of the dissemination of the message and re-adjust if necessary. While it may be more difficult to track exposure through certain media, it is possible, for example, to track the number of impressions a target audience receives on web-based media. Additionally, if a campaign goal is to increase visits to the communication center website, it is useful to use a service such as Google Analytics that allows tracking of items such as the number of visits to a particular URL per day and the sources of those visits (e.g., whether web traffic typed the communication center URL directly or if they came from particular pages like Facebook where you may be posting advertisements). It is also possible to track the percentage of visitors to a web page who click on a particular link within the page to help determine how much exposure visitors are getting to particular information on the site. For messages being disseminated across all forms of media, it may also be helpful to evaluate whether a sample of individuals in the target audience recall the messages to determine whether the message was processed.

Conclusion

Persuading students to utilize communication center services is an important activity communication center personnel must consider when seeking to maximize communication center effectiveness and success. If students do not come to the communication center, it does not matter how beautiful the space is, what state of the art technology is available, or how many consultants are available; justifying your existence will be difficult. Thus, we must be concerned about maximizing student usage of communication center services (e.g., increasing the overall number of student appointments, helping more students use on-line tutoring, or distributing more best practices or communication center handouts).

In sum, this chapter described the process of using theory to design persuasive message campaigns in an effort to increase student utilization of communication center services. Although research and assessment can be a challenging process, using persuasion theory may be a tool that can facilitate assessment efforts and provide important data that can be used to improve communication center programs. Furthermore, this research may be shared with external audiences such as administrators, accreditation review teams, and external advisory boards. By conducting formative evaluation research and assessing campaign efforts, communication center personnel may find persuasion an effective tool for assessment efforts and increasing student usage of communication center services.

Notes

1. To assess perceived norms for communication center usage, a question such as, "What percentage of students do you think would visit the communication center this year?" would be useful in identifying perceived norms about using the center. Actual norms could be assessed with a survey question asking students (using a 7-point Likert scale with endpoints of strongly agree to strongly disagree) if they intend to use the communication center in the coming year. For an excellent, highly detailed description of employing the social norms approach for creating messages, please see the document titled *Challenging High-Risk Drinking at MSU: A Social Norms Approach* at http://socialnorms.msu.edu/index.php?page=resources-downloads

References

Armitage, C. J., & Conner, M. (2001). Efficacy of the theory of planned behaviour: A meta-analytic review. *British Journal of Social Psychology, 40,* 471–499.

Atkin, C. K., & Freimuth, V. S. (2001). Formative evaluation research in campaign design. In R. E. Rice & C. K. Atkin (Eds.), *Public communication campaigns* (pp. 125–145). Thousand Oaks: Sage Publications, Inc.

Azjen, I. (1991). The theory of planned behavior. *Organizational behavior and human decision processes, 50*, 179–211.

Azjen, I., & Fishbein, M. (1980). *Understanding attitudes and predicting social behavior.* Englewood Cliffs, NJ: Prentice Hall.

Berkowitz, A. D. (2005). An overview of the social norms approach. In L. Lederman, L. Stewart, F. Goodhart, & L. Laitman (Eds.), *Changing the culture of college drinking: A socially situated prevention campaign.* Cresskill, NJ: Hampton Press.

Cross, J., & Peisner,W. (2009). A social norms campaign to reduce rumor spreading in a junior high school. *Professional School Counseling, 12*, 365–377.

Goldstein, N. J., Griskevicius, V., & Cialdini, R. B. (2007). Invoking social norms: A social psychology perspective on improving hotels' linen-reuse programs. *Cornell Hotel and Restaurant Administration Quarterly, 48* (2), 145–150.

Greene, K., & Brinn, L. (2003). Messages influencing college women's tanning bed use: Statistical versus narrative evidence format and a self-assessment to increase perceived susceptibility. *Journal of Health Communication, 8*, 443–461.

Hocking, J. E., Stacks, D. W., & McDermott, S. T. (2003). *Communication research* (3rd ed.). Boston, MA: Allyn and Bacon.

Krueger, R. A. (1994). *Focus groups: A practical guide for applied research* (2nd ed.). Newbury Park, CA: Sage.

Lapinski, M., & Rimal, R. (2005). An explication of social norms. *Communication Theory, 15*, 127–147.

Lewin, K. (1951). *Field theory in social science; selected theoretical papers.* New York: Harper & Row.

Mattson, M. (1999). Toward a reconceptualization of communication cues to action in the Health Belief Model: HIV test counseling. *Communication Monographs, 66*, 240–265.

Morgan, D. L. (1998a). *The focus groups guidebook.* Thousand Oaks, CA: Sage Publications, Inc.

Morgan, D. L. (1998b). *Planning focus groups.* Thousand Oaks, CA: Sage Publications, Inc.

Olin Health Center and Health and Risk Communication Center (2008). Challenging high-risk drinking at MSU: A social norms approach. Retrieved from http://socialnorms.msu.edu/index.php?page=resources-downloads

Park, H. S., & Smith. S. W. (2007). Distinctiveness and influence of subjective norms, personal descriptive and injunctive norms, and societal descriptive and injunctive norms on behavioral intent: A case of two behaviors critical to organ donation. *Human Communication Research, 33*, 194–218.

Perkins, H. W. (2003). The emergence and evolution of the Social Norms Approach to substance abuse prevention. In H.W. Perkins (Ed.), *The social norms approach to preventing school and college age substance abuse: A handbook for educators, counselors, and clinicians.* San Francisco: Jossey-Bass.

Primmer, E., & Karpinnen, H. (2010). Professional judgment in non-industrial private forestry: Forester attitudes and social norms influencing biodiversity conservation. *Forest Policy and Economics, 12* (2), 136–146.

Rosenstock, T. (1990). The Health Belief Model: Explaining health behavior through expectancies. In K. Glanz, F. Lewis, & B. Rimer (Eds.), *Health behavior and health education: Theory research and practice* (pp. 39–62). San Francisco,

Stewart, C. J., & Cash, W. B., Jr. (2008). *Interviewing: Principles and practices* (12th ed.). Boston: McGraw-Hill.

Wenzel, M. (2004). An analysis of norm processes in tax compliance. *Journal of Economic Psychology, 25*, 213–228.

Witte, K., Stokols, D., Ituarte, P., & Schneider, M. (1993). Testing the Health Belief Model in a field study to promote bicycle safety helmets. *Communication Research, 20*, 564–586.

Chapter 10

Focusing on Faculty: The Importance of Faculty Support to Communication Center Success

Michael L. King and Wendy Atkins-Sayre

Communication centers are important to the academic and professional success of many students, but such success hinges on students scheduling and attending tutoring sessions. To enable centers to attract these students, it becomes important to identify exactly what influences their decision to use center services. Communication centers often assume that students constitute the most critical target audience for advertisement campaigns. After all, students are often left to decide on their own if they will use center services. Although students may hear about these services as part of their college orientation, campus communication, or classroom discussion, many fail to take advantage of such support systems. The problem that many communication centers face, however, is finding the most effective method for reaching students and encouraging them to take advantage of the services. Thus, it becomes important to understand what motivates the decision to use a communication center.

Previous research (King & Atkins-Sayre, 2010) indicated that undergraduate students are most likely to attend a tutoring session when their instructors suggest they do so. This finding highlights the importance of including faculty members as a target of communication center advertisements. To make such efforts as effective as possible, the current study employs Ajzen's (1991) theory of planned behavior (TPB). The TPB provides a helpful framework with which to identify factors motivating an instructor's suggestion to attend a tutoring session at a communication center. Toward this end, this chapter first reviews TPB literature and its application to communication centers. Next, a methodology designed to identify specific factors contributing to suggesting center usage is presented. Finally, following the presentation of results, recommendations for increasing faculty support of communication centers are discussed.

The Theory of Planned Behavior

For centuries scholars have worked to better understand how people influence others with words alone (Dillard & Pfau, 2002). Contributing significantly to this endeavor is TPB (Ajzen, 1991), which subsumes its well-established precursor, the theory of reasoned action (TRA) (Fishbein & Ajzen, 1975). Generally speaking, these theories describe volitional behavior as a rational and cognitive process that directs intention, which in turn affects behavior (Ajzen, 1991; Ajzen & Fishbein, 1980, 2005; Fishbein & Ajzen, 1975). With these theories of behavior, researchers can more effectively study what Dillard and Pfau (2002) called "one of the most intellectually exciting areas of persuasion literature . . . [i.e.,] the impact of message style, structure, and content" (p. x).

In the development and application of TPB and TRA, two assumptions are made. First, intention is sufficiently related to its corresponding behavior (Fishbein & Ajzen, 1975; Sutton, 1998). Specifically, if people intend to do something, they are likely to engage in the behavior. Although not a perfect association, evidence supports the intention-behavior relationship (Armitage & Conner, 2001; Sheppard, Hartwick, & Warshaw, 1988; Sutton, 1998). The second assumption asserts that volitional behavior is predictable. Ajzen and Fishbein (1980) explained that "human beings are usually quite rational and make systematic use of the information available to them" (p. 5). This relatively consistent process results from various combinations and intensities of three individual components called direct determinants. These determinants are 1) attitude toward the behavior, 2) subjective norms, and 3) perceived behavioral control.

Attitude toward the behavior is the simple evaluation (positive/negative, good/bad) of a behavior. Generally, if a behavior is deemed positive, people are more likely to engage in the behavior (Ajzen & Fishbein, 1980). The subjective norm component addresses the perceived importance of social influence. The theory indicates that actions are, in part, determined by what people believe others (especially important others) think about the behavior in question. Similar to the attitudinal component, people will more likely engage in behaviors supported by those whose opinions are valued (Ajzen & Fishbein, 1980). Perceived behavioral control, Ajzen's (1991) individual contribution to the theory, incorporates the personal assessments of one's ability to enact a behavior in a given situation. Relative to the individual and the behavior in question, each of these direct determinants may have a rational and direct impact on a person's intention to enact a volitional behavior (Ajzen, 1991; Fishbein & Ajzen, 1975).

Beneath each direct determinant reside sets of two contributing factors that when considered together, create indirect determinants, a process explicated with the expectancy-value approach (Ajzen, 2010; Fishbein & Ajzen, 1975). Specifically, attitudes are defined as the multiplicative combination of a person's belief that a behavior will bring about a particular outcome (i.e., expectancy) and his or her evaluation of that outcome (i.e., value) (Ajzen & Fishbein, 1980). The subjective norm is a multiplicative combination of an individual's normative beliefs and his or her motivation to comply with these beliefs (Ajzen & Fishbein, 1980). Simply stated, the actions that important others find favorable or unfavorable (i.e., normative control) and their relative influence on the person (i.e., motivation to comply) combine to impact a behavior (Ajzen & Fishbein, 1980). Finally, perceived behavioral control is determined by the multiplicative combination of a person's belief regarding his or her controllability of an action and the degree to which he or she thinks the specific belief will assist or impede the behavior (Ajzen, 1991).

Researchers have conducted several meta-analyses reviewing the theory's application in the areas of general health-related behavior (Godin & Kok, 1996), exercise behavior (Hausenblas, Carron, & Mack, 1997), and condom use (Albarracin, Johnson, Fishbein, & Muellerleile, 2001), just to name a few. To date, Armitage and Connor (2001) provided the most comprehensive TPB meta-analysis. They found the combination of the three main TPB components accounted for approximately 39 percent of the variance explaining intention to enact volitional behavior (Armitage & Conner, 2001).

Communication Centers

In order to enable centers to attract students, it is important to identify what influences their decision to use center services. This understanding would maximize the persuasive effects of future message campaigns (Hardeman et al., 2002; Webb & Sheeran, 2006). Contributing first to the success of these campaigns were Clark-Hitt, Ellis, and Bender (2008). These authors argued that attitudes, subjective norms, and control beliefs were all significant predictors of accounting graduate students' intentions to use a communication center.

With the desire to expand the generalizability of these results, King and Atkins-Sayre (2010) also employed a TPB framework, but investigated both student and faculty motivators for using or suggesting the use of the communication center. This data suggested that students are more likely to attend a tutoring session when they believe their instructors want them to attend the communication center. Effective allocation of advertising efforts, they concluded, would then be directed at instructors as well as students. Therefore, to improve the efficiency of a faculty-focused advertising campaign, this chapter identifies and discusses specific factors motivating educators to suggest their students attend a communication center tutoring session.

In their first steps toward identifying factors contributing to instructors' communication center use, King and Atkins-Sayre (2010) employed qualitative procedures designed to inductively identify salient beliefs (Ajzen & Fishbein, 1980) regarding instructors encouraging students to use the communication center. Six attitudinal, three normative, and three control salient beliefs were identified (see table 10.1). Additionally, King and Atkins-Sayre reported that despite the possibility that some faculty members may have a discipline-specific mindset (see Dannels, 2001), instructors did not express concern that a communication center consultation may impede disciplinary-specific styles of speaking among students. Although this issue did not appear as a salient belief, it may have a latent effect on communication center use, and was thus included as a salient belief.

Table 10.1. Instructors' Salient Belief Categories

Component	Thematic Category	Definition
Attitudinal beliefs		*Instructors believe students attending a tutoring session may or may not result in these outcomes:*
	Feedback	receiving feedback about speech from tutor
	Tips	receiving tips (not specific to their speech)
	Presentation	improving the speech
	Affect	becoming more confident and less anxious
	Motivation	becoming motivated to work on their speech
	Discipline	receiving non-disciplinary speaking advice
Normative beliefs		*Instructors believe these groups influence their behavior:*
	Students	students in their classes
	Administration	chairs, deans, provosts, etc.
	Department	other faculty members within their dept.
Control beliefs		*Instructors feel these factors will impact their ability to suggest use of the center:*
	Knowledge	a lack of knowledge about center services
	Student resistance	students will actively resist such suggestions
	Availability	the center's hours and location

The emergence of salient beliefs, however, does not indicate a generalizable effect on the behavior in question (Ajzen & Fishbein, 1980). Therefore, the following study identifies the relative influence of each direct and indirect determinant on instructors' intention to suggest communication center usage. Accordingly, the following research questions are offered:

1. What direct determinants (i.e., attitude toward behavior, subjective norm, and perceived behavioral control) contribute to instructors' intention to suggest students attend a tutoring session at the communication center for an oral assignment?
2. What indirect determinants (i.e., salient instructor beliefs) contribute to instructors' intention to suggest students attend a tutoring session at the communication center for an oral assignment?

Method

Participants

Participants were instructors from a midsized Southeastern public university, and were solicited with direct email messages and reminders posted in the university's faculty announcement email. Through these announcements, respondents followed a link to an online survey. Eighty-one instructors (49.4 percent male, 49.4 percent female, and 1 percent unidentified) completed the questionnaire. Of these respondents, most were assistant (37 percent) or associate (32.1 percent) professors, and 79 percent of the sample reported having over five years working experience in higher education. Finally, all colleges within the university were represented.

Questionnaire

The creation of the questionnaire administered during this study followed procedures prescribed by previous TPB practitioners and theorists (i.e., Ajzen, 2006; Ajzen & Fishbein, 1980; Francis et al., 2004; Godin & Kok, 1996). The questionnaire measured the relative contribution of respondents' attitude, subjective norm, and perceived behavioral control on their intention to suggest the use of the communication center. Each component (including intention) was measured with a three-item scale and was summed to create a composite score. One item was removed from the attitude scale to improve its reliability. Table 10.2 presents the descriptive statistics for the scales.

Indirect determinants were measured with 7-point Likert-type scales. A single item assessed the degree to which the respondent agreed with a specific salient belief. A corresponding item assessed the perceived importance of this belief. Thus, sets of two items represented each category listed in table 10.1. Scale reliabilities are not reported for indirect determinants because different individuals may have, relative to each other, inconstant beliefs (Ajzen, 2010).

Table 10.2. Direct Determinants: Descriptive Statistics

Scale	Instructors			
	Range	Mean	SD	α
Advice Effectiveness	3–21	12.58	3.89	.84
Attitude	2–14	12.93	1.60	.85
Subjective Norm	3–21	16.39	3.27	.71
Perceived Control	3–21	18.99	2.60	.63
Intention	3–21	18.01	3.55	.89

Procedure

Participants were provided basic information about the Speaking Center[1] and the services it provides. Instructors not planning to assign an oral assignment that semester were asked to imagine themselves doing so in one of their classes that semester. Manipulation checks verified these hypothetical mindsets were maintained. Participants then completed the questionnaires.

Analysis

Multiple regression was used to determine the relative influence of each direct determinant on the subjects' intention to use the Speaking Center. Specifically, intention to suggest center use was regressed on attitude toward the behavior, subjective norm, and perceived behavioral control. Next, correlation tests identified the relationship between each direct determinant and sets of indirect determinants (i.e., the summed products of each corresponding belief and evaluation scale). Significant results for these tests support the validity of each set of salient beliefs. Finally, a series of logistic regressions[2] identified specific indirect determinants that reliably predict subjects' intentions to suggest student use of the communication center. For this procedure, intention is dichotomized at the sample's median score.[3] Intention is then regressed on the products of each belief and evaluation. Significant results indicate a reliable relationship between a salient belief and an intention to act.

Results

Direct Determinants

A standard multiple regression was used to assess the effects of attitude, subjective norm, and control on instructors' intention to suggest the Speaking Center. An examination of the independent variables indicated negatively skewed attitude and control distributions. Both variables were reverse coded and transformed using the log of 10. Note that reverse coding this data (needed when transforming negatively skewed data) affects the polarity of the coefficient. Specifically, after this transformation, a negative coefficient is interpreted as a positive relationship and vice versa. Assumptions and diagnostics were again checked, and one case was identified as an outlier and removed.

With these transformed data, intention was regressed on the log base 10 of attitude, subjective norm, and the log base 10 of control. Subjective norm was centered on its mean. The model was statistically significant, $F(3, 76) = 35.365$, $p < .000$, and accounted for 56 percent of the variance ($R^2 = .566$). Results of this regression are summarized in table 10.3. The model indicated that each direct determinant contributed to instructors' intent to suggest Speaking Center usage. All direct determinants contributed to intent to suggest usage and did so with moderate to large effect sizes (Keith, 2006). Attitude toward the behavior yielded a large effect ($\beta = -.319$), $t(76) = -3.319$, $p < .01$. The subjective norm component also displayed a large effect ($\beta = .445$), $t(76) = 5.362$, $p < .000$. Finally, perceived behavioral control produced a medium effect ($\beta = -.183$), $t(76) = -1.974$, $p = .052$. In other words, although instructors' decisions to suggest Speaking Center usage are based on each component, it seems subjective norm has the largest contribution, followed by attitude, and then control beliefs. The following tests determine which specific beliefs contribute to instructors' intention to suggest Speaking Center use.

Table 10.3. Regression Analysis Summary for Direct Determinants Predicting Intention

Variable	Instructors		
	b	SEB	β
Constant	17.71	.28	
Attitude	-4.47	1.34	-.31**
Subjective Norm	.54	.10	.44***
Control	-2.00	1.01	-.18

Note. $*p < .05$. $**p < .01$. $*** p < .000$

Indirect Determinants

Logistic regressions were run to identify specific indirect determinants that predict instructors' intention to use the Speaking Center. All three indirect determinant sets were validated with strong correlations between each direct determinant and the corresponding summed products of each set of indirect determinant items: attitude ($r = .67$), subjective norm ($r = .42$), and control ($r = .50$). These strong correlations suggest the elicited beliefs are appropriate direct determinant proxies to be tested against intention (Ajzen & Fishbein, 1980).

The intention variable was dichotomized to indicate group membership (i.e., those who are highly likely or those who are not as likely to suggest Speaking Center usage). The intention variable was split at the median, where low and middle scores (3–18) were coded "0" and high scores (19–21) were coded "1." Because each set of indirect determinants represents a conceptually distinct contribution affecting intention, three separate regressions were run. Unless otherwise noted, intention was regressed on the products of each set of belief and evaluation pairs. The attitude regression, however, required a hierarchal regression, which controlled for the perceived effectiveness of an instructor's in-class suggestions.[4]

The first set of indirect determinants analyzed were the attitudes toward the behavior. First, a test of logistic assumptions and diagnostics suggested the removal of three cases that had undue influence on the dataset. Next, inspection of each predictor variable revealed a positively skewed and leptokurtic distribution of the discipline variable, thus these scores were adjusted with a log base 10 transformation. Finally, a hierarchal logistic regression was run to control for instructors' beliefs regarding whether or not students follow through with their advice. Respondents' perceived advice effectiveness scores were entered into block one of a hierarchical logistic regression and block two was populated with the product terms of each attitudinal indirect determinant pair.

Results of the attitude regression indicated first that instructors' advice effectiveness produced a viable model (-2 log likelihood = 96.89, $\chi^2(1, N = 78) = 11.19$, $p < .01$) and accounted for 17 percent of the variance (Nagelkerke's pseudo $R^2 = .178$). The addition of the indirect determinants, however, increased the explained variance to 64 percent (Nagelkerke's pseudo $R^2 = .645$) with a viable model (-2 log likelihood = 56.574, $\chi^2(8, N = 78) = 51.506$, $p < .000$). The final model correctly classified 79.5 percent of the cases. One indirect determinant (i.e., feedback) was found to reliably predict intention to suggest the Speaking Center. In other words, instructors are more likely to suggest Speaking Center usage when they believe their suggestion will result in tutors providing feedback on assigned presentations. A summary of these results is presented in table 10.4. Finally, advice effectiveness was also a reliable predictor. Instructors who believed their students would follow through with their suggestion were more likely to make the suggestion.

A simple logistic regression was used in the analyses of subjective norm and control components. The regression for the subjective norm indirect determinants did not produce a reliable model (-2 Log Likelihood = 106.718; $\chi^2(3, N = 81) = 5.461, p > .05$). Although indirect and direct determinants were strongly correlated ($r = .65$), it seems that instructors do not necessarily consider students, department members, or university administration when considering suggesting their students attend a tutoring session.

Table 10.4. Significant Indirect Determinants

Component	Variable	B	Wald	Sig.	Exp(B)	95% CI for Exp(B)	
						Lower	Higher
Attitude	Feedback	.16	5.91	.015	1.33	1.05	1.67
Control	Knowledge	.11	7.79	.005	1.11	1.03	1.21
Control	Availability	.13	10.42	.001	1.14	1.05	1.24

Note. N =81 CI=Confidence Interval.

The final logistic regression concerned the impact of perceived behavioral control beliefs on intention. Results indicated that the informed model was statistically reliable in predicting intention (-2 log likelihood = 65.098; $\chi^2(3, N = 81) = 47.081, p < .000$) and accounted for 58 percent of the variance (Nagelkerke's pseudo $R^2 = .588$). The model correctly classified 79 percent of the cases. Two indirect determinants were significant: knowledge and availability. In other words, instructors' perception of Speaking Center availability, as well as their own knowledge of the center, significantly contributes to their intention to suggest its usage.

Discussion

This study focused on understanding why instructors suggest students attend a tutoring session at a communication center. The results of this study identify specific beliefs that influence suggestions to use the communication center. Generally, instructors' decision to suggest the center was affected by their attitude toward the behavior, subjective norm, and perceived ability to control the behavior. Inspection of the underlying beliefs revealed one attitudinal and two control oriented indirect determinants (i.e., feedback, knowledge, and availability, respectively) that motivate instructors' intention to suggest their students attend a tutoring session.

Instructor attitudes toward the center are affected by their belief that students will receive feedback from peer tutors regarding their oral assignment. This finding suggests that the tutoring experience may be viewed as a way to supplement teacher-student interaction with an additional outlet for interested students. The results did not show that instructors were necessarily motivated by beliefs that students would become more confident, start working on their assignments earlier, receive speaking tips, or even improve the oral presentation itself.

The importance of emphasizing specifics about feedback should be explored more thoroughly, however. Because results indicated this belief was so important to faculty, faculty support for a center may hinge on this very issue. Centers should highlight the assistance students would receive by using a communication center, persuading faculty (and students through those faculty) that a tutoring session is a worthwhile use of their time. In order to share with faculty more specific information about what kind of feedback experience students receive, centers might consider providing examples of this experience.

For instance, centers could provide sample speech outlines with comments from a staff member or videos of a conference. It would be particularly effective to provide examples at different stages of a presentation (e.g., feedback on speech ideas, research, outlining, delivery of the speech, and visual aids) and from different disciplines. Testimony from students regarding feedback that they have received in tutoring sessions would also be effective in communicating what feedback communication centers provide. Sample outlines or videos of speeches before and after receiving feedback would provide more concrete examples of center work. Finally, it would be worthwhile to recruit a student in a speaking-intensive class to follow over the course of a semester. This student could journal about experiences using a center and provide examples of different stages of their project, including their final work. Paired with testimony from the faculty member assessing that student's work, this would be a particularly effective example of how communication centers help students. Although providing this type of information to faculty might be time-intensive work, this research shows that information about feedback tutors provide would be most effective in convincing faculty to suggest using communication centers.

One final implication of this research concerns the tutors and their sessions. From this study, we know instructors send their students to the center so they can get feedback on their presentation. Tutors should be well trained to fulfill this expectation, but their efforts should not end there. Clark-Hitt et al. (2008) argued that students do not fully recognize the importance of communication ability within business and professional communities, and the findings presented in the current study imply that instructors share a similar sentiment. In an effort to emphasize more fully the importance of oral communication competence, both tutors and instructors should infuse "real-world" application along with the assistance they provide. For example, when providing examples, they could do so in terms of the learner's major. Even explicit statements that highlight the importance of superior communication ability may be worthwhile.

Beyond the attitudinal determinant of feedback, two control beliefs affected intention to suggest the communication center: knowledge and availability. Instructors who are knowledgeable about center services and believe it is readily available to students are more likely to suggest its use. Based on these findings, centers have to discover the best way to reach all instructors. Centers must actively inform instructors about their services and when they are available; it is not enough to merely provide information on a web site or to send out general emails. Perhaps in the form of a well-designed brochure or guide sheet, web site, or course management system (such as WebCT or Blackboard) course shell, centers should provide full-time faculty, adjuncts, and graduate teaching assistants with basic information about the communication center (e.g., the center's location, available hours, scheduling procedures, etc.). Importantly, these findings suggest that despite the cost of creating professional looking web sites or brochures, the use of center funds is well worth the investment.

While thinking about the best means of communicating with faculty, centers should also consider context. Are there particular modes of communication that would work best on particular campuses and with different faculty? If all faculty use course management systems regularly, perhaps enrolling them in a communication center course would afford the best access to center information. If Facebook or Twitter is widely used, this might provide the best medium for reaching every individual. The possibility of a mobile application might even be worth the time and effort for a center. If it is a low-technology campus, perhaps walking over packets of information to each departmental office, meeting with departments or colleges individually, or holding faculty orientations/open houses might be the best options. Centers should spend time researching the most effective means of communicating with the faculty on particular campuses.

Despite initial indications of the importance of subjective norms, individual subjective norm beliefs did not produce significant results. As indicated in table 10.1, instructors reported that students, department colleagues, and university administration would care whether they suggested their students use the center. The current study, however, failed to identify one of these groups as truly influencing instructor behavior. Two explanations are possible. First, instructors may instead respond to the collective influence of these groups, rather than a single contributor. Another possibility is that the truly "important other" that does motivate their behavior did not emerge in the elicitation process. Follow up research should further investigate this finding.

This study also included the belief *discipline-specific expectations*. Few instructors within this sample raised concerns that a communication center may undermine speaking expectations for their respective field. Given previous arguments that discipline-specific standards are an important part of communication across the discipline guidelines (Dannels, 2001), it is noteworthy that faculty did not seem concerned about the center undermining those specific expectations.

Conclusion

This study is not without its limitations, and two areas in particular must be recognized. First, the sample used in this study was drawn from only one university. Thus, the cross-organizational generalizability is limited to the degree to
which other universities are similar to that used in the present study. Second, the
dependent variable, *intention to suggest center usage*, was measured by asking
respondents whether they strongly agreed or strongly disagreed with statements
like, "I intend to encourage my students to use the communication center for
their oral assignment." Perhaps due to a social desirability bias, most respondents indicated fervent support of the university communication center, thus
creating a significantly skewed distribution with limited variation. Future research should account for this possible bias and take steps to increase the variability of responses by, for example, replacing the response poles with *mostly
agree* and *definitely agree*.

Future studies should also identify indirect determinants for specific colleges or disciplines. Due to inadequate variability in the instructor demographics,
participants of the current study were treated as an isomorphic group. Gathering
data from a wider variety of university faculty, however, could provide an even
more targeted analysis of what motivates faculty members to encourage student
use of communication centers.

Finally, additional research should test the applicability of the findings presented here. The full application of TPB suggests that instructors will more likely suggest the use of communication centers when they 1) believe their students
will receive presentation feedback and 2) are more knowledgeable of center services and its availability. Using these specific topics, centers can redirect advertising efforts toward instructors and subsequently survey instructors to see if
these efforts are responsible for their behavior.

Although student attitudes toward use of a communication center are important to understand, previous research (King & Atkins-Sayre, 2010) indicated that
faculty influence on students was the most significant contributor to students'
decisions to use the center. Consequently, this study has attempted to answer
some of the questions about best practices for successfully convincing faculty to
support communication centers. The findings presented here suggest a targeted
public relations campaign. Such a campaign would focus on the value of oral
communication feedback provided by communication centers as well as information about center services and availability of such services.

Notes

1. Although we speak more broadly about "communication centers," our study is
specific to our campus where the communication center is called the "Speaking Center."
When discussing this study, we will use that language.

2. Linear regression assumes homoscedasticity and a normality of errors. Our dataset, however, violates these assumptions. Therefore logistic regression was favored over linear regression because it does not require these assumptions be met (Meyers, Gamst, & Guarino, 2006).

3. Although dichotomizing continuous data results in a loss of information, such a maneuver is acceptable when "the distribution of a count variable is extremely highly skewed, to the extent that there is a large number of observations at the most extreme score on the distribution" (MacCallum, Zhang, Preacher, & Rucker, 2002, p. 38). Such is the case concerning the strong negative skew of the intention variable (a Kolmogorov-Smirnov test indicated a significantly skewed distribution of the variable, $D(81) = .231, p < .000$).

4. Regarding the attitudinal data, King and Atkins-Sayre (2010) noted that during salient belief solicitation procedures, without exception, respondents did not accurately answer the posed questions: "What do you see as the advantages/disadvantages of your suggesting that your students attend a tutoring session/consultation at the communication center for an oral assignment this semester?" Instead, respondents provided attitudinal beliefs as if the question read, "What do you see as the advantages/disadvantages of your student attending a tutoring/consultation at the communication center for an oral assignment this semester." Because these respondents provided responses that did not consider the effectiveness of their responses, an *advice effectiveness* scale was constructed to control for such variation. The scale consisted of three 7-point Likert-type items ($\alpha = .84$), and included the following items: "If I encourage my students to attend a tutoring session at the Speaking Center for help with their oral assignments, most will follow my advice," "Most of my students would heed my advice to attend a Speaking Center tutoring session for help with their oral assignments," and (reverse coded) "Most students would not follow through with my suggestion that they should attend a tutoring session at the Speaking Center." Each item was anchored with *strongly disagree* and *strongly agree*. These results are discussed in the results section.

References

Ajzen, I. (1991). The theory of planned behavior. *Organizational Behavior and Human Decision Processes, 50*, 179–211.

Ajzen, I. (2006). Constructing a TPB questionnaire: Conceptual and methodological considerations. Retrieved from: http://people.umass.edu/aizen/pdf/tpb.measurement.pdf

Ajzen, I. (2010). "Frequently asked questions." Retrieved from http://www.people.umass.edu/a

Ajzen, I., & Fishbein, M. (1977). Attitude-behavior relations: A theoretical analysis and review of empirical research. *Psychological Bulletin, 84*, 888–918.

Ajzen, I., & Fishbein, M. (1980). *Understanding attitudes and predicting social behavior.* Englewood Cliffs, NJ: Prentice-Hall.

Ajzen, I., & Fishbein, M. (2005). Influence of attitudes on behavior. In D. Albarracin, B. T. Johnson, & M. P. Zanna (Eds.), *The handbook of attitudes* (pp. 173–221). Magwah, NJ: Lawrence Erlbaum Associates.

Albarracin, D., Johnson, B. T., Fishbein, M., & Muellerleile, P. A. (2001). Theories of reasoned action and planned behavior as models of condom use: A meta-analysis. *Psychological Bulletin, 127*, 142–161.

Armitage, C. J., & Conner, M. (2001). Efficacy of the theory of planned behavior: A meta-analytic review. *British Journal of Social Psychology, 40,* 471–499.

Clark-Hitt, R., Ellis, J. B., & Bender, J. (2008, November). *Increasing student use of center services: Formative message research using the theory of planned behavior.* Paper presented at the National Communication Association Convention, San Diego, CA.

Dannels, D. P. (2001). Time to speak up: A theoretical framework of situated pedagogy and practice for communication across the curriculum. *Communication Education, 50,* 144–158.

Dillard. J. P., & Pfau, M. (2002). Introduction. In J. P. Dillard & M. Pfau (Eds.), *The persuasion handbook: Developments in theory and practice* (pp. ix–xix). Thousand Oaks, CA: Sage.

Godin, G., & Kok, G. (1996). The theory of planned behavior: A review of its applications to health-related behaviors. *American Journal of Health Promotions, 11,* 87–98.

Fishbein, M., & Ajzen, I. (1975). *Belief, attitude, intention and behavior: An introduction to theory and research.* Reading, MA: Addison-Wesley.

Francis, J., Eccles, M., Johnston, M., Walker, A., Grimshaw, J., Foy, R., Kaner, E., Smith, L., Bonetti, D. (2004). *Constructing questionnaires based on the theory of planned behaviour: A manual for health services researchers.* Report to ReBEQI: Research Based Education and Quality Improvement.

Hardeman, W., Johnston, M., Johnston, D. W., Bonetti, D., Wareham, N. J., & Kinmonth, A. L. (2002). Application of the theory of planned behavior in behavior change interventions: A systematic review. *Psychology and Health, 17,* 123–158.

Hausenblas, H. A., Carron, A. V., & Mack, D. E. (1997). Application of the theories of reasoned action and planned behavior to exercise behavior: A meta-analysis. *Journal of Sport & Exercise Psychology, 19,* 36–51.

Keith, T. Z. (2006). *Multiple regression and beyond.* Boston, MA: Pearson.

King, M., & Atkins-Sayre, W. (2010, November). *If you build it they 'might?' come: Empirically identifying motivations surrounding the use of communication centers.* Paper presented at the meeting of the National Communication Association, San Francisco, CA.

MacCallum, R. C., Zhang, S., Preacher, K. J., & Rucker, D. D. (2002). On the practice of dichotomization of quantitative variables. *Psychological Methods, 7,* 19–40.

Meyers, L. S., Gamst, G., & Guarino, A. J. (2006). *Applied multivariate research.* Thousand Oaks, CA: Sage Publications.

Sheppard, B. H., Hartwick, J., & Warshaw, P. R. (1988). The theory of reasoned action: A meta-analysis of past research with recommendations for modifications and future research. *The Journal of Consumer Research, 15,* 325–343.

Sutton, S. (1998). Predicting and explaining intentions and behavior: How well are we doing? *Journal of Applied Social Psychology, 28,* 1317–1338.

Webb, T. L., & Sheeran, P. (2006). Does changing behavioral intentions engender behavior change? A meta-analysis of the experimental evidence. *Psychological Bulletin, 132,* 249–268.

Part III:
Alternative Models for Communication Centers

Chapter 11

Communication Center Ethos: Remediating Space, Encouraging Collaboration

Russell Carpenter and Shawn Apostel

During a recent tour of Eastern Kentucky University's (EKU) Noel Studio for Academic Creativity with leaders from EKU and another local college, EKU's President, Dr. Doug Whitlock, remarked that with the opening of a new space of this size and scope, expectations often exceed reality; however, the Noel Studio is the rare case where reality has exceeded expectations. Not only has the Noel Studio furthered the objective of creating informed students who communicate effectively, but it has also become a meeting ground for collaboration across the disciplines for the development of communication skills.

Industry demand for our college graduates suggests that students' oral communication skills are related to success. Given this increased focus, we take this opportunity to explore communication centers in the process of remediating spaces and encouraging collaboration. In many communication centers, students can record and discuss their speeches with a consultant; however, the way a center is designed and the use of that space to facilitate small-group and one-on-one interaction is a topic that merits further consideration. By facilitating collaboration and feedback, space impacts the communication-design process and, in the case of the Noel Studio, the communication-design practices of an entire university. Although this chapter offers a case study of oral communication design in public and private spaces within the Noel Studio, a broad range of communication centers can benefit from the questions and concepts we consider. Even for communication centers with spatial constraints, the concepts offered in this chapter can inspire progressive collaborative efforts that enhance ethos on campus.

In September 2010, the Noel Studio opened in the heart of the EKU libraries complex. The 10,000-square-foot facility offers an integrated learning space, adding new communication services on campus where none existed before, while encouraging collaborative efforts that span the campus. The Noel Studio combines the resources of library staff with English and communication departments to create an innovative space where students can invent, research, write, and present speeches with trained consultants. In addition to its collaborative function, the Noel Studio has increased the feedback students receive on their speeches through its use of new multimedia technologies and public, small-group, and private spaces. The variety of spaces available for student use in the Noel Studio creates a dynamic environment; intersections of public and private emerge as complementary, offering students areas to compose and then move to areas that provide a safe and supportive place to practice delivery.

The Noel Studio offers students an engaging, dynamic space. The different areas were designed purposefully with each one complementing the other. Areas include the invention space, an area where ideas are born with writable walls, colorful manipulatives, writable tiles, and visual messages; the greenhouse, a large, open space at the center of the Noel Studio where ideas grow and mature; breakout spaces, which provide areas for small-group collaboration, presentations, and displays; presentation practice rooms, which offer students a more focused space where communication is refined; the presentation suite, which allows students to bring communication into a public forum for further discussion or revision; the Discovery Classroom, a space where Noel Studio pedagogy is integrated with the campus community; and a conference room where video technologies allow visitors to foreground group dynamics.

Pedagogical goals—and the role of technology—remain central to the design process and should be considered in determining the size and layout of practice rooms. For example, the arrangement of a room, placement of technology, and positioning of tables and chairs encourage some activities and discourage others (Selfe, 2005). This concept is clearly illustrated in the Noel Studio where many spaces are arranged with technology and dry-erase boards as centralizing features to encourage students to project ideas for individual or collaborative use. High-tech monitors and low-tech dry-erase boards both become complementary writable and visual spaces for envisioning and refining communication design. The placement of a camera, monitor, or microphone informs the use of that space. These technologies might encourage collaboration in a larger space and prompt focused revision of details in a smaller private space. Each area facilitates a different phase of the speech-composing process. Many students begin their experience in the invention space—developing ideas from their early stages—before they know exactly where they want to go with the project. Others feel comfortable bringing in a draft and growing their ideas in the greenhouse, a large space that encourages students to sit side-by-side with one another to develop ideas. Breakout spaces (ideal for four or five students) and presentation practice rooms (appropriate for up to three students) offer spaces where students can think about the delivery of their products while recording their practice sessions and interacting with visual messages that complement and extend their presentations through multimodal communication (a slideshow, video, or electronic portfolio). Foregrounding the ways technology complements spatial designs should prove particularly useful as communication centers continue to evolve and develop.

The Noel Studio is designed as a focused, collaborative initiative to develop informed, critical, and creative thinkers who communicate effectively. Through usage of the Noel Studio, students are expected to increase their understanding of the foundational elements of all communication, see connections between appropriate information and effective communication, work with student consultants to organize and refine ideas, develop research strategies that inform communication, deliver articulate presentations, create high-quality communication products, and hone teamwork skills in order to effectively communicate in group situations. Further, the Noel Studio views the definition of communication broadly to encompass multiple ways of engaging in and expressing meaning.

The Noel Studio space provides an environment where all students can actively participate in the discovery and creation of communication products and practices. Studios, by design, encourage active participation in and awareness of the natural processes of communication, which are supported by consultants, spaces, and technologies. Consultants reinforce the significant ways in which writing, speaking, and research are interconnected. The space encourages fruitful collaboration and beneficial feedback, and the technology facilitates multiple learning styles as well as the ability to share in the communication-design process. When combined, the consultants, space, and technologies all work together to facilitate the ethos of the Noel Studio as a communication center.

Using results from a study conducted in the Noel Studio, we argue that remediating space and encouraging collaboration enhances a center's ethos among students and within the university community by offering students small rooms where they can meet as groups to practice their communication presentations, rather than focusing on traditional one-on-one consulting in a large, open space. Through this inquiry, we offer suggestions for space use in centers that promote the design of effective oral communication products and practices.[1]

The Communication Center as Dwelling Place

In this section, we discuss the role of ethos within the context of the Noel Studio as a communication center, situating the communication center within the extant literature that has served to inform practices within the Noel Studio. Drawing from central scholars in rhetorical and new media theory, the literature surveyed here reveals that ethos does not solely apply to a presenter but can be applied to the facility within which the presentation is created and refined. We argue that space and ethos are inherently connected and that attention to space in the communication center can lead communication center directors to remix their space to enhance the development of argument and student confidence.

The role of ethos in the communication process as discussed by Hyde (2004) suggests that we reexamine the role of space: "The ethical practice of rhetoric entails the construction of a speaker's *ethos* as well as the construction of a 'dwelling place' (*ethos*) for collaborative and moral deliberation" (p. xviii). For Zulick (2004), ethos represents the "locus of convergence of ethics and aesthetics in the subjective act of invention" (p. 20). These approaches to ethos remind us that while it is important for a speaker to project a credible ethos, the term ethos also applies to the way a speech is crafted to establish a safe place for the exchange of ideas. Just as a speech should create an intellectual space of collaboration, the communication center should also fulfill the need for a safe, collaborative environment so that such a speech could be crafted in the first place. This space should facilitate and nurture the speech-composing and practicing process through feedback from individuals or groups while also allowing students to move from public to private places.

Remediation and Remix

Addressing this connection between the use of space and ethos, the concepts of remediation and remix offer a framework for making the changes needed to facilitate the collaboration students and faculty desire. Lessig's (2008) concept of remix, in a read/write culture, encourages us as communication center directors to incorporate previous practices and ideas as we search for new approaches to providing quality feedback for a rapidly changing audience, context, and media. Remediation, to use Bolter and Grusin's (1999) term, suggests that new technologies incorporate approaches established from existing technology. These terms, remediation and remix, are useful in that they encourage the examination of perspectives for designing or redesigning the twenty-first century communication center to facilitate how students use this space to compose various projects and assignments. These terms also reveal that students build on the available modes of communication to develop their ethos as presenters and rhetoricians. In the communication center, students often integrate writing, oral communication, and electronic communication in one presentation, but a dynamic space encourages a close relationship between remix and remediation by also revealing the relationships between writing, oral communication, and electronic communication that students use in a wide variety of academic presentations and collaborative arrangements. This move toward remix within an academic space like a communication center, and remediation within a technologically sophisticated space, embraces youth culture's comfort with the free-flow of ideas through multimodal communication—including video, music, or aural communication, electronic art, and performance.

Remixing the Center

The Noel Studio attempts to remediate—or refashion and improve upon—the communication center concept. Just as Bolter and Grusin (1999) argue that new media are doing exactly what their predecessors have done by "presenting themselves as refashioned and improved versions of other media" (pp. 14–15), the Noel Studio sees value in integrating complementary areas of communication—oral, written, and research—together in one space to exemplify their reciprocal nature. Doing so creates an environment that inspires students to refashion themselves as communicators within the practices at work in the space itself. In other words, integrating oral communication with writing and research in a technologically sophisticated environment encourages students to see these two aspects of communication as complementary while expanding and honing their understandings of the speech writing and practicing process.

Communication centers provide valuable space for feedback on the creation and presentation of a speech, yet they also have the potential to become a location to transition those who seek answers into those who create possibilities. Burke (1968) sets out a relationship between form and audience; form is the "creation of an appetite in the mind of the auditor, and the adequate satisfying of that appetite" (p. 31). More recently, Crick (2010) explores the Sophists' epistemology, showing us their commitment to form. As Crick explains, "The great accomplishment of the Sophists was to adopt an experimental method toward language that allowed them to channel the logical power of abstract thought through novel poetic forms and to generate the possibility for political action capable of bringing forth reward and fulfillment in the shared life of the *polis*" (pp. 41–42). The spirit of experimentation—the process of asking questions rather than constantly seeking answers—makes communication centers unique intellectual spaces where practices are remixed and technologies remediated. In them, students employ provisional methods to language by exploring their own communication styles in relation to the situation's rhetorical context to build a relationship with the audience. The communication center's ethos is built within the development of a *polis*, a shared social intellectual space where communication is invited into a public forum. Using the space, consultants are intentional in their strategies for discussing and demonstrating communication options side-by-side with students.

The design of the Noel Studio encourages movement and fluidity from one space to the next. In some cases, consultants and students move together from the invention space to the greenhouse or from the greenhouse, where the discussion on developing a speech outline began, back to the invention space as it becomes clear that the student could use feedback on generating ideas about a relevant topic or generating support for a presentation.

Studying Remix

In order to explore the role of space in the presentation consultation, this study investigated students' preferences for using three different sized rooms while preparing an oral presentation. Specifically, it examined how students use smaller "breakout spaces" and "presentation practice rooms" as well as larger open areas to see how these spaces affect confidence levels as well as facilitate feedback provided by consultants and peers from the communication course on oral communication projects. The benefits of a shared intellectual space were examined by studying the amount of feedback students received on their communication projects. Finally, this research investigated the way consultations within these different spaces encouraged students to receive a wider variety of feedback and enabled students to overcome speech anxiety as they prepared for their final presentations in the classroom.

Method

Two introductory-level oral communication classes participated in this study. One class was encouraged to schedule one-hour consultation sessions individually; the other class was encouraged to schedule one-hour consultations in groups of five. This element of the study allowed for an investigation into collaboration and ethos in the communication center. Primarily, it illuminated the potential for group consultations to build the ethos of the space, creating a more public forum for the development of communication practices. The structure of the study, with one class registering for consultations as individuals and the other class registering for consultations in groups of five students, provided some variety in terms of spaces used. Small groups scheduled sessions in the breakout spaces and presentation practice rooms, and individuals utilized the large, open greenhouse. We predicted that students who practiced in the smaller rooms with their group members in attendance to provide feedback would feel more prepared than if they met in a large, open room by themselves with a single consultant. Thus, the following hypotheses were warranted:

1. Students who had consultations in groups will report receiving more feedback during the visit than students who visited individually.
2. Students who practiced in the smaller rooms will report feeling more prepared than if they met in a large open room.

During all consultations at the Noel Studio, a record of consultation form is completed by the consultant and given to the student. A copy of that form is kept in the Noel Studio for assessment, usage analysis, and training purposes. These forms were analyzed, in addition to the collected surveys, for this research. The authors considered spaces used during the consultations, type of project, the number of times a particular student visited the Noel Studio for a consultation, and the feedback provided on the form. These forms commonly offer rich and detailed information about the consultation, including ideas discussed during the meeting, concrete and specific suggestions for the student to pursue next, and questions that might guide further exploration by the student. They also provide a space for consultants to document where they worked in the Noel Studio. Consultants are welcome to use more than one space when working with a student, therefore multiple options are included on the form. Additionally, results and discussions of this research using pre- and post-consultation surveys from two communication classes to investigate the relationship between space and oral communication are offered.

Participants included two undergraduate introductory-level oral communication classes numbering 25 students in each class for a total group of 50 students. Classes varied in terms of age, gender, and ethnic background, but all participants were 18 years or older. These students were included in the sample because they utilized the Noel Studio to work on class presentations and projects.

At the beginning of the semester, before visiting the Noel Studio with their speech materials, students were asked to complete a pre-consultation survey. The purpose of this survey was to see how confident students felt about developing an oral presentation and giving a public speech. Researchers also asked how much feedback students normally received on speeches as well as their practicing methods (i.e., by themselves or with an audience). Students in the same undergraduate communication courses were then asked to complete a survey after having consultations in the Noel Studio. This second survey allowed for an investigation into students' confidence in presenting their oral communication products, the space in which students meet with a consultant to receive feedback, and the amount of feedback students felt they received during their consultations as they were preparing for presentations. Students were also asked how they felt about the space they used, and if they felt it helped them build a more effective, convincing presentation. Designing the surveys in this way allowed researchers to see how students would normally approach the oral presentation process and contrast this practice with a consultation in the Noel Studio.

Results

Pre-consultation data suggests that, on average, students in both groups were between somewhat confident and confident about developing oral communication pieces (M=1.48, SD=.90), and they were between somewhat confident and confident about giving a public speech to a class (M=1.43, SD=1.02). This survey also finds that half the students practiced their speeches in a public space, 32 percent in a private space, 11 percent never gave a speech, and 7 percent did not practice at all.

Hypothesis 1 predicted that students who participated in group consultations would report receiving more feedback than those who participated in individual consultations. While the survey found an increase in reported feedback from students who participated in group consultations, the difference was not statistically significant. This may have resulted in part because a few students from the group consultation class met individually with consultants due to scheduling conflicts within the groups.

Hypothesis 2 predicted that students who practiced in the smaller rooms with their group members in attendance to provide feedback will feel more prepared than if they met in a large, open room by themselves with a single consultant. The survey shows a significant difference between the spaces used (small room or large open room) and students' perception of how the space affected their preparation, $F(3,36)$=4.76, p <.01. This finding supports Selfe's argument that space plays an important role in influencing the activities students perform in a communication center setting and adds to his argument by showing that small rooms are useful and productive for facilitating collaboration.

The study also found that the relationships between variables on the pre-consultation survey indicate positive correlations between students' confidence in developing oral communication pieces and comfort giving speeches in class (r=.58, p<.001). Confidence in developing oral communication pieces is related to frequency of giving speeches (r=.56, p<.001). Students' comfort with giving speeches in class is related to the amount of feedback they receive (r=.43, p<.01) as well as their frequency of giving speeches (r=.72, p<.001). There were also positive correlations showing that the amount of feedback students receive is related to the frequency with which students give speeches (r=.40, p<.01). Furthermore, there was also a significant positive correlation between confidence as a result of the consultation and amount of feedback received (r=.43, p<.01).

Although this study involved a small sample size, the data suggests the potential for space to facilitate the communication-design process within collaborative settings. While students who visit the Noel Studio often come as individuals, more students are choosing or are required to visit the space in groups to discuss their oral communication products and practices. Due to this research, the Noel Studio is continuing to focus on maintaining and developing its ethos through initiatives that integrate collaborative pedagogies into sessions, using an integrated approach that provides students with feedback on their oral communication while also highlighting the process-oriented nature of developing rhetorically effective speech products. Since this focus began, consultants are now being trained in basic small-group communication skills in addition to the interpersonal communication training they normally receive.

Implications for Space and Pedagogy Design

Lefebvre (1991) explains that "social space is what permits fresh actions to occur, while suggesting others and prohibiting yet others" (p. 73). The most popular spaces for refining oral communication in the Noel Studio—the breakout spaces and presentation practice rooms—promote small-group collaboration, creating an intimate yet collaborative environment. Specifically, they allow groups of five to seven students to gather comfortably. Breakout spaces and presentation practice rooms, for instance, allow students to maintain a collaborative approach but offer areas where they can develop communication in a social setting, in many cases with a group of peers and a consultant.

As Hyde (2004) suggests, the ethos of rhetoric directs us back to architectural functions, providing intellectual spaces for student communication to emerge and develop. This research suggests that these spaces work best when consultants and peer group work together to address what Bitzer (1968) calls the "rhetorical exigence" of the situation as peers rehearse presentations and fellow group members have the opportunity to provide immediate and beneficial feedback. Collaborative spaces are, therefore, central to the design of communication centers, as they increase opportunities for students to share their work in a social setting, allowing the feedback process to occur naturally.

Given the increased interest in small group sessions, communication centers might explore opportunities to develop more collaborative spaces. These spaces would allow students to work collaboratively on their individual presentations as well as their group presentations. Through this relatively simple adjustment, students might find that the space promotes communication center ethos: a nurturing environment in which peers and consultants can express ideas and speakers can evaluate, and perhaps implement, changes. The discourse among students, often involving consultants, becomes transformational, as remixed space encourages students to move from seeking help to asking questions while engaging the communication process.

In this study, group members were instructed to be part of the feedback process. Therefore, peers became an integrated part of the space's ethos and not simply accessories. Credibility comes with the sense of community that the space helps develop. Remediated spaces encourage the critical practice of obtaining feedback as one that involves not only a communicator but also an audience; thus, communication centers might design environments that encourage collaboration. Communication centers, as generative academic spaces, can encourage discourse by considering collaboration as part of its pedagogy.

As Hart and Daughton (2005) argue, "A basic fact about speaking often goes unnoticed: It is an activity. That is, by addressing another, a speaker both says something *and does something*" (p. 40). The architectural functions of a space should facilitate the activity of oral communication, as Hart and Daughton suggest, which entails roles for presenter and audience. In a supportive space, presenter and audience engage in collaboration that yields productive feedback and conversation. This communication is what Sawyer (2007) might call "group flow"—freewheeling, spontaneous conversations in an informal setting (p. 43). Small groups allow students to receive feedback from their peers in addition to a trained staff member. This social setting allows information to flow from one student to another, providing students with important opportunities to refine practices.

Spaces that foster collaboration capture the spirit of remediation and remix, two theories employed in the development of the Noel Studio space as a new communication center. Both remediation and remix suggest that collaboration is critical to the design of new communication messages. They attempt to respect the original while creating the new, which implies the sharing of ideas, texts, and thoughts. It also suggests that communication centers should strive to remediate and remix their spaces to encourage the flow of communication from student to student and faculty member to student in a reciprocal fashion. Spaces remediated and remixed consider the relationship between student and communication, suggesting an attention to student-centered learning while preparing college graduates to deal with the complexities of a digital age. Remediation and remix also foreground the importance of creativity in our spaces and the design of environments where students are encouraged to explore and re-energize communication products and practices. Perhaps most importantly, communication centers must remain innovative. Remediation and remix suggest innovation—taking an old space and creating a new message with it. Communication centers can embody this creative spirit of innovation by embracing change and collaboration and inviting new experiences for students, staff members, and collaborators. Change should involve collaboration, which could yield concepts for remixing space or remediating practices that re-energize an appreciation and respect for communication.

Conclusion

Communication centers convey an ethos. This ethos can be developed through the concepts of remediation and remix, as this chapter suggests. Remixes, for example, give old songs a second chance. When space and pedagogies are remixed, they also receive a second chance. The process, when applied to space, facilitates reinvention and revitalization. In addition, remixed space suggests an integration of old and new, along with a relationship between people and communication.

This chapter attempts to construct the communication center as a public space integrated tightly into the fabric of communication across diverse campus communities. Developing communication center ethos can be a complex process involving students, staff, and faculty across many departments on campus. This research suggests that space does play an important role in the amount of feedback students receive and the level of comfort students feel before they present their speeches in the classroom. The design of space and the arrangement of productive methods for feedback situate students at the center of discussions about what communication centers are and could become. Ethos involves not only the development of productive and generative spaces for students but also for the faculty and the staff working in the communication center. A collaborative space might have as part of its vision and mission the goal of involving faculty members in the design of pedagogy.

Limitations for the study include a relatively small sample size as well as the study of only one assignment. While this study addressed the quantity of feedback students felt they received, the quality of feedback provided by consultants and peers stands further investigation as well. Although this study focuses on the relationship between space and presentation confidence levels, further research could highlight the role of collaboration within the communication center beyond the scope offered here. As a logical extension of this study, more research should be conducted that explores the potential benefits of group consultations. However, the material presented here is sufficiently rich and provocative to suggest future directions for a variety of communication centers. Interestingly, during the group tour mentioned at the beginning of this chapter, we were asked what future changes we would like to see. Without hesitation, we answered that we would like more breakout spaces and presentation practice rooms because they are so popular with students. This research shows that these spaces are not only popular, but they also significantly contribute to the communication-design process.

Collaborative efforts at work in the Noel Studio, such as this one involving an oral communication course, have helped to remediate the space and remix the pedagogy. Noel Studio administrators and consultants have applied these concepts as a lens for thinking about how the room sizes inform practices and the practices inform the Noel Studio's development. What members of the Noel Studio team are learning about consultations and collaboration points this space, vision, and mission to the future. Communication center design and pedagogy will both benefit from collaborative efforts that continue to promote remixed practices of consulting. Collaboration builds ethos among members of the Noel Studio team, students, and faculty members by involving all parties in the process. Remediation and remix, as creative strategies for adjusting space and pedagogy design, provide ways to keep communication exciting and the staff learning. Communication center ethos involves a collaborative spirit and a culture of inquiry with campus-wide impact, providing a meeting ground for designing and refining communication from across the disciplines.

Notes

1. The authors would like to thank Leslie Valley for reading multiple drafts of this chapter and Michele Goltz and Drs. Rose Perrine and Eric Meiners for assistance with data analysis.

References

Bitzer, L. (1968). The rhetorical situation. *Philosophy and Rhetoric, 1*(1), 1–14.
Bolter, J. D., & Grusin, R. (1999). *Remeditation: Understanding new media.* Cambridge: MIT Press.
Burke, K. (1968). *Counter-statement.* Berkeley: University of California Press.
Crick, N. (2010). The sophistical attitude and the invention of rhetoric. *Quarterly Journal of Speech, 96,* 25–45.
Hart, R. P., & Daughton, S. (2005). *Modern rhetorical criticism.* (3rd ed.). New York: Allyn and Bacon.
Hyde, M. (2004). Introduction: Rhetorically, we dwell. In M. Hyde (Ed.), *The ethos of rhetoric* (pp. xiii–xxviii). Columbia: University of South Carolina Press.
Lefebvre, H. (1991). *The production of space.* Malden: Blackwell Publishers.
Lessig, L. (2008). *Remix: Making art and commerce thrive in the hybrid economy.* New York: Penguin.
Sawyer, K. (2007). *Group genius: The creative power of collaboration.* New York: Basic.
Selfe, R. (2005). *Sustainable computer environments: Cultures of support in English Studies and Language Arts.* Cresskill: Hampton.
Zulick, M. D. (2004). *The ethos of invention: The dialogue of ethics and aesthetics in Kenneth Burke and Mikhail Bakhtin.* In M. Hyde (Ed.), *The Ethos of Rhetoric* (pp. 20–33). Columbia: University of South Carolina Press.

Chapter 12

The Combined Centers Approach: How Speaking and Writing Centers Can Work Together

Casey Malone Maugh

In 1991, Donald Bushman reported that 90 percent of U.S. colleges and universities supported a writing center. While communication centers are less pervasive on college campuses than writing centers, in the past decade we have seen an increase in stand-alone communication centers, as well as a handful that have partnered with writing centers (Agnes Scott College, North Carolina State University, Colgate University, Chadron State College, Texas A&M, Young Harris College, to name a few). Of those few centers that have the unique opportunity to work together, little evidence exists of a combined tutoring strategy, shared tutoring staff, or a holistic approach to tutoring writing and speaking. These centers vary in form from those that share a common web site but tutor entirely independently of one another, to centers that share a similar tutoring philosophy or mission but keep the tutoring processes separate. The unique approach offered in this chapter demonstrates how pedagogical approaches to tutoring oral and written communication can be combined to offer a singular tutoring approach that enhances the overall tutoring of both writing and speaking, while reinforcing the strengths of each subject area.

In the fall of 2008, the author was newly appointed as assistant professor and the director of a Speaking Center on a satellite campus of about 3,200 students, 70 miles from the university's main campus. At that time, the speaking center shared a large open room with the writing center within the library, one of only two buildings rebuilt three years after Hurricane Katrina had destroyed the campus. The centers, though housed under the same roof, functioned entirely independently of one another, with individual tutoring staff, different operating structures, and very unique sets of training procedures and session reporting. During the fall semester the two centers faced inefficiencies of space, time, and effort which resulted in minimal growth in terms of clientele as well as a lack of identity on the campus as a whole. The two centers were directed independently of one another while sharing the same physical space and the same client base. This configuration led to increasing difficulty in maintaining the daily operations of the speaking and writing center and in recognizing the strengths and weaknesses of the other. The writing center did not employ a director, as the speaking center did; rather a coordinator served as the liaison between the two campuses with the director residing on the main campus. Aside from the myriad communication difficulties associated with the distance, what had formerly been a permanent coordinator position in the writing center shifted into a temporary appointment under the pressure of academic reappropriation and tightening budget strings.

Byron L. Stay (2006), discussing the work of writing centers at small colleges argues that "writing centers at small institutions have unique limitations, the ambiance of a small institution can present the writing center director with creative opportunities as well. These writing center directors need to find innovative ways to train tutors, staff, and budget their centers" (p. 147). Stay, an advocate of creative problem-solving, influenced the author to begin developing ways to utilize the small campus environment advantageously by being thoughtful about resources. For example, interpreting the shared physical space as a creative opportunity allowed for a reframing of what was originally a profound limitation into a chance for use of shared resources. Additionally, the relatively small population from which tutors were recruited was re-imagined as a way to redefine tutor training and develop a training protocol that would address the needs of both speaking and writing tutoring simultaneously. Although the process of rearticulating the purpose and mission of a combined communication and writing center lasted the course of several years, ultimately it strengthened the tutoring approach and offered the students a better opportunity to work closely with well-trained tutors who were proficient in the skills associated with both speaking and writing.

This essay argues that universities with the desire to create communication centers have only to look toward partnering with existing writing centers. For institutions with neither a writing nor a communication center, a combined approach provides a format for the development of communication across the curriculum. For centers that already operate within a shared physical space, this essay offers an alternative way to think about tutor training and tutoring methodologies. The combined approach provides a coherent template for enhanced interaction with faculty and students, efficient use of student consultants, and a holistic approach to written and oral communication as a means of partnering with clients and promoting the efficacy of the center to the university at large. This essay will detail the rationale for the combined centers approach as a model for other colleges. The author will outline the training model designed for a combined center and provide insight into the ways in which a center of this nature can flourish under the model as well as share a few of the potential disadvantages of a combined approach.

Rationale for the Combined Approach

The rationale for combining the two existing centers on our campus was born not only out of a need for coherence and consistency but also brought about by a sense that writing and speaking were fundamentally similar pursuits in many ways. We did not want to create a center that offered tutoring in speaking and writing, rather we strove to provide universalized tutoring related to communication concepts. Though communication scholars have focused on the importance of distinguishing between the principles of speaking and writing, the combined centers approach recognizes the important differences when appropriate but begins by recognizing the points of convergence.

In prior decades, writing experts argued that approaches to speaking and writing differed in such fundamental ways that they should be treated as separate pursuits. John T. Morello (1990) concludes in his analysis of writing across the curriculum and speaking across the curriculum programs that the differences between writing and speaking should be the specific area of focus, as these distinctions provide insight into the development of effective programs. He states that "[w]ithout focusing on the unique contributions a speaking-focused across the curriculum program can make, SAC practitioners run the risk that oral communication activities will be appropriated as a supporting part of the WAC approach and little more" (p. 111). And, Jean Halpern (1984) argues that writing and speaking fundamentally differ in that "good writing . . . functions without the supports of the speech context. Furthermore, writing functions over time. It must therefore contain within itself enough contextual background and specific detail to insure accurate interpretation by readers living and yet to be born" (p. 353). From the writing perspective, in earlier decades scholars found that the process of writing was often minimized by suggesting that writing was merely a translation of the spoken word onto paper. However, Kroll and Vann (1981) suggest that, "[t]he underlying assumptions are that writing is highly dependent upon speaking and that speaking is primary, not only in the obvious sense that it is acquired earlier than writing, but also that it is somehow closer to 'true' language" (p. vii).

The combined centers approach follows a different logic, one that is born out of the work of writing center experts who assert that the similarities between writing and speaking can be a space for strengthening both oral and written communication practices. This approach assumes that what is beneficial to the developmental process of writing can be integrated into the speech preparation process. The combined center approach begins with an emphasis on process over product, which has been articulated repeatedly throughout the literature on speaking and writing across the curriculum. Barnes (1983) suggests, "the discovery mode of communication helps students use talk as a way to explore new ideas, to think creatively and critically, and to learn in collaboration with others" (p. 42). Rafoth and Rubin (1992) support the integration of writing and speaking into college curricula for the purposes of enhancing both. They argue that, "speech teachers have a single, fast-fading performance to observe, and speech classes often become preoccupied with performance-*cum*-product . . . Writing teachers, by contrast, are privy to students' notes, jot lists, journal entries, and drafts, often relying more on in-process evaluations than on summative evaluations of final products" (p. 19). Rafoth and Rubin also recognize that as writing loses touch with good conversation, it too loses its focus. And, Melanie Sperling (1996) asserts that "the two language modes, writing and speaking, are mutually informing, and writers and speakers have much to learn from each other" (p. 53).

From the perspective of a combined center approach, speaking and writing share common starting points from which the tutoring process begins before the differences are addressed. Several reasons for this decision exist. First, starting with similarities provides a common space from which both the tutor and the client can work. Second, the clientele become familiar with the tutoring approach, which mutually reinforces the benefit of speaking and writing by starting with "global issues" and moving toward "local issues."

Training Tutors for the Combined Center

Training tutors to work with both written and oral assignments is a formidable challenge. The combined centers approach asks the tutors to begin with global issues. These issues are akin to what Reigstad and McAndrew (2001) call higher-order concerns, including: thesis, clarity of focus, purpose of the work, audience, voice, argument development, organization, supporting material, introductions, conclusions, transitions, citation style, and referencing. The discussion of global issues focuses on general matters facing students of both writing and speaking.

Though the tutor may encounter a variety of written and oral assignment descriptions, she or he should always rely on the fundamental concerns, or the global issues. By reinforcing the commonalities of the two disciplines, tutors have a base from which to work. Emphasizing the global issues allows the tutor and the student to recognize the similarities between writing and speaking. This also provides a space for the tutor to help the student step back from the work and examine the framework of the assignment.

Assisting the client in understanding the global issues, the tutors utilize rhetorical strategies throughout the session that allow oral communication to guide the tutoring process. John P. Harrington (1988) suggests that because speech is one of the "principle products" demanded of students at the university level, writing centers could incorporate the act of speaking into the tutoring process (p. 3). Harrington argues that having students talk the tutor through a written composition means that the process will not be inhibited by surface errors that generally become distractions in the process of tutoring. Rather than turning directly to the written essay or speech outline, the tutors would have the student describe the aims, scope, and then specificities of the assignment aloud, without reading the work or over-relying on the already constructed work.

For the clients who come to the center to work on a writing assignment, the tutor opens the session not by reading a draft of an essay, rather the tutor begins by asking questions about the assignment and moves toward having the client explain his or her thesis statement, the function of the essay, and the overall structure. The tutor takes notes as the student speaks. Eventually, when the tutor and client turn toward the draft, the tutor uses the conversation with the client as a means of assessing the clarity of the written work. Harrington (1988) argues that using speech in a writing tutoring model allows "invention and the intricacies of addressing an audience" to shine, which can be particularly challenging concepts in writing tutoring (p. 3).

Similarly, students needing help with a speaking assignment begin speaking from the onset of the tutoring session as they also address global issues concerning argument and organization. This model reinforces the notion that ultimately the student is adapting the message to an audience. If the client has difficulty explaining the basic tenets of the oral presentation, then the tutor will have a clear sense of not only the global issues but also the "local issues" which can be defined as delivery and anxiety in speaking and grammar, syntax, and style in writing.

Having the clients speak with the tutor often illuminates issues of anxiety with both writing and speaking. Though the focus of the session may not lead toward having the student perform the speech, the tutor can provide the student advice and feedback related to delivery or anxiety in a low-stakes environment. Speech and writing anxiety plague many students (Daly 1978; Daly & Wilson, 1983; McCroskey, 1984, 2009; Pajares & Johnson, 1994), which becomes evident when the client is asked to speak about the work with the tutor. These clients often have difficulty expressing themselves concisely or they become visibly uncomfortable when asked to speak. The tutor is asked to make a mental note of expressions of such apprehensions and to address these later in the session.

The tutors are asked to listen carefully not only to the ideas expressed but also to how those ideas are communicated. Local issues such as grammar, delivery, and anxiety are revealed through the oral communication of the session. The term "local issues" essentially defines the space where great differences emerge between writing and speaking. When local issues arise, and they inevitably do, the tutors are trained to work with the performative differences between written and oral communication. For example, tutors might notice consistent grammatical problems, excessive vocal pauses, or issues of articulation while the student is speaking. Often, when the conversation turns to the written work, similar issues of grammar emerge, as the student's writing can be reflective of his or her speaking style. Similarly, if the session centers on a speaking assignment, the client's difficulties with articulation or diction and even issues of grammar are presented to the tutor at the outset of the meeting as points of interest.

Bruffee (1995) suggests that "what peer tutor and tutee do together is not write or edit, or least of all proofread. What they do together is converse. They converse about the subject and about the assignment. They converse about, in an academic context, their own relationship and the relationships between student and teacher. Most of all they converse about and *pursuant to* writing" (p. 94). The challenge of inviting the client to articulate his or her work immediately encourages the student to be responsible by asking him or her to do the majority of the speaking in the session and allows the tutor to gain a sense of the global operations of the assignment from the outset. As the client speaks, the tutor sketches out an outline of the work, which serves to assist the tutor in understanding the global functions of the work, such as structure, argument development, audience, and clarity of focus. Working from this position, the tutor becomes the Socratic guide and the listener. As the scene is recreated through note-taking, the tutor can then identify a set of questions that will direct the client toward the overall work.

When working within this framework, especially as a new tutor begins his or her work, the tutors may experience a lack of confidence in either their speaking or writing abilities. When recruiting tutors, it is vital that the process be explained and during training sessions tutors must be reminded that good tutors are not perfect writers nor the most dynamic speakers. In fact, because the tutors are asked to work with many different types of assignments and have varying backgrounds, the tutor may feel as if his or her skills in a particular area are not developed enough. Certainly, tutors who consider themselves decent writers may not consider themselves adept public speakers. Shamoon and Burns (2001) argue that generalist tutors with strong interpersonal skills are preferable as they are often labeled, "friendly, supportive, nurturing, and responsive" by clients (p. 66). Strong communication skills certainly aid in the development of strong tutors overall.

At our center, in order to minimize the anxiety of our tutors, we set the stage for the process by deemphasizing the distinctions between writing and speaking and taking a holistic approach to communication. In our training session, we extracted tutoring from the context of speaking or writing by focusing globally. We advanced the idea that the art of tutoring relies on the skill of reading and understanding the clients' state of mind and then working with the knowledge the client already possesses to advance their written and spoken ideas. We emphasize that a great tutor is someone who has competence in the skills of asking the right questions to draw information out of the client, rather than being the best writer or speaker on campus.

Creating a Combined Center

A combined center approach consists of a communication center and a writing center, working in concert methodologically, pedagogically, and organizationally to provide tutoring services that advance a holistic, process-oriented approach. A combined center approach does not include simply creating consistencies in paperwork or basic functions of a center. The combined centers approach means that speaking and writing are treated as part of the same whole, a unified set of communication practices. To this end, tutors are trained to work with any writing or speaking assignment, faculty and classroom workshops are conducted on this combined principle, and daily operations at such a center are treated as one. This model diverges from many "combined" centers which operate in the same physical space, but continue to treat speaking and writing as fundamentally different concerns.

The Structure

Structurally, a combined center approach must take into account several major issues, such as the administrative structure of the center, the human and financial resources, and training and reporting protocol. In the case of the authors' center, there was much duplication of effort and burden of oversight between the director of the Speaking Center and the coordinator of the Writing Center. Duplication occurred while attending to many of the same duties across centers such as working with faculty, recruiting and training tutors, arranging workshops and orientations, completing payroll, and other administrative tasks. With the combined center approach, a more practical division of labor exists. To ensure that the newly proposed center fulfilled the goals of the university, both speaking and writing expertise needed to be represented in the combined leadership of the director and coordinator. For example, if the director's background was in writing, then the coordinator's background should be in speaking, or vice versa. This mandate ensures that any combined center maintains credibility in the areas of both speaking and writing. Maintaining the ethos of the center should be significant in any rationale for the combined centers approach, as it reinforces a commitment not only to quality tutoring but also to servicing the faculty of the university.

Human and Financial Resources

The second facet of creating a successful combined center is to make more efficient use of human and financial resources in terms of the tutoring staff. Under the model, all tutors are hired and trained to tutor any writing or speaking assignment, creating flexibility in meeting the needs of walk-in appointments as well as changes in demand for writing and speaking throughout the semester. In our case, the new model was necessary because budgetary issues and the lack of cross-disciplinary training caused compartmentalization between the two centers, even as they shared the same physical space. And, at our center, much like other small colleges, we do not have a communication studies department; therefore, we have no institutional structure for recruiting tutors. For centers with similar limitations, drawing tutoring staff from a variety of majors not only is an efficient use of human resources but also is a way to diversify the tutoring staff, which becomes significant in emphasizing the process of writing and speaking across the curriculum (Lunsford, 1991/2; Neuleib, 1992).

Staffing and Training

Some of the other considerations related to human and financial resources are the efficiencies of staffing; employing one director and one coordinator and a handful of tutors is far less expensive than two tutoring corps. With the combined approach, more can be done with fewer tutors. For example, at our center, we previously employed two writing tutors and one speaking tutor to meet the greater demand for writing help. However, we found at times that because the tutors were not cross-trained, students in need of help with a speaking assignment were turned away because we were understaffed, even in cases where one or both of the writing tutors had openings in their schedules. This not only frustrates the student who cannot be assisted, but also frustrates the tutor who, given the proper training, would have been able to help.

Central Reporting System

Finally, with the combined centers approach the training, scheduling, and reporting procedures are unified, creating one central system, where clients operate under the same procedures whether receiving assistance in speaking or in writing. Having a unified system of procedures is particularly important when a common space is being shared. In our case, we found that students perceived the centers as "one" place and even minor differences in procedure were confusing. For example, if a student visited the writing center, they would make an appointment by phone, enter the center for the appointment and complete paperwork to record the session. On the other hand, if a student needed an appointment for speaking assistance, they would visit a web site and make their own appointment. When the student came for the session, there would be no paperwork and the post-session survey was conducted online. We found that the incoherence of having two different operating procedures in one physical space caused confusion for many students and for the staff and tutors working at the center. Streamlining the scheduling and reporting processes creates a great sense of unity and cohesion for the students and faculty of the college.

In order to make a cogent argument about why a combined center approach works, emphasis must be placed on administrative structure, the conservation of human and financial resources, and coherence of the daily operations of the center. Though not every center currently operating within the same physical space or under the same general mission may encounter the difficulties of our center, these three areas of emphasis may prove instrumental in rationalizing a combined center approach.

After operating as a combined center for one full academic year, challenges of consistency and coherence of method remain. The tutoring staff has developed adeptness at holding lengthy conversations about the work before turning to the work itself. While this means that some tutoring sessions end without much attention paid to the document written by the student or the prepared presentation, it does not mean that many of the concerns existent in the work itself have not been addressed. Quite the opposite happens; clients express gratitude for the work that results from critical listening and critical thinking, even if they are surprised by the approach initially.

For small institutions who find themselves recruiting tutors from a wide variety of programs, this is an opportunity to build a diverse tutoring staff, which will provide a breadth of knowledge from which the tutors can work and to use those experiences to their advantage. At the same time, a coherent model for tutoring incorporates the strengths of the tutors (i.e., knowledge of various style manuals, intimate knowledge of expectations of faculty across the disciplines, and a depth of expertise in areas within which we do not often see in writing and speaking centers). Our belief is that students need not be the perfect writer or a brilliant, engaging public speaker to be a great tutor. And, although we employ excellent tutors, the depth and breadth of assignments they work with during a given week challenges even the most gifted tutor. In order to combat this challenge, our approach focuses on being humble and recognizing the benefits as well as the limitations of peer tutoring.

For colleges or universities considering the combined center approach, a clear focus on methodological direction must be taken seriously. The training of a tutoring staff in a way that maximizes the efficacy of the session and minimizes the anxiety of the client and tutor should be central to the mission of a combined center. Choosing to emphasize process over product and begin with the similarities between writing and speaking allows a combined center the unique advantage of reinforcing communication and writing across the curriculum.

Conclusion

A combined center approach provides many benefits to the campus community and at the same time presents some unique challenges. The consistencies in administration, budgeting, scheduling, and coherence of pedagogical practice create a streamlined system whereby the center flows smoothly. Workshops with faculty concerning communication across the curriculum feel organic as the symbiotic relationship between speaking and writing emerges as two elements of the same whole. Faculty are able to see the commonalities of process and are able to adapt their assignment descriptions and grading rubric in ways that reinforce the global approach to oral and written communication practices. Clients benefit from a combined approach in that they become better writers and speakers simultaneously. Because the tutoring sessions emphasize process over product, the students begin to understand that working from the global down toward the local issues results in a more coherent message overall. Despite these benefits, the challenges of a combined centers approach should also be noted.

A major challenge presented in a combined center is a resistance to our tutoring approach. Most clients, begrudgingly or not, cooperate with the tutor's request to "just talk" about the project. However, we have encountered clients who simply will not speak. When asked questions, they respond with a question such as "I don't know, what do you think?" These clients resist the process for many different reasons, and the tutors are trained to be sensitive to this. At the same time, part of our job is to familiarize the client with our method. If a student does not want to talk, the tutor will try to be much more direct in questioning or give an example for the client as a model. If the client seems to want the tutor to do the work for them, then the tutor continues to engage the student as well as she or he can. And, if after many attempts at engaging the client she or he is insistent that all that is needed is someone to read over the essay or check an outline or bibliography for structure, then the tutor does the best job possible of doing just that.

The client is not the only partner who challenges the new tutoring method. The model we prefer is not easy to implement. Now and again we overhear tutors slipping back into the "old way" of tutoring. Rather than asking guided questions and listening to the student, they opt to read the essay or study the speech outline. This is mostly a result of old habits or frustration with an uncooperative student. But, ultimately, the tutors understand and appreciate the model because it makes the work of bringing speaking and writing together easier.

The combined centers approach has radically changed the face of our center; it has brought together two seemingly different centers, enhancing our ability to offer tutoring services across the curriculum in a more coherent way. It has improved the communication between client and tutor. Additionally, the combined centers approach has provided a space from which we can justify needs and expectations more clearly for purposes of growth and assessment. Finally, it has brought the center into the spotlight amongst faculty and administration.

Other campuses interested in such a model, should consider the specific mission set forth by the college or university concerning writing and speaking across the curriculum. This model may not work on a larger campus or on a campus where writing and communication are institutionalized in ways that do not conform to working together. On a campus where strong tutoring pools in both writing and speaking exist, the idea of combining centers might also not be attractive. However, if a pedagogical approach to tutoring that advocates a holistic approach to tutoring based on the process of speaking and writing and communication (both oral and written) is advanced across the curriculum, then a combined approach certainly would be worth considering.

Developing a combined center, though it takes dedication from the administration and staff and radical reformulating of the way we think about the process of speaking and writing tutoring, can result in many benefits for the institution: an efficient use of human and financial resources, a pedagogical framework that will ultimately enhance communication across the curriculum, and engagement of faculty and students alike in the mission of the center. For those who share a similar vision for the future of writing and speaking, the combined approach provides a space for moving toward holistically addressing communication, both written and spoken.

References

Barnes, D. (1983). Oral language and learning. In R. Rubin (Ed.), *Improving speaking and writing skills* (pp. 41–54). San Francisco, CA: Jossey-Bass.

Bruffee, K. A. (1995). Peer tutoring and the "conversation of mankind." In C. Murphy & J. Law (Eds.), *Landmark essays on writing centers* (pp. 88–98). Davis, CA: Hermagoras Press.

Bushman, D.E. (1991). Past accomplishments and current trends in writing center research: A bibliographic essay. In R. Wallace & J. Simpson (Eds.), *The writing center: New directions* (pp. 27–37). New York: Garland.

Daly, J. A. (1978). Writing apprehension and writing competency. *The Journal of Educational Research, 72*(1), 10–14.

Daly, J. A., & Wilson, D. A. (1983). Writing apprehension, self-esteem, and personality. *Research in the Teaching of English, 17*(4), 327–341.

Halpern, J. W. (1984). Differences between speaking and writing and their implications for teaching. *College Composition and Communication, 35*(3), 345–357.

Harrington, J. P. (1988). The idea of a center for writing and speaking. *The Writing Lab Newsletter, 12*(10), 1–3.

Kroll, B. M., & Vann, R. J. (1981). *Exploring speaking and writing center relationships.* Urbana, IL: National Council of Teachers of English.

Lunsford, A. (1991/92). Collaboration, control, and the idea of a writing center. *Writing Lab Newsletter, 16*(4–5), 1–5.

McCroskey J. C. (2009). Communication apprehension: What we have learned in the last four decades. *Human Communication, 12*(2), 179–187.

McCroskey, J. C. (1984). The communication apprehension perspective. In J. A. Daly & J. C. McCroskey (Eds.), *Avoiding communication: Shyness, reticence, and communication* (pp. 13–38). Beverly Hills, CA: Sage Publications.

Morello, J. T. (1990). Comparing speaking across the curriculum and writing across the curriculum programs. *Communication Education, 49*, 99–113.

Neuleib, J. (1992). The friendly stranger: Twenty-five years as "other." *College Composition and Communication, 43*, 231–243.

Pajares, F., & Johnson, M. J. (1994). Confidence and competence in writing: The role of self-efficacy, outcome expectancy, and apprehension. *Research in Teaching English, 28*(3), 313–331.

Rafoth, B. A., & Rubin, D. L. (1992). Speaking-writing curricula: New designs on an old idea. *WPA: Writing Program Administration, 15*(3), 17–29.

Reigstad, T. J., & McAndrew, D. A. (2001). *Tutoring writing: A practical guide for conferences.* Portsmouth, NH: Boynton/Cook-Heinemann

Shamoon, L. K., & Burns, D. H. (2001). Labor pains: A political analysis of writing center tutoring. In J. Nelson & K. Evertz (Eds.), *The politics of writing centers* (pp. 62–73). Portsmouth, NH: Boynton/Cook-Heinemann.

Sperling, M. (1996). Revisiting the writing-speaking connection: Challenges for research on writing and writing instruction. *Review of Educational Research, 66* (1), 53–86.

Stay, B. L. (2006). Writing centers in the small college. In C. Murphy & B. L. Stay (Eds.), *The writing center director's resource book* (pp. 147–151). Mahwah, NJ: Lawrence Erlbaum Associates.

Chapter 13

Course Management Systems: Creating Alternative Avenues for Student Access to Communication Centers

Luke LeFebvre

Computer-assisted instruction has altered the practices and learning experiences of institutions of higher education like no other previous media technology (De-Lacey & Leonard, 2002; Radcliffe, 2002). Computer-mediated communication allows the user to easily do message transmission, exchange, and interaction processing. Paralleling the rapid diffusion of the Internet has been the Internet-based course management system (Fredrickson, 1999). A course management system (CMS) is a platform that allows for computer-assisted instruction, which is defined as, "computer-presented instruction that is individualized, interactive, and guided" (Steinberg, 1991, p. 2). Communication centers have an opportunity to expand their influence through the use of course management systems; integration of the course management system allows the center to reach students who might not feel comfortable attending the center for face-to-face consultations through computer-mediated communication (see Griffiths & Miller, 2005).

Computer-mediated communication, available through a CMS, "involves two or more computer users who use their machines to share messages" (Kuehn, 1994, p. 173). Computer-mediated communication, a standard and accepted mode of communication at college and university campuses (McCollum, 1998), has the potential to create an avenue for centers to network and communicate with students in a habituated virtual environment. Moreover, institutional socialization of course management software has become standard in higher education (Ellaway, 2006; Lane & Shelton, 2001), allowing for access at any time

187

from any computer (Gibson & Barrett, 2003; Wood & Fassett, 2003), and requiring minimal overhead and limited training for adaptation into the communication center's arsenal to provide service to students seeking assistance to develop their communication skills.

Given the potential for computer management systems to change the face of higher education, this chapter argues for the integration of a CMS into the communication center. This chapter first examines CMSs by describing the basic components, financial investments involved in course management software, student use of the technology, and the potential use of the software for computer-mediated communication. Next, the communication center is introduced and its primary student-learning objective is defined. Finally, suggestions for incorporating a CMS into the communication center are described.

Course Management Systems

Course management systems have seen a robust growth since being introduced in the late 1990s and have become essential to the institutional framework of higher education institutions (see Allen & Seaman, 2010; Angelo, 2004; Morgan, 2003). A CMS is a software program or integrated platform, specifically marketed to university and college campuses, that contains a series of customizable web-based tools (Severson, 2004) to support the instructional design and strategies for learning in traditional and online courses. The core group of tools available for use in CMSs include: synchronous and asynchronous communication, content storage and access, announcements, quiz and survey tools, grade books, email, chat, discussion boards, and virtual classroom environments with audio and video features. Blackboard, Angel, WebCT, Moodle, eCollege, and Desire2Learn are all examples of course management systems.

The power of the CMS for colleges and universities is in its ability to create e-learning environments that reach learners beyond the traditional brick and mortar classroom (Green, 2001). The appeal for the CMS is in its ability to generate interactivity and individualized control to the user. Above all, the system is a computer technology that allows for computer-mediated communication. Computer-mediated communication describes "synchronous and asynchronous computer connections between participants in an instructional context" (Kuehn, 1994, p. 173). Synchronous communication allows participants to immediately and simultaneously interact (i.e., chats, Internet phone calls, video conferences, etc.), while asynchronous communication occurs at different times (i.e., email, discussion boards, etc.) (Ko & Rossen, 2004). Each of these modes of communication allows participants to choose the avenue of communication that best suits them at a convenient time and for however long is needed to solidify meaning. Therefore, reaching out to these new populations provides institutions of higher education with the ability to increase their overall financial capital; however, the use of the CMS comes with a financial cost.

The Campus Computing Project (2003) and the Educause Center for Applied Research found in their 2003 study that more than 80 percent of colleges and universities in the United States utilize a CMS. The systems involve a sizable investment for campuses. For example, full-feature packages "start at around $50,000 and range through the six figures, depending on institutional enrollment and the advanced features selected" (Wagner, 2003, p. 2). Due to the ubiquitous nature and nearly mandatory use of the systems the starting cost is nearly always surpassed because of upgrades, outsourcing, faculty use, student demand, and strategic administrative decision-making.

Unfortunately, little research exists on the cost and benefits of CMSs use in higher education. According to Harrington, Gordon, and Schibik (2004), "much of this research is hampered by the exceedingly difficult prospect of gathering accurate measures of the costs" (p. 3). Moreover, most of the operational costs for CMSs are spread over multiple departments on campus, which makes interpreting bottom-line financial investments difficult to ascertain. What is known is that students are being exposed to CMSs and are required to use this technology almost immediately when enrolling at an academic institution.

Widely Disseminated Technologies in U.S. Colleges and Universities

Over 8,800 colleges and universities in the United States use Blackboard, and WebCT has in excess of 2,600 colleges and universities in more than 80 countries worldwide using its course management system software (Park, Lee, & Cheong, 2008). Additionally, more than 5.6 million students were enrolled in at least one online course during the fall 2009 semester (Allen & Seaman, 2010). Harrington et al. (2004) found in their online national survey of academic departments that 90 percent report that their department currently uses a course management system. Furthermore, the majority of these departments primarily use the CMS for traditional face-to-face courses. According to this information the vast majority of the undergraduate student population seems to be fully assimilated into the use of CMSs at institutes of higher education.

The Educause Center for Applied Research found that nearly three out of four students have used a CMS for at least one class (Katz, 2006). Additionally, more than three-quarters of those who had used a CMS rated their experience as positive or very positive. These numbers clearly indicate that the educational technology revolution has required and continues to require students to access and be exposed to the systems. It would also seem that, as Katz observed, "Familiarity with these systems breeds contentment" (p. 5). Since students are already familiar with their CMS the communication center need only to adapt the software use from the traditional classroom use to a more non-traditional utilization of the software.

Purpose of the CMS: Traditional vs. Non-traditional

The original purpose of the CMS was to allow students and teachers to interact outside the classroom in virtual spaces (McGee & Leffel, 2005). CMSs allowed faculty additional methods of communication with students and students had additional methods of communication with faculty and other students (Harrington et al., 2004). These forms of interaction between faculty-student and student-student are traditional purposes of online education and were anticipated by the advent of the CMS. However, higher education institutional members are utilizing CMSs in non-traditional, innovative, and evolving ways that were not foreseen.

For example, departments are using CMSs to communicate and interact with colleagues (i.e., faculty-faculty), and human resource departments use the systems to communicate with institutional faculty and administration (i.e., administration-faculty, administration-administration). CMSs are "affected by social, organizational, economic, and cultural factors that surround the system" (Park, Lee, Cheong, 2008, p. 164) and are not limited by the original intentions behind the technological design. Understanding that premise, the CMS has the ability to be manipulated as a technological tool to be used beyond the "one size fits all" service to assist communication centers in meeting student needs in a personalized and supportive manner.

Communication Centers and CMSs

The primary goal of communication centers is to assist students in the development of their oral communication abilities and skills. The communication center allows for individualized and reflective learning that can be augmented and enhanced by the use of CMSs and is characterized by (a) increased availability, (b) demonstrated caring, and (c) inclusion of outside assistance (see McComb, 1994). The center could be available beyond regular location hours when students are developing their speech topics or communication strategies. The center's CMS allows for another resource beyond the classroom's walls and at various times not predicated by institutional hours. Inherently this communicates that the institution, particularly the center, cares for students' needs as it relates to the development of communication competencies. Time and attention is dedicated to the student via computer-mediated communication within the CMS. Finally, outside assistance providers (i.e., tutors and center staff) have the opportunity to assist learners to develop communication knowledge and skills. The dialogue is carried beyond the classroom and enacted during convenient times and places for the student. Therefore, the system becomes another avenue to provide flexible and tailored instructional support to students to develop competent communication skills. Furthermore, when integrating a CMS into the communication center both resources complement and magnify the college or university's ability to allocate resources for learning opportunities engaging students beyond the classroom.

Previous research indicates that two components lead to high levels of student engagement: (1) amount of time students dedicate to their studies and (2) the ways the institution allocates resources and organizes learning opportunities and services to foster student participation (Astin, 1991; Chickering & Reisser, 1993; Kuh, Schuh, Witt, & Associates, 1991; Pascarella & Terenzini, 1991, 2005; Tinto, 1975, 1987). The CMS functions as a resource to provide faculty and students with an additional avenue for communication so that students can extend their learning beyond the physical classroom. Moreover, faculty report increased communication with students by way of the CMS (Morgan, 2003). The same type of increase in student communication and usage can be replicated for the communication center via the CMS.

Regarding the second component, resource allocation, the communication center functions as a resource for students to improve oral communication. To fulfill their mission, communication centers must choose how to allocate available resources to organize learning opportunities that induce student engagement. The CMS is an established and readily accessible resource for the communication center to encourage and create encounters for students. These encounters are critical to student engagement, especially if the student experience is to be satisfying and rewarding (Tinto, 1975, 1987).

Course management systems have been shown to significantly increase student involvement in multiple aspects of courses (Stith, 2000). The merging of the communication center and CMS resources provide increased student engagement in the learning opportunities provided by the communication center. The CMS meets today's students, digital natives (viz., people who grew up in the digital world using technology to communicate, record, educate, and understand), where they are. Communication centers maximize learning opportunities by reaching out to students using CMSs. Plus, centers will find that student users will seek more versions of electronic sources because they like to receive information very quickly (Prensky, 2001). This provides an opportunity for communication centers to create a connection with the student and introduce other available resources the center offers beyond the CMS.

Communication Center + CMS = Personalized Instruction

Students' needs vary; consequently, the instructional support must accommodate the varied characteristics of learners. The key component of the communication center is the individualized instruction provided to students with diverse needs. The CMS for the communication center is no different, and should be designed as an open-ended learning environment (Azevedo, 2005) where both experienced and inexperienced students are able to find assistance to improve their communication competencies (Vovides, Sanchez-Alonso, Mitropoulou, & Nickmans, 2007). The CMS becomes an interactive resource with a "live" guide (i.e., tutor) to engage the student. Providing a CMS also allows access to students who may not yet feel comfortable with face-to-face interactions (Griffiths & Miller, 2005). Additionally, all students have access to the same instructional materials and the same web-based tools with personalized support from the center staff on the CMS. This allows for a personalized learning experience for the student, and a potential opportunity for the communication center to move from online assistance to face-to-face for future consultations.

Implementation of a CMS for the Communication Center

Utilization of the CMS as an extension of the communication center is a relatively new innovation. Depending on which CMS tool is used, its usage alters the traditional preparation and training approaches required for face-to-face consultations with the center director and tutors. The ultimate technological goal of the CMS integration is to make the technology transparent, which will allow those involved to concentrate on the academic task at hand (Goodyear, 2000). Therefore, what follows are suggestions for directors and tutors when using a CMS to assist students.

Adapting the CMS to the Communication Center

Directors of communication centers must coordinate a number of primary responsibilities when bringing a CMS online for the communication center. These duties are similar to those identified by Hobgood (2000) for creating a traditional communication center: "information gathering and needs assessment, faculty training and support, and training of student staff" (p. 340).

First, the information gathering of course syllabi is essential for preparing the CMS. All course syllabi should be made available on the CMS, at the very minimum to the tutorial staff. Syllabi, specific course materials, assignments, exercises, rubrics and evaluation forms can all be stored in electronic folders (identified by course and instructor's name) on the CMS for quick and easy access. By creating such a database tutors are able to provide specific and tailored assistance nearly instantaneously to students who may not have all the required materials to provide to the tutor. Moreover, this resource is highly beneficial for both e-tutoring and face-to-face sessions. In essence the director is responsible for creating and maintaining a warehouse of communication competence support information and materials. These documents should be uploaded as reference material for tutors.

Examination of the information presented in the course syllabi and materials should provide valuable information for identifying what students may need from the communication center. This needs assessment should include three logical steps: (1) clarify the objective or desired goal of achievement, (2) ascertain the existing performance level, and (3) determine the gap or need that must be minimized or eliminated (Dick, Carey, & Carey, 2005). To provide the most effective and efficient service to the students, the director must do both a thorough examination of the syllabi and an assessment of the needs of the communication center. This is especially important if instructors have specific assignments and requirements to complete those assignments that the center staff may not have been aware of prior to the CMS integration.

Next, faculty support is imperative for CMS center effectiveness. Without faculty cooperation the CMS will have limited faculty-provided resources (such as those described above). When interacting with faculty, the communication center director can emphasize that the CMS for the center is a supplemental resource, just like the center itself. Open dialogues with faculty and find key players who are willing to integrate course activities that might include the center's CMS. Student success should be a common interest and priority of both the faculty and the center (Hobgood, 2000).

Tutor-training modules can be embedded into the course management system. Modules, resources, and links to training materials should be made available to tutors via the CMS and quizzes for staff members could be created in order to check understanding of the material. The director should be the administrator of the CMS, tutors should have access to nearly all the training and course materials, and the students should have access to the tools and functions that will allow for interaction with the tutors.

The elegance of the CMS is that its operations can be tailored to multiple parties simultaneously without other parties having access to the information. However, center directors should decide whether to have all students enrolled within one CMS, or whether separate CMSs should be used for center staff and for students and faculty, in consultation with their campus CMS technology managers. Faculty comfort with open accessibility to their teaching materials, as well as staff comfort level with open access to discussion forums, should also be considered when making this decision, especially when diverse faculty from across-the-curriculum programs are involved. If enrolling all students in one CMS, the director should make sure all tracking devices are activated for each content area available in the CMS to allow for assessment and reporting purposes, including what information is being accessed by which populations.

Tutors should be coached and made aware of the transition in skills needed to provide assistance electronically. E-tutoring and face-to-face tutoring differ significantly due to the lack of nonverbal communication (Allan & Lewis, n.d.; Deketelaere, Degryse, DeMunter, & DeLeyn, 2009; Richmond, McCroskey, & Hickson, 2008). E-tutors are tutors who assist learners electronically. Therefore, tutors should be prepared to adapt to the virtual environment.

An excellent training process for tutors is to simulate e-tutoring sessions, just as with face-to-face student consultations. With an e-tutoring simulation, tutors learn to use the technology including how the software functions, advantages and limitations, and are able to brainstorm options among themselves for handling various situations. Each tutor should take turns experimenting with the technology and de-brief as a group after each simulation. This type of training allows the director to identify gaps in the technology and provides an excellent opportunity for those involved to discuss what was effective and ineffective during the simulations.

The shift to a CMS can be facilitated for tutors by incorporating the use of the telephone or similar electronic vocal communication technologies when video conferencing is not available. The communication center's phone number or Skype address (discussed more below with video conferencing) should be placed on the CMS and made available to the student by the tutor once contact has been initiated via the CMS. Tutors who use electronic vocal communication devices are able to make sure their feedback is being clearly interpreted by the student. The interaction is easier for the tutor because the e-tutoring session is similar to the face-to-face tutoring session. Despite the benefits of e-tutoring, it is important to understand that e-consultations are more time consuming than face-to-face interactions (Griffiths & Miller, 2005), although the phone helps economize time needed during an electronic session. In addition to time concerns, it should also be noted that while the phone assists the tutor to a certain extent, it is essential that tutors have good written communication skills when providing electronic feedback to students to avoid misinterpretation (Deketelaere et al., 2009).

Video conferencing may also be used to facilitate group conferencing with students who are working on a group presentation. For example, visual aids created in PowerPoint can be designed in a collaborative effort allowing text and/or picture additions with all the students while the tutor offers suggestions and feedback. If video conferencing is available via the CMS, directors should spend a great deal of time assisting the tutors to become familiar with using and assisting others with this technology. Most video conferencing tools (i.e., Wimba) on the CMS are similar to Skype Limited, which permits a user to make computer-to-computer telephone and video calls over the Internet (Bates, Chadwick, Stevens, Goldman, & Gillett, 2011). The tutor and tutee have the advantage of interacting both verbally and nonverbally with this tool. Also, this channel of computer-mediated communication is an extremely familiar way for the tutors to interact with students who need assistance because it has nearly all the qualities of a face-to-face interaction.

Preparing tutors for the transitions listed above allows the tutor to approach the process in a more prepared manner when consulting with students via the CMS. To facilitate the transitions, the director might create a discussion board forum for tutors to post issues and discuss their experiences (Deketelaere et al., 2009). This type of dialogue will not only help the tutors but will also allow the director to identify potential areas of improvement when updating procedures and protocols for using the CMS as an extension of the communication center. The effectiveness of the center's CMS relies on the tutors who interact with the software and students daily, so building feedback mechanisms into your center's program is imperative.

Additional Recommendations for the Center's CMS

A number of strategies can be employed to assure success when integrating the CMS into a communication center's resources. One of the key areas is marketing. During the first week of each semester, center directors should reach out to the student population to make them aware of the CMS resource and the communication center itself via the system email. Post the communication center hours of operation and contact information on the opening page of the CMS. Make sure this information stands out to students and is easily found on the system. Also, have the consultation forms available for student access.

Foster a supportive and welcoming environment for students. For example, integrate video introductions of the director and tutors to reach students and to limit anxiety about attending the center. This is also a way to reach students in courses that may not tour the communication center. Training video clips or video examples of speeches may be embedded or linked as resources for students and/or faculty. If possible, ensure these examples are universally agreed upon as competent and effective illustrations of the communicative behaviors faculty would like to see developed by students in their courses.

Develop a frequently asked questions page for students who use the center's CMS by asking tutors to keep track of recurring questions that occur during e-consultations. In the long run this will help tutors be more effective with their time when interacting with tutees regarding common or reoccurring questions. Note that if you choose to integrate a discussion board for students it should be monitored for appropriateness. Remember the communication center CMS will include *all* students from many different sections and, possibly, from a variety of courses. Use the discussion board feature with caution.

Beyond focusing on student usage of CMS within the communication center, it is politically critical to enroll important stakeholders into the system. Include your department chair, faculty colleagues who support the center and include center activities as part of their course(s), and other individuals specific to your institution who might be potential collaborators or important figures as you garner support for the communication center. By including these individuals, they will have the opportunity to see for themselves the amount of work and effort necessary to create, maintain, and service the student population at your institution.

Conclusion

Incorporating a CMS into the resources at the communication center has the potential to enhance avenues of support to students and improve access to learning resources without any additional technological fees. The computer-mediated communication provided by the CMS is an additional channel for students to seek assistance when developing their communication competencies. The technology is most likely already available at your institution and need only be organized to meet the center's intentions. Why not give students every opportunity to find the help they need to be successful when developing their communication skills? When moving forward, be sure to incorporate a CMS that is well-suited for your communication center. Remember to do an audience analysis of your learners and the context of the support center to determine the specific needs within your institution. This will help you to create a system that is reliable, flexible, and supportive to the communication center at your specific institution. Start small and assess the need for growth as you bring your course management system online. Once online, the computer-mediated communication available through the integration of a CMS allows students (and peer tutors), most likely digital natives, to use and interact with center resources via a communication channel they find comfortable and are probably already using on a regular basis.

References

Allan, B., & Lewis, D. (n.d.). *E-tutoring in higher education*. Retrieved from http://www-users.york.ac.uk

Allen, I. E., & Seaman, J. (2010). *Class differences: Online education in the United States*. Retrieved from The Sloan Consortium, Inc. website: http://sloanconsortium.org/publications/survey/class_differences

Angelo, J. M. (2004). New lessons in course management. *University Business: The Magazine for College and University Administrators*. Retrieved from http://universitybusiness.ccsct.com/page.cfm?p=616

Astin, A. W. (1991) Assessment of excellence: The philosophy and practice of assessment and evaluation in higher education. *American Council on Education Series on Higher Education*. Washington/New York: American Council on Education and Macmillan.

Azevedo, R. (2005). Using hypermedia as a metacognitive tool for enhancing student learning? The role of self-regulated learning. *Educational Psychologist, 40*(4), 199–209.

Bates, T., Chadwick, J., Stevens, N., Goldman, N., & Gillett, M. (2011). *About Skype: What is Skype?* Retrieved from http://about.skype.com/

The Campus Computing Project. (2003). *The 2003 National Survey of Information Technology in U.S. Higher Education*. Retrieved from The Campus Computing Project website: http://www.campuscomputing.net/survey

Chickering, A. W., & Reisser, L. (1993). *Education and identity.* San Francisco, CA: Jossey-Bass.

Deketelaere, A., Degryse, J., DeMunter, A., & DeLeyn, P. (2009). Twelve tips for successful e-tutoring using electronic portfolios. *Medical Teacher, 31,* 497–501.

DeLacy, B., & Leonard, D. (2002). Case study on technology and distance in education at the Harvard Business School. *Educational Technology & Society, 5*(2). Retrieved from http://ifets.info/journals/5_2?delacey.html

Dick, W., Carey, L., & Carey, J. O. (2005). *The systematic design of instruction* (6th ed.). Boston: Allyn & Bacon.

Ellaway, R. (2006). Weaving the 'e's together. *Medical Teacher, 28,* 587–590.

Fredrickson, S. (1999). Untangling a tangled Web: An overview of Web-based instruction programs. *T.H.E. Journal, 26*(11), 67.

Gibson, D., & Barrett, H. (2003). Directions in electronic portfolio development. *Contemporary Issues in Technology and Teacher Education, 2,* 559–576.

Goodyear, P. (2000). Effective networked learning in higher education: Notes and guidelines. Retrieved from Lancaster University, Networked Learning in Higher Education website: http://csalt.lancs.ac.uk/jisc

Green, K. (2001). *The 12th National Survey of Computing and Information Technology in American Higher Education.* Encino, CA: Campus Computing.

Griffiths, M., & Miller, H. (2005). E-mentoring: Does it have a place in medicine? *Postgraduate Medical Journal, 81,* 389–390.

Harrington, C. F., Gordon, S. A., & Schibik, T. J. (2004). Course management system utilization and implications for practice: A national survey of departmental chairpersons. *Online Journal of Distance Learning Administration, 7*(4). Retrieved from http://www.westga.edu/~distance/ojdla/winter74/harrington74.htm

Hobgood, L. B. (2000). The pursuit of speaking proficiency: A voluntary approach. *Communication Education, 49,* 339–351.

Hunt, S. K., & Simonds, C. J. (2002). Extending learning opportunities in the basic communication course: Exploring the pedagogical benefits of speech laboratories. *Basic Communication Course Annual, 14,* 60–86.

Katz, R. N. (2006). *The ECAR study of undergraduate students and information technology.* Retrieved from Educause Center for Applied Research website: http://www.educause.edu/ers0808

Knorr, E. M. (2006). *Course management system (CMS) evaluation and strategy at UBC: A viewpoint from the faculty of science.* Vancouver, BC: University of British Columbia.

Ko, S., & Rossen, S. (2004). *Teaching online: A practical guide* (2nd ed.). Boston, MA: Houghton Mifflin.

Kuehn, S. A. (1994). Computer-mediated communication in instructional settings: A research agenda. *Communication Education, 43,* 171–183.

Kuh, G. D., Kinzie, J., Schuh, J. H., Whitt, E. J., & Associates. (2005). *Student success in college: Creating conditions that matter.* San Francisco, CA: Jossey-Bass.

Kuh, G. D., Schuh, J. H., Whitt, E. J., & Associates. (1991). *Involving colleges: Successful approaches to fostering student learning and personal development outside the classroom.* San Francisco, CA: Jossey-Bass.

Lane, D. R., & Shelton, M. W. (2001). The centrality of communication education in classroom computer-mediated-communication: Toward a practical and evaluative pedagogy. *Communication Education, 50,* 241–255.

McCollum, K. (1998, October 16). Now that computers are the rule U. of Florida begins to adopt. *The Chronicle of Higher Education,* pp. A27–28.

McComb, M. (1994). Benefits of computer-mediated communication in college courses. *Communication Education, 43,* 159–170.

McGee, P., & Leffel, A. (2005). Ethics and decision-making in a course management system: Instructor and learner development. *Education, Communication & Influence, 5*(3), 265–284.

Morgan, G. (2003). *Faculty use of course management systems.* Retrieved from Educause Center for Applied Research website: http://www.educause.edu/ECAR/FacultyUseofCourseManagementSy/158560

Park, N., Lee, K. M., & Cheong, P. H. (2008). University instructors' acceptance of electronic courseware: An application of the technology acceptance model. *Journal of Computer-Mediated Communication, 13,* 163–186.

Pascarella, E. T., & Terenzini, P. T. (1991). *How college affects students.* San Francisco, CA: Jossey-Bass.

Pascarella, E. T., & Terenzini, P. T. (2005). *How college affects students: A third decade of research* (Vol. 2). San Francisco, CA: Jossey-Bass.

Prensky, M. (2001). Digital natives, digital immigrants, part 1. *On the Horizon, 9*(5), 2–6.

Radcliffe, D. (2002). Technological and pedagogical convergence between work-based and campus-based learning. *Educational Technology & Society, 5*(2). Retrieved from http://www.ifets.info/journals/5_2/radcliffe.html

Richmond, V. P., McCroskey, J. C., & Hickson, M. L. (2008). *Nonverbal behaviors in interpersonal relations* (6th ed.). Boston, MA: Pearson.

Sausner, R. (2006). *Course management: Ready for prime time.* Retrieved from University Business: The Magazine for College and University Administrators website: http://universitybusiness.ccsct.com/page.cfm?p=791

Severson, A. (2004). *Faculty support required for the implementation of a new learning management system* (Unpublished master's thesis). Simon Fraser University, Burnaby, British Columbia, Canada.

Steinberg, E. R. (1991). *Computer-assisted instruction: A synthesis of theory, practice, and technology.* Hillsdale, NJ: Lawrence Erlbaum Associates.

Stith, B. (2000). Web-enhanced lecture course scores big with student and faculty. *T.H.E. Journal, 27*(8), 21–28.

Tinto, V. (1975). Dropout from higher education: A theoretical synthesis of recent research. *Review of Education Research, 45,* 89–125.

Tinto, V. (1987). *Leaving college: Rethinking the causes and cures of student attrition.* Chicago: University of Chicago Press.

Vovides, Y., Sanchez-Alonso, S., Mitropoulou, V., & Nickmans, G. (2007). The use of e-learning course management systems to support learning strategies and to improve self-regulated learning. *Educational Research Review, 2,* 64–74.

Wagner, T. (2003). *Calling all course management systems: There's undisputed value in CMS, but you need to get the lay of the land before you invest.* Retrieved from University Business: The Magazine for College and University Administrators website: http://universitybusiness.ccsct.com/page.cfm?p=491

Wood, A. F., & Fassett, D. L. (2003). Remote control: Identity, power, and technology in the communication classroom. *Communication Education, 52*(3), 286–296.

Chapter 14

Virtual Communication Centers: A Resource for Building Oral Competency

Lynn O. Cooper

In their comprehensive study of American colleges and universities, Morreale, Worley, and Hugenberg (2010) found enrollments in the basic course to be healthy. However, after 40 years of studying the basic course, Morreale et al. found that significant challenges remain for administrators and practitioners in both two-year and four-year institutions. Most importantly, consistency and standardization across course sections, the ability to assess student learning, and adequate training of instructors was cited. The inclusion of various types of students, such as those with high levels of speech apprehension and international students who often require more help with oral skills is important, though these populations are rarely included in consideration of the basic course. Additionally, a new generation of students with technological sophistication and high expectations, but indifferent engagement in learning activities has entered the classroom (Herrington, Reeves, & Oliver, 2010). The ability to engage these varied students in creative, achievement-oriented activities that provide timely feedback is another challenge (p. 104). Finally, a dramatic increase in the use of media and technology in the basic course has occurred over the past 10 years, as distant delivery continues to expand and students face economic and financial challenges (Morreale, Worley, & Hugenberg, 2010). In talking about this longitudinal trend, Morreale et al. note:

> the use of media and technology is probably one of the most significant changes affecting the basic course over time. Pedagogically, the emergence of the digitized age has provided equipment to upgrade the recording and criti-

199

quing of student performances. In addition, innovative options for classroom instruction [. . .] DVDs, web-based videos, and other digital resources now are commonplace. And while the earlier studies did not focus on the topic of technology, the importance of technically mediated and computer mediated communication in every aspect of social life calls for greater inclusion of these topics in the course. The basic course needs to address these topics and meet students where they are in the digital world (p. 426).

In summary, the demand for greater consistency, standardization, instructor training, attention to individual student needs, technologically relevant delivery systems, and assessment of effectiveness create significant challenges for the basic course. As fewer course sections and expanding enrollments continue to put pressure on class size, the need to explore other instructional delivery options is apparent. One of these options is the utilization of a web-based system of instruction.

This chapter chronicles an attempt to meet the needs of a new generation of students by highlighting the ten-year development of a web-based communication center on a college campus. Its focus is to present administrators and faculty with a learning resource to strengthen the impact of the basic course. From an overview of mediated learning, the chapter introduces a conceptual model of a virtual communication center, along with a description of a working center and measures of effectiveness. Finally, student, faculty, and administrative implications for web-based learning are raised.

A Primer on Web-Based Learning

Instructional enhancement through web-based resources is not new. At the beginning of this century, Piccoli, Ahmad, and Ives' (2001) review of the literature highlighted advantages in technology-mediated learning environments in areas of student achievement, positive attitudes toward learning and the evaluation of the learning experience, increased convenience, flexibility, currency of material, student retention, individualized learning, and feedback. MacGregor and Lou (2004) extolled the pedagogical value of having access to current information available through websites, digital libraries, primary source documents, and multimedia presentations.

Web-based learning as a supplement to face-to-face teaching provides multimedia rich, attractive content to student learners (Baturay & Bay, 2010). The basic feature is the presentation of various lessons using multimedia materials, such as downloadable lecture notes, video examples, and various communication evaluation tools. Objectives and pedagogical strategies are key attributes to foster an effective learning environment. In a web-based learning environment, they are digitally interactive through extranet or intranet, a web of social relations imaginatively constructed to provide a stimulus for learning and cooperative social interaction. Some advantages of virtual environments include flexibility in being able to "work ahead" on assignments, the ability to repeat or review work for greater learning and retention, the establishment of minimal standards for communication performance, application of public speaking concepts, and performance activities that do not require class attendance. Prerequisites for creating a virtual environment include the selection of some standardized course materials, development of uniform training, and personnel willing to put the model into action (Carliner, 2002; Herrington, Reeves, & Oliver, 2010; Mackey & Jacobson, 2008; Seiler & Titsworth, 1999; Sherblom, 2010; Waldeck, 2008).

Piccoli, Ahmad, and Ives (2001) define several types of digital learning environments. A "virtual learning environment" involves computer-based systems such as those employed in on-line courses, which allow interactions with other participants. "Classroom-based learning environments" define a traditional course that uses different technologies as tools to support classroom activities; the most well-known examples would be Blackboard and WebCT environments. Finally, a "computer microworld" is where students individually enter a self-contained computer-based learning environment. This last definition of web-based learning will be most appropriate in understanding the virtual communication center highlighted in this chapter. Littlejohn and Pegler (2007) use the term "blended e-learning" to denote a wide choice of computer resources drawn from digital repositories that can be accessed by a single login. "E-learning" appears more frequently in educational literature after 2002, and is a broader umbrella term for "networked learning," "online learning," "computer-assisted learning," "web-based instruction," and "computer-mediated learning."

Web-based learning environments bring something extra to learning situations because they are user-driven media. That is, individuals move actively around the system of using computer-based hypertext by choosing which links to follow (Graff, 2006). Graff suggests that cognitive style is the pertinent factor when considering successful student engagement with web-based learning systems. Graff found that awareness of the student's cognitive style, or the way people perceive, remember, and use information from their environment influenced how successful web-based environments were. A mixed hyper-text architecture appeared to be the most effective way of structuring learning material. This may be because students view hypertext as a kind of physical space where they recall only a few of the places they visit, but will remember landmarks, routes, and key information. Some information is arranged hierarchically so that superordinate pages are linked to lower order pages, and some pages are networked, or connected to other pages to form a complex structure with many links.

However, mere exposure to Internet resources cannot improve student learning; the instructional design and learning environment is critical. Accessibility is one of the main design requirements for web-based content, a student's ability to navigate through the site, and find the information needed to complete tasks. The site itself must provide a structured framework for student learning, interesting background information, step-by-step procedures to follow, and an evaluative rubric to assess the student's work (Guo & Zhang, 2009). Students may have different background knowledge of a subject, need more explanations, be differently motivated, or have different cognitive learning styles, but personalization and adaptation are possible in a web-based learning system.

Benoit, Benoit, Milyo, and Hansen's (2006) meta analysis of existing research on web-assisted (online) learning looked at cross-disciplinary courses, including 28 studies on learning (N=2,361) and 10 studies on satisfaction (N=768). While some disciplines would not adapt as well to a web-assisted format, no significant difference was seen in learning from traditional and web-assisted instruction. The Benoit et al. meta-analysis found slightly less satisfaction for web-assisted courses than traditional instruction, although there is a trend of greater satisfaction in more recent studies. They conclude that growing technological sophistication on the part of both faculty and students, increased media use for social networking, and improvements to institutional equipment for hosting and accessing web-assisted course software may explain why both learning and satisfaction with web-assisted instruction appear to be increasing incrementally over time. Obviously, non-content technology issues (e.g., being able to access content) can influence student satisfaction.

Other findings suggest that coordination of web content with course content, appropriate interactive features in instructional modules, and uniformity in the look and feel of web modules ensure a consistency in the delivery of course content. In a separate study that limited participants to introductory communication courses (N=2,062), Benoit et al. (2006) found web-based materials consistently added to the quality of instruction and were as effective as a traditional classroom in terms of student learning. Web-assisted instruction also reduced communication apprehension (time one versus time two). However, overall, students in this study preferred traditional learning over web-assisted instruction. Sherblom (2010) concluded that when it comes to computer-mediated instruction, the faculty member's ability to choose the appropriate medium and develop a social presence within it is critical to student satisfaction. This means that the instructor must give time and effort to develop communication strategies for effective interaction. Faculty must not only be acquainted with the technology, but consider how students learn best in online settings, and develop their instruction to promote learning that can take place effectively outside face-to-face interactions.

Timmerman and Kruepke (2006) conducted a meta analysis that looks at the overall effects of computer-assisted instruction (CAI) compared to traditional instruction. This study included 118 studies that appeared from 1985–2004 (N=12,398). The courses in this analysis engaged instructional technology used by the instructor or student-operated computer technology for delivering or supplementing content included in courses with regular, face-to-face instruction. CAI showed higher levels of student performance, though this difference was not as large for language and humanities courses as it was for courses in the natural or social sciences. CAI showed higher results when comparing lecture to hard text activity, for undergraduate rather than graduate students, and when used multiple times instead of just once. Timmerman and Kruepke concluded that students who used CAI fared better than their traditional counterparts, and that it did not make a difference whether student feedback was provided. They also found CAI delivered with an audio channel was associated with the highest performance gains, followed by text, and text with graphics, video and physical apparatus. Downs, Boyson, Alley, and Bloom (2011) concluded that the effects of technology on learning are significant, and that learning improved when lessons applied to two rather than one sensory method. In their study, pairing audio and video led to the most effective learning outcome.

Conceptual Model for the Virtual Communication Center

The communication competency classroom model by Morreale and Hackman (1994) was adapted within the author's academic department after a ten-year curricular review highlighted the need for systematic procedures of evaluation and assessment. In the first stage of implementation, this meant standardizing textbook, assignments, and speech evaluation across course sections and individual speeches using *The Competent Speaker* evaluation form (Morreale, Moore, Surges-Tatum, & Webster, 2007).

When personnel shortages stemming from a program change and budget cutbacks produced a reduction in the number of public speaking sections as well as backlog of students for the basic course, the second stage of Morreale and Hackman's (1994) model was implemented. This involved a pilot program involving a master lecture/break-out performance format for the basic course. Although most sections of the basic course remained as traditional stand-alone courses, piloted sections of the eight-week courses first appeared in the fall of 2003. Early piloted sections featured lectures taught by senior faculty with two to four accompanying performance sections taught by adjunct instructors, since this institution does not employ graduate teaching assistants. By 2006, seven small group sections were offered concurrently under one "master" teacher. The master teacher was responsible for course policies, syllabus, testing, lectures, and training. Individual small group instructors listen to and record student speeches, provide individual skill development, and grade assignments. A limited (four to eight hours per week) low-technology communication center staffed by peer coaches chosen from upper-divisional majors and area alumni comprised a level of support for the piloted course.

The Development of a Virtual Communication Center

With the large number of adjunct faculty and student helpers now involved in the basic course, department and administrative leadership quickly saw the advantage in the third component used in Morreale and Hackman's (1994) model, the introduction of a technology-based speaking laboratory. With an on-line communication center, the department could provide standardized 24/7 access to learning resources for skill enhancement through a series of user-friendly, online learning modules consistent with fundamental oral competencies. Initial research[1] began in 2002 to explore options for designing an online communication center. Using specific phrases ("communication lab," "communications lab," "communication center," "communications center," "speech lab," "speech center," "speakers lab," "speakers center," "media lab," "media center"), 21 college and university locations were bookmarked for further investigation. This preliminary research revealed that while writing centers were prevalent, the concept of a communication center was not; if it existed, the most common campus arrangement would be a combined writing and communication center.

Examination of Other Campus Innovations

Since department faculty did not have a clear vision of how computer-assisted learning would work on campus, several innovative programs and instructional models were examined. Compiling information from other campuses (Burnette, 1997; Cronin & Grice, 1993; Flores, 1997; Ganschow, 1997; Grice & Cronin, 1992; Hobgood, 1999; Miller, 1997, 2000; Morello, 1997; Sandin, 1997) gave valuable perspective about how centers could develop consistently with course curriculum and sequencing, measures of content-based competencies, and measures of performance-based criteria to assess students' communication competency skills.

Of the 21 bookmarked communication lab sites, none was completely online. Instead, most of the communication center websites acted to inform Internet visitors of their physical facility. For example, the University of Pennsylvania included help sheets on structure and organization, delivery, visual support, debate, and discussion. The University of North Texas communication lab website, which focused on anxiety and apprehension, had McCroskey's Personal Report of Communication Apprehension available in a "quasi-online" format, consisting of an Excel spreadsheet that students could fill in, print out, and bring to a lab consultant for analysis. Most centers offered help in topic selection, research, organization, outlines, audience analysis, visual aids and use of PowerPoint, delivery, speech anxiety or apprehension, and interpersonal skills. Some group and organizational topics were covered, including conflict and negotiation, power, assertion/aggression, nonverbal behavior, self-disclosure, appropriate language (specifically, awareness of and sensitivity to all forms of diversity), group and business presentations, and interviewing. An essential element of these communication centers was the ability to record and review student presentations with a trained lab consultant. Audio and video recorders, playback equipment, computers (equipped with PowerPoint, still and digital projectors), and media libraries (including helpful books, videotapes, and CDs) were the norm.

Personalized systems of instruction (Seiler & Fuss-Reineck, 1986) were applied to communication courses in the mid-1970s, and these systems provided another instructional model. The structured model of competency-based instruction at the University of Nebraska (Seiler & Titsworth, 1999) focused on the idiosyncratic needs of a performance-based or skills-oriented course, and provided an alternative to the small, self-contained classroom. Its success was dependent upon standardization, a personnel hierarchy, competency-based evaluation, use of the classroom to apply course material, and reliance on undergraduate teaching assistants. Similarly, another early model proposed by Grice and Cronin (1992) at Radford University implemented a comprehensive laboratory as part of its oral communication across the curriculum emphasis. By combining the use of computerized interactive video instruction and peer tutoring, the program offered quality, convenient, and cost-effective oral communication instruction, practice, and evaluation for students throughout the university.

Sawyer and Behnke (2001) proposed technological innovations as a way of standardizing sections of communication performance courses at Texas Christian University. They cited several trends in communication education, including the use of reliable and valid tools such as the *Competent Speaker Evaluation Form*, as well as computer delivery of speech criticism. Sawyer and Behnke argued that computer-assisted instruction increased quality, reliability, speed, and efficiency of feedback, encouraged extensive, friendly, and well-worded commentary, and had the ability to store this information for later recall. This type of software in higher education, available since 1993, resulted in fewer student complaints about the inequities in grading between sections and more information about how to improve future performance. Sawyer and Behnke's work seemed relevant since it used the *Competent Speaker Evaluation Form* to evaluate videotaped or "live" speeches with instructor feedback. Similarly, observations of the communication center at Mary Washington College addressed the dialectic tensions of providing students with feedback as well as evaluation (Buske-Zainal & Gurien, 1999).

Consideration of Campus-specific Needs
At the time of decision-making, computer-supported learning systems such as Blackboard and WebCT were not available on campus. Therefore, the department did not have a good frame of reference for a web-based teaching and learning resource with administrative features. The desire for a user-friendly student interface with easy access to courses had to be designed. Features such as digitized speeches, course materials, and on-line assessments needed integration with the college's existing communication systems. One model seen was Gardner, Sheridan, and White's (2002) computer-supported learning system (CECIL)

at the University of Auckland in 1995. CECIL included responses to student quizzes and email feedback, as well as organization of text and multimedia learning materials. Self-assessment was highlighted as one of the most popular options.

With the perspective of other programs in hand, the primary audience, design, and features of the proposed communication center could be approached. It was determined that the primary audience for the on-line communication center would consist of those students enrolled in the general education public speaking courses. The traditional course would continue to be the norm, but determining how much this communication center would replace or duplicate regular course content was still debatable. Since the proposed communication center was a purely online format, and at least initially there would be no consultants, the system would need to compensate for lost face-to-face interaction. Finally, if an essential element of most of the labs is the ability to record student presentations and review them with a trained lab consultant, a way to compensate for this feature would need to be determined.

The technological demands at the time made the creation of a virtual communication center challenging. Therefore, the vision and goals for this learning resource ended up being a collaboration led by the Communication Department and aided by Computing Services, Media Resources, Marketing Communications, and Institutional Research personnel.[2] It was agreed that the communication center would be made more real for students if actual students in classroom situations were taped instead of actors. Due to the high learning curve, there was an initial desire to use fewer interactive elements. Rather, there could be independent course support through sample speeches, full-sentence outlines for different types of speeches available, links to relevant tutorials (e.g., PowerPoint instruction, library research aids), and grading templates for each assignment. The possibility of a self-assessment tool for listening competency, and online speech critique were enhancements planned for the future. Beginning with the overarching question "What do we want students to be able to get out of the lab that they can't get in the classroom?" possible modules and learning resources were proposed.

Modules

Returning to Aristotelian roots, three fundamental competencies were outlined for the basic speech course—invention, organization, and delivery. Audience analysis and adaptation were incorporated as part of each core competency. To insure the correct sub-components would be included, leading public speaking textbooks were examined first, and then departmental members were consulted for consensus. Each module sub-component was edited to adapt to an on-line audience's need for succinctness and clarity.

A diverse group of students representing various speaking styles, topics, and cultural backgrounds were then recruited to tape speech segments to illustrate these principles, which were eventually edited to play anywhere from 10–

120 seconds in length. Many of the student speech segments were created in parallel construction to provide a good or "competent" example alongside a poor or "incompetent" example. A faculty "coach" worked with these student speakers to coax a credible and relevant performance for the center.

Currently, 19 modules are housed on the campus intranet as part of an online communication center to help with speaking competencies, and seven listening modules have been produced. The modules are connected by hyperlinks on the students' web-based speech evaluations (Cooper, 2011) to help students who received average to poor scores understand why they received the score they did, or to summarize the key ideas behind this particular aspect of invention, organization, or delivery. That is, the student not only receives feedback through campus email on the speech, but also is guided to the on-line speech center for future improvement. In most cases, this feedback comes within 24 hours of delivering the speech, well before the next speaking assignment is due. Hyperlinks access video excerpts as well as text so that "incompetent" as well as "competent" messages are illustrated for the student.

Besides modules highlighting the invention, organization, and delivery of extemporaneous speeches, the website has additional learning resources for the basic course. These include sample outlines created by students, full-length student speeches illustrating three informative and persuasive speaking assignments, and a student presentation using visual aids. Grading templates for each of these assignments is also included. Links to relevant tutorials (e.g., PowerPoint), interesting web sources, and the campus library provide information on primary research strategies and finding statistical data. Finally, a listening self-assessment is available to students.

Measurements of Effectiveness

Littlejohn and Pegler (2007) believe the most important considerations behind the decision to incorporate e-learning to the curriculum are 1) widening student participation and interest, 2) enhancing the quality of instruction, and 3) controlling costs. Before embarking on a virtual communication center, basic course administrators and practitioners should first determine who or what is driving changes toward e-learning formats (i.e., why consider a virtual communication center in the first place?). Second, there needs to be a way to evaluate the outcome of this change, so the drive toward standardization is not at odds with good theory and practice (Morreale, et al., 2010).

Can a Virtual Communication Center Widen Student Participation and Interest?

Before the creation of the virtual communication center described in this chapter, student focus groups were conducted to determine why the on-campus communication center was under-utilized. Several consistent patterns emerged, but the overwhelming reason given by students was the lack of perceived need for this help. A second response cited hours that the communication center was available as a limiting factor. While the flexibility of peer tutoring hours was a legitimate complaint, faculty questioned the lack of perceived need when instructors' office hours were in demand, and clearly many of their students would benefit from extra coaching. Even with heavy class advertising and extra credit as an incentive, on average only 60 students would use the physical communication center each year.

The potential of the virtual communication center was seen in the first year the center was digitized. Several hundred visitors came each year, far surpassing the number of face-to-face visits with peer coaches or individual appointments with faculty. In the last few months of preparing this chapter, there were 237 visitors to the website. This number does not take into account the students who access the Communication Center through links in their speech critiques, since this information is not currently collected. When students taking the general education courses were asked on the post-assessment survey whether they had visited the on-line communication center because they were prompted to do so by their electronic speech critique form, more than a third answered, "yes." That is, of the 561 students who responded to this question over a two-semester period, 190 students said they did visit the online communication center when prompted. Since only students receiving scores of "1," "2," or "3" on a five-point scale would receive this prompt, it is not clear whether the majority did not visit the on-line communication center because they did not receive a prompt to do so or because they did not want to do so. However, to put this number in perspective means that *one out of three* students enrolled in the basic course visited this site, as compared to the roughly 1:9 ratio of students who visited the physical communication center.

The good news gets better, since the majority of visits occur in the first three weeks of the course when learning and intervention is most critical. Significantly, the number of visits from class members increased over each of the last three years. While the data does not currently show what specific pages or resources were used, within the last six months the "outline" resource alone logged 84 "hits." Current improvements are underway to collect more information about these web visits, such as which modules are most popular and how much time students spend on-line. The virtual Communication Center also includes information highlighting the oral competency exam on campus. Not surprisingly, some identifiable traffic from students not enrolled in courses occurs here, specifically in the period that precedes the campus' oral communication validation examination.

Liu (2010) talks about "self efficacy," the student's judgment of his or her capacity to use any technological tool. Liu's findings suggest that the perceived ease of use and perceived usefulness of that tool determine a student's behavioral intent to use a technology, which in turn, influences subsequent behavior. Similarly, King, Schrodt, and Weisel (2009) believe that students' orientation to instructional feedback consists of four relevant dimensions: utility, retention, confidentiality, and sensitivity. When relevant individual differences are high-lighted, this kind of feedback can significantly improve the practice of teaching as well as student satisfaction. With the increase in the use of the virtual Communication Center over physical peer evaluation on this campus, student comments on post-assessment reviews suggested that the feedback received online seemed to enhance student participation and interest. This may be because the feedback from this technology was perceived as useful, easy to obtain, memorable, and less threatening, thus meeting standards of confidentiality and functionality.

Can a Virtual Communication Center Enhance the Quality of Education?

A virtual communication center offers distinct advantages to student learners. It fosters learning in different spaces. It is flexible in terms of time; that is, students can participate when they want to, and thereby balance work and co-curricular activities with course study. Mackey and Jacobson (2008) consider the web a collaborative medium for communication and instructional design and find that even as formats continue to change, core principles can be promoted. As students are challenged to think critically about the information they research and synthesize, technology becomes a tool in enhancing their basic knowledge and skills.

Likewise, the virtual center opens up a range of media resources, as well as activities in which different kinds of students can learn. Students can create their own resource banks, and integrate formal library materials with other knowledge. Ultimately, the locus of control shifts from the teacher to the student. On a macro level, time can then be spent on periodic measurements of effectiveness in order to clarify programmatic differences that ultimately created a credible, financially accountable, and responsive program of instruction.

One example of how the virtual communication center enhanced the quality of education is in the area of listening assessment. Because of the author's work with the *Organizational Listening Survey*, or *OLS* (Cooper & Husband, 1993), a listening self-assessment was readily available for online use. The *OLS* consists of a 30-item Likert-type questionnaire that reflects various listening attitudes and behaviors indicated in the literature. Early work tested a two-factor model that included accurate listening and supportive listening. Accuracy items included discriminating and recalling behaviors that enable the listener to *confirm* her understanding of the message; support items included attending, clarifying, affiliating, and accommodating behaviors that *affirm* her interest in the speaker. Later work (Cooper, Seibold, & Suchner, 1997) suggested that a single factor (general listening competency) model could account for what others perceive to be effective listening, regardless of the communication target. Data collected from the online listening self-assessments provide useful feedback to students on oral strengths and weaknesses, as well as furthers this research agenda by identifying campus norms for general listening competency. The "big five" listening skills are seen in the communicator's: 1) openness or willingness to listen, 2) ability to read nonverbal cues, 3) ability to understand verbal cues, 4) ability to remember relevant details, and 5) ability to respond appropriately (Cooper & Buchanan, 2010). Now these skills are applied to individual training and practice sessions in the classroom.

Virtual communication centers can also help with the "instructor's dilemma," the problem of engaging in two different processes at the same time: being a good listener, while critically evaluating speaking behaviors (Sawyer & Behnke, 2001). Since rhetorical analysis is important in helping students become better speakers themselves, the idea of creating an interactive module where students can view speeches and critique them against faculty evaluations and average scores from other student graders was pursued. Visitors could watch a video clip of an actual student-delivered speech in the upper portion of their Web browser window and in the lower portion answer questions related to the speech. After completing their rating, students go to a webpage where their evaluation was listed alongside those of faculty. This kind of online critique tool is relatively easy to set up, requiring only basic video editing and computer programming.

Kaya (2010) highlights a video-sharing platform at Baruch College used in distance-learning courses to bring students virtually face-to-face with their instructors. While not currently used on the author's campus, software can now be purchased to accomplish this purpose.

Scholars have also explored use of on-line learning through iPod tests. Downs, Boyson, Alley, and Bloom (2011) used iPods for a 15-item, multiple-choice test and found learning varied significantly with only one exposure to the content, when the instructor, lecturer content, and length of the lecture were all held constant. They found that audio only was less effective (56 percent accuracy) than when this medium added text/audio (60 percent), and audio/visual (71 percent). Since digital editing software enables instructors to add graphics, highlight key portions of a frame, or add textual overlap, learning can be enhanced. The work of setting up a camcorder with SD card that uploads to a computer file is no longer outside the experience of most instructors.

The original Web was based on hypertext linking and relationships among and within documents that traditional printed documents did not contain. Web 2.0 technology includes such things as blogs, wikis, podcasts, and RSS feeds, as well as free on-line resources. It encourages students to solve problems, be creative in the design of their own materials, and participate in collaborative learning. Web 2.0 is less static because it is based on how people communicate rather than on the structure of information in linked documents. This influences how students locate, evaluate, exchange, and synthesize information. In partnerships with faculty and librarians, the availability of easy-to-use production software also expands content options and personalizes instruction for students (Mackey & Jacobson, 2008). Is the new way of educating *better*? Most research report no significant differences between the teaching quality of courses that used new technology and those that did not, but there are quantifiable improvements for this generation of students that comes through the use of e-learning (Littlejohn & Pegler, 2007).

Can a Virtual Communication Center Cut Costs?

Although the creation of these modules represented a significant amount of work in the beginning, maintaining and updating a virtual communication center is cost-effective. Much of the initial costs of development came out of faculty release time and generous staff support from other departments. Only small stipends from the department's budget were tapped; for example, for student performers, or for advertising. Periodic updates to the system incur costs outside the department; while there is additional work to "sync" the new technology, little "down" time occurred between transitions. Web content is reviewed each year by interested faculty, but this process usually results in minor text or digital changes that can be completed with student employees. Every few years, greater attention goes to web content and revision, and during this process the department can usually rely upon small institutional grants to make these changes.

As technology has become more accessible and affordable, effective learning in virtual environments has improved. Since the 2003 development of the virtual communication center described in this chapter, WebCT and Blackboard systems came to campus and provided other user-friendly options for teachers and students. Butler (2010) reports use of the Blackboard Learning Management System along with online/blended academics in a secondary school system in Northern Ohio in 2004. It was popular because it could expand the classroom day, reinforce an important technological skill, and build time-management ability. However, online and blended learning demands ongoing support; once the instructor created and customized a course, it had to be updated, so web links, audio, and video excerpts were added. The advantages included course continuity for absent class members, automatic access to tutorials, access to review content prior to testing, differentiated instruction, multisensory learning, customized content for students' learning styles, and electronic feedback for analysis. Drawbacks in these management systems is that access to the system is limited to students enrolled in the course, and the institutional costs of on-going upgrades and fees for this technology.

Beyond support of Web 2.0 technologies, Mackey and Jacobson (2008) highlight the wide availability of many free resources online to enhance virtual experiences. They outline a variety of institutions and disciplines that have successfully utilized virtual partnerships on campuses. While not claiming greater engagement and satisfaction among all users, these virtual experiences nonetheless creatively convey core information in a cost-efficient way.

While finances should not be the major consideration for going digital, the lack of standardization, assessment protocol, and graduate teaching assistants certainly made an online choice an easy one for the author's campus. The relatively low cost of a virtual communication center has had a huge payoff in terms of connection with the today's student. As technology veterans who routinely utilize new modes of communication and online collaborations, students have connected well with the virtual communication center and shown priceless improvement in their speaking and listening abilities.

Conclusion

The effectiveness of a virtual communication center in delivering specific information for students' oral presentations on campus should be considered when the opportunity for a physical communication center does not exist. Data must continue to be collected to evaluate its effectiveness in providing best practices for training both students and instructors, and in assessing growth in communication skills. While the virtual communication center may not completely bridge the instructional gap in the same way face-to-face interaction does, it provides a unique opportunity to enhance learning for the next generation of students.

Notes

1. Early research was conducted by Mark Klinski, with later review by Jordan Whilden. Former colleague Scott Hale was significant in the conception and creation of the physical communication center that existed on campus between 2002 and 2006.
2. The creative contributions of Les Barker (Marketing Communications), Jun Collado, Beth Johanson, David Kletzing, Bruce Knowlton, and J.R. Smith (Media Resources) were critical in developing the modules, digitally capturing and editing speech excerpts, and posting these materials on-line. Jessie Awig Johnson and Celeste Elsenheimer Barnett recruited many of the students to perform the speech excerpts, and colleagues Ken Chase and Christy Gardner coached these students into credible online oral performances. Nancy Falciani White (Library) prepared library resources for hyperlink, and all such resources were programmed by Brian Hurley (Computing Services). Gary Larson (Institutional Research), and Stan Jones (Provost) provided time and financial resources. Finally, Jonathan Harrell's skill and creativity brought all this work together into an accessible format that comprises the current virtual communication center.

References

Baturay, M. H., & Bay, O. F. (2010). The effects of problem-based learning on the classroom community perceptions and achievement of web-based education students. *Computers & Education, 55*, 43–52.

Benoit, P. J., Benoit, W. L., Milyo, J., & Hansen, G. J. (2006). *The effects of traditional vs. web-assisted instruction on student learning and satisfaction.* Columbia, MO: University of Missouri Press.

Burnette, A. (1997, November). *Southwest Texas State University Center for Communication Excellence materials.* Paper presented at the National Communication Association, Chicago, IL.

Buske-Zainal, P., & Gurien, R. (1999, November). *Dialectical tensions of running a speaking center at a college without a required communication course.* Paper presented at the National Communication Association, Chicago, IL.

Butler, J. W. (2010). 24/7 on-line learning: Lessons learned. *Techniques, 85*(6), 33–36. Retrieved from http://www.acteonline.org/tech_archive.aspx

Carliner, S. (2002). Designing e-learning. Alexandria, VA: ASTD.

Cooper, L. O. (2011). *WebGrader*: An on-line instrument for evaluation and assessment of oral competency. *Communication Teacher, 25*, 68–80.

Cooper, L. O., & Buchanan, T. (2010). Listening competency on campus: A psychometric analysis of student listening. *International Journal of Listening, 24*, 3–18.

Cooper, L. O., & Husband, R. L. (1993). Developing a model of organizational listening competency. *Journal of the International Listening Association, 7*, 6–34.

Cooper, L. O., Seibold, D, & Suchner, R. (1997). Listening in organizations: An analysis of error structures in models of listening competency. *Communication Research Reports, 14*, 312–320.

Cronin, M. W., & Grice, G. L. (1993). A comparative analysis of training models versus consulting training models for implementing oral communication across the curriculum. *Communication Education, 42*, 1–9.

Downs, E., Boyson, A. R., Alley, H., & Bloom, N. R. (2011). iPedagogy: Using multimedia learning theory to identify best practices for MP3 player use in higher education. *Journal of Applied Communication Research, 39*, 184–200.

Flores, N. L. (1997, November). *How Golden West College is addressing pedagogical, assessment, and accountability concerns through integrated spoken communication labs.* Paper presented at the National Communication Association, Chicago, IL.

Ganschow, J. (1997, November). *A dialogue: Blueprints for communication labs that address pedagogical, assessment, and accountability concerns.* Paper presented at the National Communication Association, Chicago, IL.

Gardner, L., Sheridan, D., & White, D. (2002). A web-based learning and assessment system to support flexible education. *Journal of Computer Assisted Learning, 18*, 125–136.

Graff, M. (2006). Constructing and maintaining an effective hypertext-based learning environment: Web-based learning and cognitive style. *Education & Training, 48*, 143–155.

Grice, G., & Cronin, M. (1992). *The comprehensive speech communication laboratory: We have ways of making you talk.* Paper presented at the Southern States Communication Association, San Antonio, TX.

Guo, Q., & Zhang, M. (2009). Implement web learning environment based on data mining. *Knowledge-Based Systems, 22*, 439–442.

Herrington, J., Reeves, T. C., & Oliver, R. (2010). *A guide to authentic e-learning.* NY: Routledge.

Hobgood, L. (1999, November). *Establishing a communication lab or speaking center.* Paper presented at the National Communication Association, Chicago, IL.

Kaya, T. (2010, October 15). Wired Campus: Using web video to fine-tune student performance. *The Chronicle of Higher Education.* Retrieved from http://chronicle.com/blogs/wiredcampus/using-web-video-to-fine-tune-student-performance.

King, P. E., Schrodt, P., & Weisel, J. J. (2009). The instructional feedback orientation scale: Conceptualizing and validating a new measure for assessing perceptions of instructional feedback. *Communication Education, 58,* 235–261.

Littlejohn, A., & Pegler, C. (2007). *Preparing for blended e-learning.* London: Routledge.

Liu, X. (2010). Empirical testing of a theoretical extension of the technology acceptance model: An exploratory study of educational wikis. *Communication Education, 59,* 52–69.

MacGregor, S. K., & Lou, Y. (2004). Web-based learning: How task scaffolding and website design support knowledge acquisition. *Journal of Research on Technology in Education, 37,* 161–175.

Mackey, T. P., & Jacobson, T. E. (Eds.). (2008). *Using technology to teach information literacy.* NY: Neal-Schuman.

Miller, P. C. (1997, November). *The mission of the Speaking/Listening Center of De-Pauw University.* Paper presented at the National Communication Association, Chicago, IL.

Miller, P. C. (2000, November). *Speaker's lab: New uses, new populations.* Paper presented at the National Communication Association, Seattle, WA.

Morreale, S. P., & Hackman, M. Z. (1994). A competency approach to public speaking instruction. *Journal of Instructional Psychology, 21,* 250–257.

Morreale, S. P., Hugenberg, L., & Worley, D. (2006). The basic communication course at U.S. colleges and universities in the 21st century: Study VI. *Communication Education, 55,* 415–437.

Morreale, S. P., Moore, M. R., Surges-Tatum, D., & Webster, L. (Eds.) (2007). *"The Competent Speaker" Speech Evaluation Form.* Retrieved from http://www.natcom.org/uploadedFiles/Content/Research/CardCall-2009-2-Rubric%20and%20Assessment%20Report%20%28Tate%29.pdf

Morreale, S. P., Worley, D. W., & Hugenberg, B. (2010). The basic communication course at two-and four-year colleges and universities: Study VII – The 40th anniversary. *Communication Education, 59,* 405–430.

Morello, J. (1997). *Handbook for speaking center consultants.* Unpublished manuscript. Speaking Center, Mary Washington College, Fredericksburg, VA.

Piccoli, G., Ahmad, R., & Ives, B. (2001). Web-based virtual learning environments: A research framework and a preliminary assessment of effectiveness in basic IT skills training. *MIS Quarterly, 25,* 401–426.

Sandin, P. J. (1997, November). *Launching the Speakers Lab at Butler University.* Paper presented at the National Communication Association, Chicago, IL.

Sawyer, C. R., & Behnke, R. R. (2001). Computer-assisted evaluation of speaking competencies in the basic speech course. *Journal of the Association for Communication Administration, 30,* 104–110.

Seiler, W. J., & Fuss-Reineck, M. (1986). Developing the personalized system of instruction for the basic course. *Communication Education, 35,* 126–133.

Seiler, W. J., & Titsworth, B. S. (1999). Individualized approaches to instruction. In A. L. Vangelisti, J. A. Daly, & G. W. Friedrich's (Eds.), *Teaching communication,* 2nd edition (pp. 375–392). Mahwah, NJ: Lawrence Erlbaum.

Sherblom, J. C. (2010). The computer-mediated communication (CMC) classroom: A challenge of medium, presence, interaction, identity, and relationship. *Communication Education, 59,* 497–523.

Smith, C. D., & King, P.E. (2004). Student feedback sensitivity and the efficacy of feedback interventions in public speaking performance improvement. *Communication Education, 53,* 302–216.

Timmerman, C. E., & Kruepke, K. A. (2006). Computer-assisted instruction, media richness, and college student performance. *Communication Education, 55,* 73–104.

Waldeck, J. H. (2008). The development of an industry specific online learning center: Consulting lessons learned. *Communication Education, 57,* 452–463.

Chapter 15

The Implementation of Computer Mediated Communication in Communication Centers

Alyssa Davis

Computer Mediated Communication (CMC) is a growing area of study, as the use of the Internet has increased for business, educational, and personal communication. A study conducted by the Pew Internet and American Life Project showed that 74 percent of American adults used the Internet in 2010, which is a marked increase from 66 percent of adult Americans using the Internet in 2005 (Rainie, 2010). Not only are the numbers of users rising, but the uses of the Internet are diversifying as well. For example, besides the general public increasingly using computers and the Internet for entertainment and research purposes, email and instant messaging have become supplemental options to the conventional use of telephones and postal service for business communication. The increasing diversity of Internet use in virtually all sectors of society is manifested in the variety of articles listed by the Pew Research Center between January and May of 2011 alone: the research center posted articles discussing Internet use for such purposes as dissemination of health information, pursuit of philanthropic goals, promotion of political campaigns, as well as for participation in social networking and collaborative information sites such as Wikipedia (Pew Research Center, 2011).

Another novel application of Computer Mediated Communication (CMC) use is in the area of peer tutoring in communication centers. Using CMC to help students to increase their communication competence when working on papers, assignments and speeches are all ways that the Internet has impacted peer tutoring in communication centers. Implementing CMC in communication centers helps to enhance the services offered by extending the way peer tutors can help speakers from solely face-to-face interaction to the widely growing area of Internet communication.

However, along with the advantages of increasing avenues of service through CMC, there also exist challenges such as the absence of nonverbal signs normally utilized to convey meaning in face-to-face interaction and an increased risk of unintentional rudeness during the peer tutoring process. Such advantages and challenges are discussed in this chapter by reviewing existing CMC research and reflecting on the pilot experiences of one communication center's online program.

The Online Communication Center

The University of North Carolina at Greensboro Online Speaking Center was inaugurated in the fall of 2010. It sought to implement findings of prior CMC research and to test the theory that access to online services would enhance the experiences of both the clients and the peer educators (consultants). The online program consisted of two sections of an Introduction to Communication course that required students to consult the center twice over the course of the semester. These two sections had a total of forty-six students enrolled.

Initially, there were four consultants trained to handle online consultations but at the end there were a total of twelve. As the need arose, the four initial consultants trained more consultants throughout the trial period in order to better accommodate the volume of appointments being made. This process of continuous training throughout the trial created a unique opportunity to evaluate how the system was working and to both troubleshoot and question if there were better ways of handling situations as they arose, from both experienced and novice perspectives. The outcomes of this learning process will be discussed in sections covering the topics of advantages and challenges of the Online Speaking Center.

But first, an understanding of the procedures practiced within these online consultations is needed. Although other alternatives such as Skype, WCOnline, and WIMBA exist, the communication center currently uses Gmail and Google Documents because of the consultants' familiarity with the programs, in addition to the programs being free to the public. The consultant begins the online session by logging into the Speaking Center's Gmail account. The university uses a form of Gmail, called iSpartan, as the official email for faculty, staff, and students. The University Speaking Center does not have an iSpartan account, but because iSpartan is a form of Gmail, the students' accounts and the Speaking Center's account can communicate with each other through chat. Therefore, the consultant begins the session by inviting the student to chat online. When the student accepts, the consultant greets the student, provides him/her with an overview of what to expect in the consultation, and asks the student to send the speech document to the Speaking Center email account as an attachment. This document can then be converted for online editing by viewing the document through Google Documents and sharing it with the student. Then, both parties can make changes to the document and communicate through a chat box in real time.

If the consultant highlights a part of the text, the client can see it, and if the client makes any changes, they appear immediately for the consultant to review. Other options included for the consultations are the use of webcams and the "Call Phone" option of Gmail which can be used instead of the chat option. As the consultation ends, the client is provided with a link to an online survey which is designed to give feedback on the consultant and the Speaking Center's services. The feedback obtained in this manner is the material used throughout this chapter to report the clients' opinions of both the advantages and disadvantages of the Online Speaking Center.

Advantages

When studying the benefits of adding an online program to communication centers, consultant, workplace, and client advantages were all taken into account. The list of advantages was compiled from client and consultant comments, previous literature, and experiences from the beta test of the new online center. The advantages were diverse, but the main benefits found were convenience, more productive and interactive consultations, increased accessibility, and decreased anxiety.

Advantages for Consultants

There are many advantages, both personal and professional, for consultants in learning how to conduct consultations online. The most commonly stated remarks from consultants and clients alike addressed the convenience of the online speaking center. One consultant said, "I prefer online appointments because I feel they are more convenient for students. I myself have a busy schedule and prefer to do things online. That way I can still wind down and relax but still complete my work." Another consultant remarked, "Speakers can now get help with whatever they need at home in their pajamas!"

In addition to the convenience online consulting can provide, consultants can learn to be well-versed in CMC in order to become better prepared for their future careers. Santra and Giri (2009) discuss how using CMC helps facilitate more effective communication in the workplace. The authors say, "Computer-based communication not only facilitates new means of educating students, it also prepares a large segment of the next generation to enter the workplace able to use CMC and, by doing so, serves to increase their value as organizational employees" (p. 104). One consultant said, "I am not technology savvy, so a lot of the things we use for the Online Speaking Center I did not know how to do. Using the Online Speaking Center is always a learning experience for me." She went on to explain that she feels much more comfortable with the technology now and believes that it will serve her well in the future, for her classes, and for her career.

Additionally, research has also shown that some of the impersonality of CMC can help facilitate more productive work sessions. Joseph Walther (1996) states, "Take away these interpersonal and social hindrances through "socio-technical" arrangements, and the resulting impersonal orientation to ideas via CMC increases process effectiveness" (p. 6). For example, reducing superfluous interpersonal and social cues such as visual indicators of class or race that can be distractions as the consultant is working with the client, can help to increase the amount and quality of feedback that the consultant can provide.

Finally, an advantage of online sessions for consultants is the interactivity that these consultations inspire. One online consultant expressed this by saying, "I liked that the client was able to see exactly what I was talking about through use of highlighting, and I was also able to see what directions the client was 'adjusting' to when editing." This consultant liked that he was able to give more personalized information as the client was changing his outline while they chatted. In a face-to-face consultation, it is rare that the consultant ever gets to see the actual changes that the client makes to his presentations as he will usually take notes and change his outline after leaving the consultation. This ability to actually see the changes gives the consultant a stronger feeling that he has helped the client and that the client actually understood what he was talking about.

Advantages for Clients

In addition to advantages for consultants, client advantages were also explored through research and comments. The University Speaking Center uses Survey Monkey to provide the clients with a link to an online survey at the end of every consultation, face-to-face or online. The clients had overwhelmingly positive responses regarding the Online Speaking Center. One client remarked: "taking me step by step while chatting to me was highly helpful." As one consultant remarked earlier, the ability to work step-by-step and make changes in real time improved the experience of both the consultants and the clients by being able to ensure that everything was understood and that the feedback was as personalized as possible. Another client remarked in response to a question about the most important thing he learned: "I had errors I didn't see, and it took honest feedback from a peer to show me how to fix them." Another client stated in reference to this same question: "[R]eally good session. [Consultant] was amazingly helpful and this was my first time using this and I believe I will keep coming back." These clients valued the time they spent working with the consultant online and saw this as a helpful resource for presentations they may have to give in the future

Also, as stated previously, the most commonly stated remarks from consultants and clients alike addressed the convenience of the online speaking center. One client said, "It saves a lot of time to do it over the Internet than having to come in for some people. I received the same assistance that I would have if I came in. This helped a lot with my organization of the speech." As this student said, holding a consultation online can save a lot of time, especially if the student is a distance learning student or a commuter. The students' professor also noted that she believed the online consultations to be easier to attend than the conventional face-to-face consultations; commuters must drive to the campus, find parking (which is easier said than done), and walk to the Speaking Center. Moreover, while it can be inconvenient for a commuting student to make a special trip to campus, it may be impractical or impossible for a distance learning student to come to campus if she lives in another state or country.

In addition to convenience, the alternative to a conventional face-to-face interaction with a consultant opens the door for clients who might not ordinarily consider making an appointment. One of these kinds of clients is addressed in an article by Durkin, Conti-Ramsden, and Walker (2010), who argue that CMC, "in terms of its less stringent language demands and its reduced-cues environment, can provide a medium for positive adaptation of adolescents with communication challenges" (p. 1). Communication challenges could include such things as a stutter, hearing impairment, severe anxiety, or other such challenges that impede communication with one's peers. In this instance, a client could focus entirely on the content of her presentation and outline with a consultant, and could later focus on her "communication challenge" in relation to delivery, personally or with a consultant. The online program provides a lower stress environment for this type of client to begin the process of creating her presentation.

Among communication challenges, one specific challenge is the existence of hearing impairments. Research shows that "adolescents with hearing impairments used the Internet more intensively than did peers with normal hearing" (Durkin et al., 2010, p. 3). When a client must attend a face-to-face consultation with an interpreter, the logistics of obtaining an interpreter and making an appointment, combined with the stress of communicating with the consultant through the interpreter, can become a strong deterrent from making an appointment. By attending an online consultation, the audio and vocal challenge is removed through the medium of online chat. This option reduces the stress and the inconvenience that members of the deaf community may face when looking to make an appointment for a face-to-face consultation.

Another set of clients who experience a communication challenge and may be reached more conveniently through an online program are those who suffer from a high level of speaking, or social, anxiety. Amichai-Hamburger and

McKenna (2006) explain that interaction anxiety can be greatly reduced when the interaction takes place over the Internet in a text-based format instead of face-to-face. This is because the student has more control over how he presents his views and himself. Also, the anxiety-producing elements inherent in face-to-face interaction of having to respond on the spot and feeling as if one is being evaluated visually is not present in a text-based environment

In a related article, McKenna, Green, and Gleason (2002) explain that it is easier for people with extreme shyness to create relationships on the Internet because they can "share [their] inner beliefs and emotional reactions with much less fear of disapproval and sanction" (p. 10). Reduction of fear is an important factor in the consultation process, as the fear of rejection or disapproval of one's work product can be a deterrent for those who have a high level of shyness or anxiety. Also, the client can avoid the anxiety of what McKenna et al. call "gating features," including physical appearance, a stigma such as stuttering, or the belief that their anxiety is visible. The absence of these perceptual cues creates more freedom and less anxiety for the client who may feel held back by them in a face-to-face interaction.

Another aspect of convenience that the online program provided was a way to clarify information with clients who are non-native speakers of English. As with students who suffer from anxiety, non-native speakers have more time to present their thoughts the way that they intend them, by looking up words or checking grammar, when compared to a face-to-face consultation situation. Also, a text-based format helps with clarification between the consultant and the client. One conversation benefited from this clarification when a vacation destination was being discussed. The international student was unsure as to the name of the country in English and she typed "philiphin" and "philippine." By these two suggestions she made in the chat box, the country was clarified as the Philippines. Both the student and the consultant benefited from understanding what was being talked about and the clarification that the text format brought, rather than having to verbalize the spellings which would add another level of difficulty for the non-native speaker of English.

Though this section has addressed students with particular communication challenges, the average student can also feel a relief from gating features in an online format. One faculty member whose class participated in online consultations remarked that her students felt less anxious about the content of their outlines, such as length and information, when having the consultation online versus having it in person. The students felt more in control of how their information was presented to the consultant when it was text based and not face-to-face, perhaps partly due to the convenience and effectiveness of sharing textual information online.

Challenges

This chapter has highlighted many advantages of implementing an online component in communication centers; however, CMC research and experiences with the trial online program have revealed many challenges that accompany its use. Solutions to these problems were sought and ideas were discovered both through reviewing existing CMC research and through trial and error. Some solutions are still forthcoming, as there are limitations to the communication channel that are particularly challenging.

Challenges for Consultants

The consultants' views of the challenges of this program largely had to do with decreased interaction with their clients. One consultant remarked, "I didn't like the isolation I felt as a consultant while being in the OSC [Online Speaking Center] area." The consultants felt a little isolated off by themselves with a computer. Eventually, they began to do online consultations together in a room in order to feel less isolated, and this greatly helped. However, in the later part of the trial when the phone option was added, noise became a problem in doing consultations together. By talking to their clients on the phone, though, the consultants again felt connected and not isolated, so doing consultations together was not an issue anymore.

Challenges for Clients

In addition to the positive comments previously mentioned, clients made some comments which led us to recognize additional areas of improvement. One client remarked, "I felt that a person to person consultation would be more effective. It was harder to get my questions answered." This refers to having to type everything in the chat boxes. For students who may not be efficient typists, using chat boxes can be an ineffective use of their time. The option to conduct the consultation over the phone has helped in these cases.

Another comment was, "It took us 20 minutes to get started." This comment came from early on in our endeavors to figure out the software and the procedure. We learned from this comment to give the technical side a ten minute limit and then to abandon it and have the student email the document and talk about it either over chat or the phone. This method is not quite as convenient, but it reduces the time taken away from the consultation to figure out the technology. We did not want the tutoring process to suffer due to technological issues.

The professor of the two sections that utilized the Online Speaking Center services also noted some challenges that she faced. She found that explaining the technology to the students was a very involved process. However, she said that handouts helped a great deal in explaining the technology and procedure. The other problem she encountered was the belief on the part of her students that they did not need to go to the Speaking Center to practice their presentation if they had worked on organization already. However, in our experience this is a problem encountered both in person and online. The only solution we have come up with is to stress the importance that speech making is a process and that practice is an integral part of that process, and one in which the Speaking Center can greatly help.

Perceived Impoliteness

Claire Hardaker (2010) defines the impoliteness most commonly found in CMC as either "non-malicious impoliteness" or "rudeness, faux pas, failed politeness" (p. 218). Non-malicious impoliteness refers to a remark given where the intention is not to produce malice but where the speaker recognizes that offense may be caused anyway. Hardaker relates this to a tutor critiquing a student's work. This is an area that consultants deal with in both face-to-face and online environments and one in which nonverbal cues help a great deal. By smiling and using friendly gestures, consultants can generally negate any potential impoliteness while giving feedback on a student's presentation in a face-to-face interaction.

The second type of impoliteness in CMC, which Hardaker calls rudeness, *faux pas*, and failed politeness, is when the speaker does not intend to be impolite, but the hearer interprets the communication as impolite anyway. This situation can arise when the speaker fails to perform some behavior marked as polite, fails to recognize a behavior that should or should not be performed in the situation, or when the speaker misjudges the degree of politeness needed in the situation. The main determinant in both of these types of impoliteness is whether the hearer recognizes the situation as unintentional on the part of the speaker or if they see it as intentional.

Avoiding instances in which the hearer may perceive the speaker as impolite is the best way to prevent these situations from occurring. Helen Spencer-Oatey (2005) defines (im)politeness as "an evaluative label that people attach to behavior, as a result of their subjective judgments about social appropriateness" (p. 97). She states that behavioral expectations are generally based on behavioral norms. Spencer-Oatey proposes two principles to stay within good behavioral expectations. Although these principles are useful in both face-to-face and online consultations, only examples relating to online consultations are discussed below.

The first principle is the equity principle. This principle holds that people have the right to not be "unduly imposed upon, that they are not unfairly ordered about, and that they are not taken advantage of or exploited" (p. 100). This can be followed in an online consultation by not telling the client to change something but asking if they would like to change something. It is not the consultants' job to make the client change anything within their presentation, but rather it is their job to suggest areas that could be made stronger or clearer. This principle can also be followed by providing examples when explaining a suggestion. This use of examples shows effort on the part of the consultant to be involved in the speech-making process with the client instead of arbitrarily dictating changes. Another simple way to implement this principle in an online consultation is to make sure that the client knows ahead of time what she can expect from the consultation and the amount of time allocated for the consultation. This will ensure that the client will not feel that her time or expectations are being imposed upon.

The second principle is the association principle. Spencer-Oatey (2005) defines this as the belief that people are "entitled to an association with others that is in keeping with the type of relationship that they have with them" (p. 100). This principle calls for maintaining the professional expectations of the consultant. For instance, a client will expect the consultant to use correct grammar and spelling while chatting with her. Ender and Newton (2000) discuss the role of the peer tutor paraprofessional, explaining that they become a type of role model for the students with whom they are working. Therefore, if the peer tutor is helping the student to create an organized and coherent outline for their presentation, they should maintain the client's professional expectations by using correct grammar and spelling.

In addition to these two principles that Spencer-Oatey suggests, Graham (2006) illustrates another way to avoid impoliteness in CMC. He suggests that, in order to avoid impoliteness, the speaker "[M]ust assign intent without prosodic and non-verbal markers, they must accommodate and anticipate the expectations and face needs of an audience that may be, at least partially, unknown, and they must be versed in the expectations of e-politeness or Netiquette" (p. 744). In order to implement this suggestion, the consultant should evaluate the needs of their clients and how to best serve those needs, use language and emoticons to mark force and nonverbal cues in online sessions, and maintain a professional persona with their client. By understanding the student's assignment, the professor's expectations, and how to use the technology required for the online consultation, the consultant can thereby show the client that they care about both them and their presentation, which will also help to reduce any potential, unintended impoliteness.

Restricted Nonverbal Cues

One potential reason for the perceived impoliteness in online consultations is the lack of nonverbal cues when using the online format, which was the most frequently addressed challenge for all participants. One consultant said, in favor of face-to-face consultations, "I like being able to have the human interaction with someone and read the nonverbals to make sure the client understands and is also engaged." It proved difficult to tell from long pauses, because of lack of nonverbal communication, if the client understood what was just explained, if she was thinking, or if she was checking her email instead of chatting with the consultant. CMC research addresses this lack of nonverbal cues in two major ways that pertain to the online program: using verbal communication to make up for the nonverbal absence and through the use of emoticons.

Walther, Van Der Heide, Tom Tong, Carr, and Atkin (2010) address the practice of using verbal communication to make up for the lack of nonverbal communication. According to their research, "individuals use language-based strategies to pursue relational goals online" (p. 325). They explain that this is done primarily through (dis)confirmation or (dis)agreement. By showing affinity towards something the other person values, it shows good feelings and intentions towards that person, and vice versa. A way of implementing this in an online consultation is suggested by Artemio Ramirez (2009), who argues that "Greater interactivity, in the form of involvement and mutuality, and more positive relationship forecasts resulted when communicators interacted and positive information was disclosed rather than when they observed and negative information was shared" (p. 319). For consultants, this means being involved in the process of improving the client's presentation and what the UNCG consultants affectionately call the "praise sandwich": Instead of explaining only what needs to be corrected in the client's speech, the consultant should tell the client what they did effectively, what the client can work on to improve their speech, and then what struck the consultant as being strong about the document (or a similar pattern of positives and negatives, as long as the student's strengths are emphasized). Therefore, the consultant is layering the negative, or what needs to be corrected, together with positive information, giving the consultation an overall positive feel while still conveying how to improve. This is a technique used in face-to-face consultations; however, it is even more important in online consultations because it is easier for the client to take any negatives more personally when they do not have the consultant's nonverbal communication to show them how the comment was meant to be taken. Also, while showing the client specific areas by highlighting the text, moving the cursor, or referencing a specific line or passage, the consultants are making themselves more involved and not being a passive observer of the process which reduces the frustration of the client created by not having nonverbal markers in the conversation.

The use of emoticons is another way of expressing information normally conveyed nonverbally. According to Dresner and Herring (2010), the emoticon was first invented in 1982 by a computer scientist at Carnegie Melon University. He suggested two symbols that are now known as the "smiley face" and the "frowning face," to clarify if a message should be read as a joke or as a serious contribution in the discussion forum used by his department (p. 249). Since that initial use, emoticons have become more diverse, innovative, and widespread in recent years and are widely used in online and text communication.

In the meetings conducted during the beta test to discuss the online trial program, emoticons were brought up as a concern for decreasing professionalism. CMC research offers an explanation and a strategy to resolve this issue. Franklin B. Krohn (2004) suggests that a generational approach be taken which he calls "Generational Recipient Determinism (GRD)" (p. 325). He explains that, as emoticons have only been around since the early 1980s, an approach based on identifying which generation the recipient of the online communication belongs to is the practical way to implement them in online communication. He suggests that Traditionalists (those born before 1946) not be sent anything with emoticons, Baby Boomers (between 1946 and 1964) should probably not be sent anything with emoticons, Generation X (between 1964 and 1980) may have some of the more common emoticons, and Millennials (after 1980 and coming of age after 2000) may be sent generous amounts of emoticons. For an online program in a communication center, this means that emoticons are welcomed, as the vast majority of clients are college students falling within the Millennial category, with a few Generation X members using the services. While Baby Boomers are occasionally encountered as clients in consultations, it is very rare. Therefore, the use of emoticons, according to Krohn, is a useful tool that may be freely used in online consultations.

After establishing that emoticons can be used, the next question is how they should be used. The problem is, as Krohn (2004) explains, "nonverbal cues tend to be more believable than verbal. In a situation where the verbal and nonverbal cues are contradictory, the nonverbal cues will tend to be believed" (p. 322). Emoticons are intentional nonverbal markers which contradict the rule that nonverbal cues are involuntary and spontaneous and therefore received as more honest. In this case, as an intentional emotional marker, emoticons cannot stand as an exact substitute for normal nonverbal cues. They can still be used to mark facial expression or emotion, but they do not express the same amount of information that face-to-face, nonverbal communication would.

Dresner and Herring (2010) identify three ways that emoticons can be substituted for nonverbal communication in text form. These are "(a) as emotion indicators, mapped directly onto facial expression; (b) as indicators of nonemotional meanings, mapped conventionally onto facial expressions; and (c) as illocutionary force indicators that do not map conventionally onto a facial expression" (p. 250). Though the use of emoticons as emotion indicators and facial expressions is important, the most relevant use of them for our study of online consultations would be their use to mark the force that a statement should convey, or to convey the intended meaning of the statement. Dresner and Herring (2010) explain this type of use by saying, "uses of emoticons as indicators of illocutionary force can be viewed as an expansion of text in the same way that, for example, question marks and exclamation marks are" (p. 264).

Additionally, the emoticon can indicate whether a comment is a joke, just playful, or truly serious. For instance, a statement such as "That is not exactly right; let me explain again" has a different force than "That is not exactly right:-) let me explain again." The former statement can be ambiguous, either read as if the writer is looking to help, or as if the writer is irritated that they are going to have to explain something yet another time. The latter statement clearly has a lighter tone, with the speaker looking to help, perhaps even as though they are taking some of the blame for the problem not being exactly right. In this case, the emoticon can be used to more clearly mark how the statement should be received. Use of the emoticon is also one way to avoid conveying unintentional impoliteness, as discussed in the previous section.

Privacy and Time Limitations

Two other challenges encountered while conducting the pilot online program were issues of student privacy and time limitations for funding purposes. In an effort to protect student privacy, the consultants were not sure about how to report the sessions to the students' professors: How much should they tell the professor about the consultation? In a face-to-face consultation, the consultant usually hands the client a paper copy of the report form to give to his professor, if he so chooses. These report forms include the day and time that the student came into the center, the name of the consultant he worked with, and the consultant's notes on what they worked on in the consultation. However, with the online program, there are no paper copies to give to the clients. Therefore the consultant must email the professor. It was decided that the best way to do this without infringing on the student's privacy was to ask the student if he would like his professor notified, and then to just tell the professor the student's name. In the future, the suggestion is to have an option in the online survey to notify the student's professor. Then, if the box is checked, a notification will automatically be sent to the professor.

Another problem encountered was the additional time commitment required for online consultations and how that affected funding. It took an average of sixty minutes to conduct a consultation online that would normally take thirty minutes face-to-face. Therefore, consultants could not take as many clients, and staffing suffered. The eventual solution to this problem was to add the voice option to consultations. With this option, the consultant would conduct the consultation through the shared Google Documents option, but they could talk to the client over the phone instead of typing. In order to do this, the consultants use the "Call Phone" option in Gmail. When clicked, this option allows the consultant to call a phone number and talk to the client over the internet through a headset. This cut the time back to the thirty minute limit of the face-to-face consultations. Then, the students who would rather do their consultation through the chat option can make an appointment with the consultants who have more flexible schedules.

Conclusion

This chapter reported on a pilot online consultation program at a communication center. Although some lessons were learned and shared, there is much research that can still be done on the implementation of CMC in communication centers. As this was a test trial of students who were required to use the online consultation format, it would be beneficial to look at a situation where the students are not required and to ask why they chose the online option. This would help us understand why some student populations self-select to use the online consultation option. Also, more research needs to be done regarding the phone option to see what different effects it may have from using chat. Use of video is also an option that future research should consider.

Overall, the results of the trial online consultation program were encouraging and we have high hopes for the future. There are still some areas that we are working on to further advance our knowledge of how this program can help the UNCG Speaking Center and other communication centers. We believe that technology and CMC has become such an integral part of American society that neglecting to implement it at our center would not help to move forward the work that we are trying to do on our campus. By adding this new program, we hope to help more students and more fully prepare our consultants for the workforce. We are also exploring new technology and other options for reducing such current challenges as the lack of nonverbal cues and perceived impoliteness. As technology and related research are continuously developing, we hope that in the future we will be able to overcome these challenges to make the online consultation an integral part of what we do at our communication centers.

References

Amichai-Hamburger, Y., & McKenna, K. Y. A. (2006). The contact hypothesis reconsidered: Interacting via the Internet. *Journal of Computer-Mediated Communication, 11*(3), 825–843.

Dresner, E., & Herring, S. C. (2010). Functions of the nonverbal in CMC: Emoticons and illocutionary force. *Communication Theory, 20,* 249–268.

Durkin, K., Conti-Ramsden, G., & Walker, A. J. (2010). Computer mediated communication in adolescents with and without a specific language impairment. *Computers in Human Behavior, 26*(2), 176–185.

Ender, S. C., & Newton, F. B. (2000). *Students helping students: A guide for peer educators on college campuses* (1st ed.). San Francisco, CA: Jossey-Bass.

Graham, S. L. (2006). Disagreeing to agree: Conflict, (im)politeness and identity in a computer-mediated community. *Journal of Pragmatics, 39*(4), 742–759.

Hardaker, C. (2010). Trolling in asynchronous computer-mediated communication: From user discussions to academic definitions. *Journal of Politeness Research: Language, Behavior, Culture, 6,* 215–242.

Krohn, F. B. (2004). A generational approach to using emoticons as nonverbal communication. *Journal of Technical Writing and Communication, 34*(4), 321–328.

McKenna, K. Y. A., Green, A. S., & Gleason, M. E. J. (2002). Relationship formation on the internet: What's the big attraction? *Journal of Social Issues, 58*(1), 9–31.

Pew Research Center (2011). *Pew Internet and American Life Project: Latest Research.* Retrieved from http://www.pewinternet.org/Static-Pages/Data-Tools/Get-the-Latest-Statistics/Latest-Research.aspx?start=11&x=x#ListContinue

Rainie, L (2010). *Internet, broadband, and cell phone statistics.* Retrieved from http://www.pewinternet.org/Reports/2010/Internet-broadband-and-cell-phone-statistics.aspx

Ramirez, A., Jr. (2009). The effect of interactivity on initial interactions: The influence of information seeking role on computer-mediated interaction. *Western Journal of Communication, 73*, 300–325.

Santra, T., & Giri, V. N. (2009). Analyzing computer-mediated communication and organizational effectiveness. *The Review of Communication, 9*(1), 100–109.

Spencer-Oatey, H. (2005). (Im)Politeness, face and perceptions of rapport: Unpackaging their bases and interrelationships. *Journal of Politeness Research: Language, Behavior, Culture, 1*(1), 95–119.

Walther, J. B. (1996). Computer-mediated communication: Impersonal, interpersonal, and hyperpersonal interaction. *Communication Research, 23*(1), 3–43.

Walther, J. B., Van Der Heide, B., Tom Tong, S., Carr, C. T., & Atkin, C. K. (2010). Effects of interpersonal goals on inadvertent intrapersonal influence in computer-mediated communication. *Human Communication Research, 36*, 323–34.

Part IV:
New Directions in Consultant Training

Chapter 16

Technology Tutoring: Communication Centers Take the Lead

Michelle A. Moreau and A. Paige Normand

Communication centers share a foundation of traditional training in public address or performance studies. But tutors may feel handicapped keeping up with the changing "rules" for creating visual support for oral messages. In addition, students as well as faculty increasingly request assistance in using technology to create clear and exciting visual aids. Especially given the growing number of online applications for creating visuals—such as Prezi, a Flash-based presentation application, and drag and drop web publishing applications, such as WordPress or Wix—students and faculty might find it difficult to choose the best way to utilize the web while responding to their audience's needs. Tutors with the appropriate training in technology tutoring can offer qualified, objective consultations.

Imagine a scenario in which a student enrolled in your university's basic communication course comes into your center to improve her PowerPoint slides and asks if she can incorporate a YouTube clip for her presentation next week. Or, a group of students practice their presentation that includes slides full of bulleted text, but they only ask for feedback on their delivery. Or, perhaps a communication major in an advanced public speaking course comes into your center because her professor has challenged the class to create visual aids that are not traditional PowerPoint slides. How would you approach these consultation scenarios?

Our center has created a training infrastructure to make sure that our team of undergraduate speech consultants is prepared to tutor in the area of communication technology. In this chapter, we provide an overview of the theoretical framework we use to assess multimedia communication and offer four illustrative consultation training scenarios.

Digital Natives in Academia

"Millennials" and "Digital Natives" are the two titles given to the generation of people who were born after 1980 and grew up during the digital age. As these digital natives work their way through college, university professors and administrators are trying to address the educational needs of a generation that has been immersed in digital technology. In 2010 the Pew Research Center published a report detailing the Millennials' use of media and technology. One of the contributors, danah boyd, a Social Media Researcher from Harvard University's Berkman Center for Internet and Society, describes how these students have grown accustomed to "a level of information persistence, information searchability, information replicability, [and] information scalability, that we've never seen before" (p. 13). To best serve these students, we must first understand their predominant skills and the impact their use of the Internet and multimedia messages has had on their communication skills.

The results from Pew's research (2010) document report that Millennials are outpacing previous generations when it comes to uploading videos to the Internet and using social media and microblogging sites; however, their proficiency with technology is primarily interpersonal, and almost exclusively limited to the social sphere. In a Pew Research Center panel on "Millennials, Media and Information," boyd (2010) asserts that the particular skills "digital natives" learn from an early age include "how to navigate textual conversations" and how to engage "in a whole multimodal way of interacting socially" (p. 7). This social technology acumen does not necessarily transfer to the academic or professional arena. Margaryan, Littlejohn, and Vojt (2011) conclude from their survey of two UK universities that "students have limited understanding of what tools they could adopt and how to support their own learning" (p. 439). Rather, these researchers found students look to educational authority figures for ideas. However, faculty members may be more likely to produce what we might think of as "standard" PowerPoint presentations for their lectures: using the software to present their lecture notes. The Pew panel concluded on this point that the Millennials' immersion in technology and multimedia messages only reinforces the importance of media literacy training in higher education.

These studies demonstrate that traditional college students, despite having ample experience utilizing technology to communicate socially in multimodal ways, commonly lack the critical skills necessary to target audiences other than their peers and to use communication technology in public speaking or academic contexts. Since professors frequently perceive Millennials as more "tech savvy," they might encourage use of videos, animations, and websites in public speaking regardless of the quality of student output. However, a Millennial student who feels comfortable making and editing a YouTube video may, when asked to make a presentation for class, recreate the same type of text-heavy PowerPoint presentations she is accustomed to seeing from her professors. Though their needs might be different, students and faculty alike need support, training, and feedback in order to harness multimedia messages to best facilitate learning and communication.

Communication centers offer the discursive and physical space for students and faculty to contemplate their use of communication technology, to model innovative visual messages not often encountered in the classroom, and to encourage digital natives and digital immigrants to contemplate the impact their multimedia messages will have on their audiences. In the following section, we detail research from modern cognitive science that communication center tutors need to understand in order to guide clients' multimedia message creation in an audience-centered way.

How the Brain Works: Modern Theories

Multimedia messages, such as PowerPoint or Prezi, require audiences to interpret multiple types of auditory and visual information. To facilitate media literacy in Millennial and non-traditional students, communication center tutors need expertise in how combinations of sights, sounds, motions, and linguistic information should be arranged to promote the audience's optimal retention. To do this, tutors must first understand how the human brain works. In his book *Multimedia Learning*, Mayer (2001) provides a structure for understanding the complex ways that humans perceive and understand information when learning. Specifically, he builds on previous theories of human cognition to forward empirically-tested ideas about how to create multimedia messages that are free from extraneous noise, structured to emphasize the essential message, and poised to generate new ideas.

Effective messages, multimedia or otherwise, are produced when speakers and writers respect the limitations of working memory and facilitate the connection of their information with an audience's existing knowledge. Before the 1950s, cognitive scientists believed the brain had an unlimited capacity to receive and process new stimuli (sights, smells, sounds, touch). They theorized that people either "got it" or did not based only on individual limitations such as intelligence or physical impairments. In the mid 1950s, George Miller altered the course of cognitive theory by proving that working memory's ability to process and integrate new stimuli is fairly limited (Mayer, 2001). In order for people to interpret stimuli, they must first be able to take in and retain this information in their working memory and then contextualize and organize it through schemas, which are the frameworks that allow a person to understand information.

The threshold for a person's ability to interpret sensory stimuli is called cognitive load. There are two facets of cognitive input: intrinsic load, or the complexity of the content, and extraneous load, or the presentation of that content (Chandler & Sweller, 1991; Cooper, 2009; Leahy, Chandler, & Sweller, 2003; Tindall-Ford & Sweller, 2006). Subject matter that requires new vocabulary and abstract relationships, such as theoretical physics, carries a high intrinsic cognitive load. Content that can be explained linearly and with minimal morphologically complex terms, such as the timeline of events leading up to the United States' involvement in World War II, would have a low intrinsic cognitive load. Though speakers can make an effort to utilize existing schemas and avoid jargon, they ultimately have little control over the message's level of intrinsic cognitive load. Extraneous cognitive load, however, is affected by the way speakers arrange and develop ideas. The material a speaker uses to convey his message has the potential to create extraneous load and inhibit the audience's attention and retention. Communication centers can utilize our understanding of cognitive load to guide students' presentation of material to best facilitate their audience's attention and learning.

Multimedia learning theory contends that, when listening to multimedia messages, humans actively select relevant auditory and visual sensory stimuli, organize their selection in working memory into either verbal or pictorial representations, and then integrate those representations with existing schemas (Mayer, 2001). Traditional research assumes that cognitive load results from the presence of too much of one type of sensory stimuli. Rather than taking a pure sensory approach, Mayer melds competing theories of human encoding by also considering the two channels humans use in cognitive processing. He names the channels "auditory/verbal" and "visual/pictorial." When humans select stimulus to enter either of these channels, the working memory then organizes them into either verbal or pictorial representations that then get linked up to schema in long term memory. Thus, a key facet of multimedia learning theory is that language usually becomes verbal representations in working memory whether it is spoken or presented as text. Both spoken words and images enter working memory via a congruous channel. Spoken words enter the auditory/verbal channel and become verbal representations; images enter the visual/pictorial channel and become pictorial representations. According to Mayer, "if words are presented as on-screen text or printed text, this process begins in the visual channel and later may move to the auditory channel if the learner mentally articulates the printed words." Written text, then, takes a more complicated route as readers "sound out" text in their mind.

Limitations in cognitive processing, then, occur when one channel is taxed by the overlap of text and oration. For example, Morett, Clegg, Blalock, and Mong (2009) found that drivers recalled more when they heard a recording of spoken directions while they viewed a map. As an image that contains little to no linguistic information, subjects can easily select and organize what they are seeing along with the auditory reinforcement. On the other hand, Leahy, Chandler and Sweller (2003) found that providing an audience with both auditory (verbal) information and visual information facilitated learning *as long as the auditory information did not overlap with the textual information.* In other words, an audience is likely to retain more information about a graph if they can hear an explanation while they look at it; however, they are likely to retain less information if they see the graph, hear an explanation, and try to read the same explanation textually. Mayer proposes that audiences learn best when hearing and seeing information because this instruction style engages two senses. However, when an audience is forced to hear and read the same information, they are less likely to retain it due to the cognitive load placed on their visual/pictorial channel. While professors and students alike will be communicating more complex messages than simple directions, speakers must be conscious of the balance between oration, text and visual images in their presentations to best facilitate retention.

We will address specifically how Multimedia Learning theory can be incorporated into Communication Center consultations in the "debrief" sections of the following scenarios. However, Mayer's (2001) findings that simultaneous use of written and spoken information can slow an audience's processing ability has particular relevance to the most prevalent multimedia software, PowerPoint. Therefore we will first examine the influence that this software has had on speakers' creation of visual aids.

Multimedia Presentational Software: History and Design

While our understanding of the human brain and cognitive processing has evolved, the fundamental design of Microsoft PowerPoint software has not. Through its long-standing slide defaults and the momentum of what is perceived as "traditional" presentations, PowerPoint software engenders visual aids that are text-centric, linear, and promote excessive cognitive load. Criticisms of PowerPoint slide design stem from the software's default settings that encourage text, which in turn encourages presenters to use their slides as speaker notes rather than engaging with their audience. The default settings for slides prompt the user to "Click to add title" and "Click to add subtitle." When a slide only prompts a user for text, and when the majority of presentations students see predominantly include text, even digital natives exhibit a lack of creative ownership. Garner, Alley, Allen, and Zappe (2009) found that 65 percent of the 1,025 slides, collected from the engineering and technical groups involved in their study followed the traditional topic-subtopic PowerPoint default format. Moreover, despite the importance of visual information for engineering, none of the slides included images.

Forward-thinking leaders of industry and government are making an effort to change this type of "traditional" PowerPoint usage and to promote new digital presentation tools. Unfortunately most advice, such as that given in the books *Presentation Zen* and *Slide-ology*, targets business and nonprofit groups, not educational audiences. Without professors feeling prepared and motivated to revise their media communication strategies or foster student innovation, college graduates will be less likely to bring new communication strategies into the professional world. Also, well-meaning instructors often perpetuate the "rules" of PowerPoint. In our communication center alone, we have seen rules about the number of slides per length of talk, the number of words per bullet, the number of bullets per slides, the use or absence of animation, the amount and quality of font and background colors, and so on. Such rules are likely well-meaning guidelines diluted from personal preferences or theoretical insight; however, these rules can handicap speakers even among generations of students who want to create novel visual aids. Because clients rarely see innovative multimedia images, we found in our communication center that clients resisted our suggestions to revise their slides. Armed with knowledge about the cognitive process and perils of technology default settings, communication center educators are better prepared to help clients use communication technology more effectively in their presentations.

Modeling and Non-directive Feedback

Communication center tutors need to have a wide base of knowledge and experience with different multimedia presentation strategies; this enables the tutors to offer their technical expertise and practical knowledge to anticipate questions and to offer strategies for maximizing the effectiveness of any media a client chooses. We focus on training our student tutors in new communication applications and software in order to integrate their media skills into the academic realm. To this end we keep a repertoire of innovative PowerPoint slides, Prezi, or specific examples for utilizing websites and video to offer as models for students. We also posted some of our most popular techniques on our website in the form of screencasts. These all serve as a starting point for a dialogue with the students about selecting a method that best suits their presentational needs and capitalize on digital natives'—both clients' and tutors'—fluency with social multimedia.

We train our student tutors in a non-directive, dialogical consultation style. This best facilitates clients' critical engagement with technology, specifically when students are in the brainstorming stage or revising multimedia presentations. Muriel Harris (1995), one of the leading scholars on writing center tutoring and pedagogy, details that the overwhelming response of students to non-directive feedback was that "they prefer to do their own work, come to their own conclusions, write what was in their own head: these students do not want to be told what to do" (p. 30). Borrowing from writing center studies, we train our tutors how to take advantage of their non-authoritarian position to address the individual concerns, assumptions, and needs of their clients by engaging in conversation about the motivation, purpose, and reasons that shaped their projects. By engaging with the student to discover his or her strengths in multimedia communication and by modeling innovative examples, our tutors can—as Harris (1995) points out—"startle a student as he suddenly 'sees' what he's supposed to do in order to achieve whatever it was he was trying to achieve" (p. 33). Our tutoring also offers an alternative route for inspiration: rather than relying on faculty as the authority or defaulting to PowerPoint, students can work with their peers to synthesize their social media knowledge and translate such skills into a professional or academic venue.

Equipped with an understanding of cognitive processing, the history and evolution of visual presentation software, and the right type of tutoring approach, communication center tutors can engender responsible and inventive technology use for the tools that exist today and tomorrow. In the following sections, we offer four illustrative training scenarios of consultations that originated from our communication center: a freshman needing assistance in revising his PowerPoint presentation for a speech; a sophomore wanting assistance in deciding what type of media would be best for her speech; a junior wanting to practice using Prezi for a presentation; a professor wishing to improve her PowerPoint presentations for her statistics class. Each section elaborates on the theory that informs our feedback, the intended impact of the consultation, and the questions we use to guide the client.

Scenario 1: Nathan the Freshman

Nathan, a freshman in an introductory communication course, comes to the communication center to practice his informative speech on columns in classical architecture. He is nervous and states that he "just wants general feedback." He begins his presentation and turns to the screen to read through his PowerPoint slides which consist of a title page, "columns," his name, and five subsequent slides that have bullet point definitions of the different kinds of columns.

Debriefing

Multimedia learning theory suggests that spoken words and written text should not be repetitive and that, when both spoken words and written text are present, audiences retain more information from what the speaker says aloud. Creating slides that contain speaking notes tempts speakers to read directly from them, which not only leads to a lack of eye contact and flattening of pitch, but also creates a cognitive load in the audience who cannot read and listen at the same time. Hence, the sum of all of these factors reduces the audience member's ability to pay attention and retain the message.

Return to the Scenario

For this consultation, the tutor focuses on preparing Nathan to make the transition from speaker-centered presentation to an audience-centered presentation. The tutor explains that a presentation that includes both visual text and verbal information typically leads an audience to focus on only one or the other. To convey this information to the client, the tutor asks Nathan what he typically does when he sees text-heavy slides. Nathan admits that he typically reads his professor's slides rather than listening to the lecture.

Sometimes PowerPoint's defaults are so ingrained in a student's mind that it takes some prodding from the tutor to get the student to consider reducing the presentation text. Nathan is at first a little stumped by the questions about his audience. Like many freshmen, he thinks the purpose of papers and speeches is to simply show his professor that he knows the information; he has not considered the importance of the presentation of that information. In order to facilitate this transition, the tutor shows one of the examples of non-traditional PowerPoints that the communication center made for instructional purposes. When Nathan sees the PowerPoint presentation that consists almost entirely of images, he says, "None of the other students' presentations look like that. I don't think that's what my professor wants." Utilizing non-directive feedback, the tutor begins the discussion by asking Nathan, "But as an audience member, I'm having trouble visualizing the differences between these types of columns. What could you do to help your audience understand these sometimes subtle distinctions?"

After they discuss this issue, Nathan agrees to incorporate images of each of the different types of columns, but wants to keep his bullet-point descriptions in his presentation. The tutor then shows Nathan how to use PowerPoint tools to visually highlight the differences in the columns while verbally explaining the chronological progression of these changes. Nathan then practices his presentation and talks through each issue as he highlights the image and realizes by the time he flips to his bullet-point slides, he has already conveyed all of this information and skips on to the next picture slide. Nathan agrees to practice the presentation with slides that are just highlighted pictures of columns labeled with their names. The tutor and Nathan discuss whether the use of text labels will encourage the audience to read rather than listen. Nathan says, "Well, they are kinda foreign words; let's keep them on the slide."

Results

The desired results of this consultation are three-fold: the student began to more thoroughly consider the needs of his audience members to facilitate their learning; the student practiced creating slides that facilitate the visualization of information rather than using his slides as speaking notes; the student began the transition from reading his slides and began speaking to his audience rather than facing the screen. When students come into a consultation with drafts of visual aids, a communication center tutor can ask:

- What do you want your audience to get out of your presentation?
- How will you keep your audience engaged and interested?
- What would help your audience learn this information?
- Is your audience going to read the text on your slide or just look at it for reference?

Scenario 2: Julie the Sophomore

Julie is giving an informative speech for her advanced public speaking course. She wants to tell her audience about the local food kitchen. Julie has already created an outline and note cards. The other students in her class made Power-Point presentations and read their speeches from the screen. Julie's teacher encourages the class to be more creative, and she needs a good grade on this speech. Julie wants to find a new kind of visual aid for her presentation to impress her professor.

Debrief

Multimedia learning theory provides ample advice to help speakers make media and style choices when they know what they want to say, but do not know how to best visually support the message. For example, audiences will learn more when media is located close to the oral message, spatially and temporally. Waiting until the end of a speech to show a video clip that supports the first main idea might leave the audience confused or distracted. Any visual should contribute to the core message. Websites, YouTube videos, and slides are relatively easy to show, but it is easy to get confused as to what part of the presentation needs illustration. Walking clients through an outline, main idea by main idea, can help them discover when an oral message needs visual support.

Further, multimedia learning theory posits that messages are easier to retain when they engage more than one sense. Choosing graphs and pictures to accentuate a message is an easy way to make the message more engaging. The admonition in the previous scenario may leave speakers thinking that slides have to be "image-only" to prevent cognitive load; however, it is possible to view linguistic information without reading. Websites, for example, might contain text, but when used in live presentations audiences are more likely to see them as an image rather than attempting to read the content. They will retain and benefit from layout, design and navigation that accentuate a speaker's talk or provide direction for additional reading separate from the speech.

Return to the Scenario

The tutor suggests that they start with Julie's outline: "If we can determine what sort of organizational pattern you've used here, we can figure out what sort of presentation will work best." Julie looks through her outline and the tutor asks, "If the main points were rearranged, would that make any difference to the presentation?" Julie realizes that aside from introducing the food bank, all of the other information—the location, hours, and volunteer programs—are all interchangeable. The tutor responds, "If your organizational pattern is topical, you probably wouldn't need a PowerPoint presentation, since the progression of slides create a linear structure. Why did you choose to discuss the food bank?" Julie explains that the website and the video from the food bank's website was very inspirational. She pulls up the site and shows the tutor the first couple of minutes of their promotional video.

After thinking it through, Julie decides that showing the video in her presentation would take too much time. The tutor suggests that instead of showing the video, Julie could at least show her audience the food bank's website. Julie asks, "Can I do that? Can I just show the website—instead of an *actual* presentation?" The tutor asks if Julie has the assignment prompt and they look it over together. They review where the professor asks for a "compelling and memorable presentation"; Julie agrees that the site is very compelling and would make an effective visual aid for her presentation. She and the tutor map out which website pages and images she wants to show the audience to support the corresponding main ideas of her speech. They also plan on when to minimize the page so the audience can focus solely on her oral message.

Results

The tutor focused on two main ideas to help this student select visual media that supports rather than detracts from her message: the student should first consider the visual support; choosing the right media for a presentation comes down to organization and purpose; and any visual media should enhance but not overwhelm the oral message in live presentations. When tutoring students who have not already created visual media for a speech, communication center tutors can provide guidance by asking:

- What are the main claims in your presentation?
- What visual aids do you need to support your claims?
- What is the organizational pattern? (For example, linear, specific to general, general to specific, spatial)
- Do you really need a slide presentation or can you use an online video or website?

Scenario 3: Dorian the Junior

Dorian, a junior communication studies major, brings in a Prezi presentation for a persuasive speech. He recently learned about the Prezi online application and, excited to have an alternative to PowerPoint, has made a presentation that utilizes many of its unique features: zooming in and out, rotating, creating spatial relationships among his images, and embedding videos. He presents his 10-minute speech, which is well written and well delivered, but his Prezi contains so many visuals and movements that the tutor is not only overwhelmed, but somewhat confused by the end of it.

Debriefing

Multimedia learning theory posits that speakers should remove interesting but unnecessary words and sounds to focus on the essential parts of the message. Encouraging students to create innovative presentations often leads even well-meaning students to fill mediated messages with non-essential extras. All PowerPoint slides, for example, contain layers of information such as color, line, font, font size, movement, design, layout, etc. Even when speakers know how to include visual images at compelling points of their speech, they still fight the temptation to clutter their presentation with extraneous elements. With new tools comes the temptation to find new ways to use exciting movement and digital extras. In keeping with the multimedia learning theory principles, any visual, auditory, and sensory information should be relevant to the core message. Just because a program or application offers exciting options for new stimuli does not mean that a presenter should use all of them.

Return to the Scenario

The tutor begins by discussing the use of movement through the presentation. Dorian is initially resistant to altering the path through his presentation since he has invested a substantial amount of time creating this portion of his presentation. The tutor suggests that Dorian sit next to her and watch the movement on the big screen as opposed to viewing it on his laptop. The spinning and zooming is clearly overwhelming and he agrees that he should change it. They discuss how best to make the movement in his presentation meaningful; in particular, they talk about the spatial connections among the images and text.

After discussing the importance of paring down the motion of the presentation, the tutor asks Dorian about his videos. Dorian anticipates the tutor's advice and states, "I don't really need that first one; I just thought it was funny." The tutor discusses the video's merits in terms of an attention-getter, but Dorian has already internalized the importance of keeping his media relevant to his message and states that he might look for another one, but will probably only keep one video in his presentation. The tutor and Dorian then go through the presentation one last time, and the tutor suggests that he pay attention to the cohesion of his images. Dorian notices that the lack of unity among the colors and dimensions of his images is also distracting. He realizes that he should focus on maintaining a more consistent look among his images in order to avoid overwhelming his audience with different shapes and colors.

Results

The tutor focused the student's attention to different aspects of his presentation (movement, videos, and images) in order to remind him of the needs of his audience and to eliminate sensory clutter. The tutor discussed three main points with this student: experimenting with new media, stripping away extra information and justifying what stays, and keeping in mind what his audience will see. When assisting clients' selection of visual media types, it can help to ask:

- What information does your media convey to your audience?
- What are the essential points to your presentation and what media do you use to convey it?
- Is any of your media distracting your audience from your message?
- If you had to spend a dollar for every color, font, line, movement, sound, background design or word, would you make the same investments?

Scenario 4: Jane the Professor

Jane, a statistics professor, visits the communication center because her students are performing poorly on her tests. She mentions that her lectures typically consist of examples, explanations, and terms. She explains that she follows the "rules" of PowerPoint slide design: no more than four bullet points per slide and no more than four words per bullet point.

Debriefing

Multimedia learning theory posits that audiences learn more deeply when they are already moderately familiar with the message terms and ideas. Understanding new vocabulary takes repeated exposure in order to attach new concepts to pre-existing schemas in long-term memory or to create new schemas. Certainly, few speakers can control what their audience knows ahead of time or reduce the inherent complexity of the material. Reducing complicated ideas to bulleted lists can make material more difficult to understand when the audience has little prior knowledge to understand terms or ideas. Also, trying to force concepts to fit a mold with a fixed number of words misdirects a speaker's energy into "constructing the perfect slide" rather than conveying meaning.

As stated above, audiences cannot listen and read simultaneously due to the mind "sounding out" phonemes as it reads. Therefore, it seems contradictory to suggest the use of full sentences. However, when an audience is not already familiar with vocabulary or concepts, bulleted phrases, which are still read, can be even more confusing due to the lack of context for the ideas. Writing out simple, active-voice sentence headlines about novel concepts, allowing time for the audience to read and absorb are both strategies to aid retention.

Return to the Scenario

Jane's course material carries a high intrinsic load due to the concept complexity and new vocabulary, so her tutor begins by asking, "Will people be able to pay attention to what you are saying while they read your slides?" Jane has assumed that the overlap of visual and verbal information would be helpful to reach different kinds of learners, so the tutor dispels the "rules" about text on PowerPoint slides and encourages Jane to think about what function the text serves in her presentations. The tutor then shows the professor examples of instructional slides with full-sentence headlines and accompanying images and explains that bullet points carry less meaning than a clear, direct sentence and encourages Jane to focus on only one idea per slide to best facilitate retention for any kind of learner.

Jane picks one chapter from her class, null hypothesis testing, to focus on for the consultation, since it contains foundational information for the course. She and the tutor work on breaking it down into parts. They return to the professor's existing slides and discuss which bullets should be written out in full-sentence format with a formula or graph depicting the concept. Jane says, "But this slide is a list of assumptions. I don't want to break that up into three slides, because it's really all one idea." The tutor shows Jane how to frame the list like a checkbox to visually reinforce the idea that the information is all connected. As the session progresses, Jane discovers that most of the images of graphs, tables, and formulas already exist on her old slides. In the process of looking for new examples, she also finds new websites to show in class.

At the end of the session, Jane is satisfied with her new slideshow, but feels hesitant to discard the old slides because, she says, "my students use these as notes." The tutor shows Jane the outline function in PowerPoint that creates a word-for-word outline from her slides that she can give to her students or keep on the course website. Jane has heard of Prezi and is tempted to begin using it for class. She sees how she can replicate the same process of sifting through her written text, visual images, and web links for the next media tool that comes along.

Results

The tutor focused on discussing three main points with the professor: write full sentence headlines for complex information, keep only one idea per slide, and dissect slides into written, visual, and linked content when redesigning old slides or creating new media. When helping clients make complex decisions about which and how much text to include in visual media, tutors would be wise to ask:

- Will people be able to pay attention to what you are saying while they read your slides?
- What function does the text serve?
- What does your audience need to see in order to understand your ideas?
- Which ideas are new? Which ones are reviewed? Can your students tell the difference?

Conclusion

Accustomed to digital communication in their social lives, Millennials can be proficient at using technology to create multimedia messages. However as these students transition into college, they will need support in transferring their social technological acumen to the academic environment. While faculty might be less apt to integrate innovative communication strategies, students still look to them as role models of public address. Communication centers are also a safe environment for faculty to try adopting new approaches, while receiving feedback from their colleagues and qualified students. Centers offer unique one-to-one and small group consultations where peers can encourage students to consider the audience and occasion of their presentation in a manner that responsibly blends theory and practice. By approaching these consultations between student tutors and student clients as a dialogue, communication centers foster the natural communication skills of these students. Adept tutoring can also offer strategies for critically assessing an audience, and the theoretical framework to understand how best to create presentations that complement cognitive processing.

References

boyd, d., Casey, D., & Lenhart, A. (2010). Millennials: A portrait of generation next; Panel 2: millennials, media, and information. *Pew Research Center*. 1–27.

Chandler, P., & Sweller, J. (1991). Cognitive load theory and the format of instruction. *Cognition and Instruction, 8*(4), 293–332.

Cooper, E. (2009). Overloading on slides: Cognitive theory and Microsoft's slide program PowerPoint. *Association for the Advancement of Computing in Education Journal, 17*(2), 127–135.

Duarte, N. (2008) *Slide-ology: The art and science of creating great presentations*. Sebastocol, CA: O'Reilly Media.

Garner, J. K., Alley, M., Allen, F. G., & Zappe, S. E. (2009). Common use of PowerPoint versus the assertion-evidence structure: A cognitive psychology perspective. *Technical Communication, 56*(4), 331–345.

Harris, M. (1995). Talking in the middle: Why writers need writing tutors. *College English, 57*, 27–42.

Leahy, W., Chandler, P., & Sweller, J. (2003). When auditory presentations should and should not be a component of multimedia instruction. *Applied Cognitive Psychology, 17*, 401–418.

Margaryan, A., Littlejohn, A., & Vojt, G. (2011). Are digital natives a myth or reality? University students' use of digital technologies. *Computers & Education, 56*, 429–440.

Mayer, R. E. (2001). *Multimedia learning*. Cambridge, UK: Cambridge University Press.

Morett, L. M., Clegg, B. A., Blalock, L. D., & Mong, H. M. (2009). Applying multimedia learning theory to map learning and driving navigation. *Transportation Research Part F: Psychology and Behaviour, 12* (1), 40–49.

Reynolds, G. (2008). *Presentation zen: Simple ideas on presentation design and delivery*. Berkeley, CA: New Riders.

Taylor P., & Keeter, S. (2010). Millennials: A Portrait of Generation Next. *Pew Research Center*. 1 – 148.

Tindall-Ford, S., & Sweller, J. (2006). Altering the modality of instructions to facilitate imagination: Interactions between the modality and imagination effects. *Instructional Science, 34*, 343–365.

Chapter 17

Using Empathetic Listening to Build Relationships at the Center

Kimberly M. Cuny, Sarah M. Wilde, and
Alexandra Vizzier Stephenson

Administrators and staff at communication centers have many responsibilities: increasing publicity, making sure things run smoothly, gaining buy-in from faculty across the curriculum, and recruiting and training staff, to note a few. Emery (2006) argued that successful communication centers are developed in line with the needs of particular institutions and their students. Services are rendered through peer tutors who are trained to review the assignment requirements and listen to the needs of students seeking their assistance, as well as to provide feedback for improvement during simulated practice sessions (Yook, 2006). Tutors at some centers also provide some instruction in the form of workshops for students. As with any job, there are unwritten responsibilities that may not appear in the job description—namely, building positive relationships with and among peer tutors.

Focusing on the work of the communication center at a mid-sized public university, our chapter seeks to show how peer-to-peer tutoring incorporates empathetic listening to build lasting relationships between peers, i.e., between staff and their speaker-clients (heretoforth referred to as speakers). Although the concept of empathetic listening has been studied predominantly in therapist-client contexts, we apply it to the relationships developed and maintained in a peer tutoring setting. Both tutoring and therapy involve face-to-face relationship-building conversations requiring an active level of listening. This chapter attempts to connect empathetic listening, unconditional positive regard, and confirmation to the success of individual peer tutors. We believe that through the employment of empathetic listening techniques including focusing, encouraging, and reflecting skills, unconditional positive regard, confirmation, immediacy behaviors, and application of the SOFTEN technique, more successful peer relationships will develop.

Empathetic Listening

In Ward and Schwartzman's (2009) empirical study of the dynamics of speaking center consultations, they note that consultant-speaker relationships are an integral part of communication centers. Though this relationship begins to evolve within minutes, it has a critical impact on the success of communication centers. Listening is a large part of that relational success.

Empathetic listening is a major communication competency utilized by peer educators at communication centers as they build relationships with speakers. Empathetic listening should be used in all situations at communication centers. This type of listening requires listeners to refrain from judging the speaker and instead advocates placing themselves in the speaker's position. Doing so allows the listener to understand the speaker's point of view.

Characteristics of empathetic listening include being aware and being in the present moment, acknowledging the other, resisting distractions, noting all of the speaker's nonverbal and verbal communication, and being empathetic to the speaker's thoughts and feelings (Burley-Allen, 1995). Empathetic listening requires that the listener show both verbally and nonverbally that listening is truly taking place. Stewart and Logan (2002) discuss three competencies in developing empathetic listening: focusing, encouraging, and reflection.

Focusing Skills

Focusing skills, the first competency of empathetic listening, entails being attentive to the person you are helping. To implement these skills, the peer tutor must make appropriate eye contact and react responsively while facing the speaker. When peer tutors are facilitating a consultation, whether it is with a group or an individual, they should make every effort to maximize eye contact with the speaker. Regardless of whether the speaker is seeking feedback on a presentation, watching a recording of themselves giving a presentation with the intent of goal-setting for future class presentations, or working on interpersonal competencies (such as conversational turn taking behaviors), the staff members should strive to maintain eye contact in order to make the speaker feel comfortable and appreciated. However, as the staff member must at times look down to write notes on the report form, the speaker should be alerted in advance so as to maintain their sense of validation. Also, with an influx of English language learners utilizing center services, it has become imperative for the staff to be mindful of the impact of cultural implications on eye behaviors (i.e., to know that some cultures may be uncomfortable with sustained direct eye contact).

Through their work at the center, the staff learns the benefits of connecting with their audience and taking the necessary measures to be attentive to their speakers. Sometimes staff find themselves facing difficult situations such as having to deal with a dysfunctional group with aggressive members, speakers who do not have a clear idea of what the class assignment entails, those who want the staff to break the honor code or academic integrity policy and write their speeches for them, or faculty members requesting a staff presentation for a time frame that is not feasible. Fortunately, staff members do not typically have to deal with such challenging situations; nevertheless, they must always be prepared to handle all communication professionally while still being attentive to the speaker. Focusing skills can make the difference in these situations. Sometimes reacting responsibly means suggesting that the speaker visit another organization on campus such as the Speech and Hearing Center, Psychological Services, or The Dean of Students (for students in distress) to receive even more specialized assistance. Serving in the role of peer tutor, the staff must know their own limits for helping others and listen carefully to make the necessary referrals.

When providing constructive feedback to a speaker, the staff members should do so in a careful manner so as not to embarrass or undermine self-worth. During consultations, peer tutors typically sit with the speaker and use an open posture in which they face the speaker throughout the entire consultation. Additionally, in attending to speakers, staff members need to be cognizant of their word choices, especially in challenging situations, to ensure that the words are constructive yet assertive. Staff members should be encouraged to employ "I" language rather than "you" language. In teaching consultants about "I" language we suggest reading the extensive review of its effectiveness offered by Proctor and Wilcox (1993). "I" language allows tutors to own their messages, rather than to assign blame. Starting a sentence with "I" instead of "you" (such as in the following sentence: "I felt . . . when you . . . because. . . ."), allows messages to be more descriptive and less judgmental. At the close of every consultation, speakers are given the opportunity to fill out feedback via an online survey. This process communicates to our speakers that we value what they have to offer and that we are listening. Feedback is carefully considered for staff performance reviews.

Encouraging Skills

Stewart and Logan's (2002) second competency involves motivating the other to talk more. In order to motivate the speaker, the peer tutor can mirror, or repeat, the speaker's words in order to encourage more elaboration on a given topic.

The peer tutor can also ask clarifying and open questions that require more than a yes/no response. By listening actively and using moderate self-disclosure, the peer tutor demonstrates interest in what the speaker is saying. For example, if the speaker discloses that they live in a particular dorm on campus, the peer tutor may also share information about the dorm in which they live. In turn this allows the speaker to become more comfortable and provide more valid information that enables the listener to ask relevant questions (Burley-Allen, 1995). This sets into motion a supportive chain of interactions in which the speaker feels more accepted and validated.

Speakers come into the center with a varying level of understanding of public, group, and interpersonal communication as well as the details of the assignment for which they are using the services of the center. Sometimes the speakers come in with a copy of their class assignment which makes it easier for the peer tutor to more effectively work with a speaker, but many times the peer tutors must motivate their speakers to talk more about the assignment and their comfort level with speaking in front of, or with, others. The staff members must listen carefully to determine how best to help individual speakers to determine whether they need help in boosting their self-esteem, being more assertive when speaking, managing their public speaking anxiety, articulating their points more clearly, connecting with their audience, or organizing their ideas. Careful listening can help the staff to determine what questions to ask in order to clearly identify the main goal of the speaker's visit.

Reflecting Skills

Stewart and Logan's (2002) final competency entails reflecting the client's perspective. The peer tutor can accomplish this competency through paraphrasing the speaker's words and/or adding an example that the peer tutor believes illustrates the speaker's perspective. To listen effectively one needs to check understanding regularly by summarizing and paraphrasing what the other has said. After summary one must wait for feedback. Following feedback, the consultant needs to either confirm that they share understanding, or offer clarification of what the speaker might have intended.

The staff of a communication center should follow this model of reflective listening during all consultations and communication exchanges. While paraphrasing, reflecting, and summarizing, staff members need to make sure that external and internal distractions do not get in the way. They also work to ensure that they paraphrase both the content and the feelings of the speaker in a non-evaluative way while accurately interpreting their understanding of what they have heard (Ender & Newton, 2000).

In addition to empathetic listening, staff members should utilize empathetic understanding, which is the understanding of another's world through their frame of reference and knowing how they think and feel in regard to the content of the message they are delivering (Ender & Newton, 2000). If a speaker thinks you are truly listening and understanding him or her, then you can help to develop better personal understanding. One way for staff to express this type of understanding is by providing examples from their own speaking experiences, which could include personal struggles. Through practicing empathetic understanding, the staff member will be able to develop a relationship with the speaker and ultimately help the speaker with his or her needs.

Confirmation and Unconditional Positive Regard

True unconditional positive regard and confirmation can only take place when empathetic listening is employed by center staff. The communication center staff helps speakers with their speech endeavors by offering suggestions as well as praise and offering guidance where appropriate. They do this while simultaneously building a relationship with individual speakers. These relationships, Ward & Schwartzman (2009) conclude, are vital to the work of peer educators in communication centers. It is through the praxis of confirmation, positive regard, and empathetic listening that these relationships are forged.

Rogers (1992) defines unconditional positive regard as "caring for the client, but not in a possessive way or in such a way as simply to satisfy the therapist's own needs" (p. 829). Communication consultants can communicate unconditional positive regard in their tutoring by increasing their use of nonverbal immediacy behaviors. Immediacy has been defined as "the degree of perceived physical or psychological closeness between people" (Richmond, 2002, p. 68).

The use of immediacy behaviors in the work of communication centers can be examined in many ways. Our focus here is on the use of face, eyes, and time to increase perceived closeness which can lead to a feeling of being positively cared for or about. Communication consultants who maintain comfortable eye contact and pleasing facial expressions during tutoring sessions while speaking and listening communicate increased unconditional positive regard. Immediate consultants also signal unconditional positive regard to speakers by arriving early for work and starting or ending consultations on time.

Verbal behaviors can also be used to demonstrate unconditional positive regard. In her essay, Wilde (2005) notes verbal immediacy behaviors that a teacher can employ when seeking to be attentive to their students during class. These verbal behaviors include regular use of a speaker's first name during a consultation, proper pronunciation of the speaker's name, verbal messages that encourage and praise (while not forgetting the importance of offering feedback), the use of inclusive language, and the avoidance of a monotone voice. Communication consultants can use these same behaviors to express positive regard when working with speakers.

Confirmation is difficult to define and has yet to be operationalized (Cissna & Anderson, 1994). Although the ways in which individuals confirm each other in relationships are different, confirmation always involves expressing recognition of another's existence, acknowledging that a relationship of affiliation exists, expressing awareness of the significance of the other, and accepting or endorsing the validity of another person's experience (Cissna & Sieburg, 1981).

Buber (1999) writes, "The basis of man's life with man is twofold, and it is one—the wish of every man to be confirmed as what he is, even as what he can become, by men; and the innate capacity in man to confirm his fellow men in this way" (p. 12). Thus, human instinct makes people want to be confirmed by others. Consultants are positioned well to confirm others given the one-on-one nature of their work.

Center staff can utilize the SOFTENS technique to communicate unconditional positive regard and confirmation. The technique in its origin represents nonverbal behaviors that can be used to mitigate the fear a speaker might experience at the initial contact (of the relationship). While Wassmer (1978) put forth the SOFTENS technique for the initial stage of relationship forming, it extends throughout the peer tutoring process. Body language is listed as one of the seven characteristics of effective listening, which also contributes to a sense of unconditional positive regard and confirmation (Cobb, 2000).

The original SOFTENS technique involves smiling, open posture, forward lean, touching by shaking hands, eye contact, nodding, and use of space. In applying SOFTENS to communication center work, we advocate changing "T" from touching by shaking hands to taking notes and omitting considerations of space. Thus SOFTENS becomes SOFTEN (smiling, open posture, forward lean, taking notes, eye contact, nodding).

Conclusion

Relationships between the center staff and speakers can be built and maintained through empathetic listening. Moreover, by listening empathetically the staff can create an atmosphere in which the speaker feels comfortable expressing fears and frustrations related to oral communication competencies, to which the staff can respond demonstrating unconditional positive regard or confirmation.

The empathetic approach to listening can be a powerful competency for improving interpersonal skills of communication consultants. Some payoffs include improved working relationships, ability to sell ideas to management, ability to handle emotional individuals, and conducting more effective interviews (Burley-Allen, 1995). Empathetic listening can be used to solve problems, reduce tension, facilitate cooperation, promote communication, develop cognition, and enhance self-concept. True listening assumes that the speaker has worth, dignity, and something to offer; as a result, this attitude ultimately helps the speaker develop self-confidence.

Communication centers are positioned well to make significant contributions to the listening literature. To further research on the topic of listening, for example, empirical studies investigating the development of listening competencies of peer tutors can be conducted. Interviews with past and present tutors could yield rich data to test the hypothesis that peer tutors' listening competencies increase as a result of tutoring at the center. Staff members in training could be given a listening self-assessment at the start of their formal training. The same self-assessment can be distributed at the end of their training and/or at the end of their center employment.

Just as many centers have naturally focused on communication apprehension as a way to get the attention and interest of speakers, listening could offer a similar allure. Centers could strategically make listening a competency that speakers could work on by coming in for a session. Centers could create interactive activities that allow for self-assessment and competency development in private or semi-private, safe environments. As with communication apprehension, center-led listening activities could allow speakers additional aid in building listening competency at the center.

Additionally, many communication centers collect basic data from their clients at the start of a consultation. This data is often used to report to the administration. Centers could easily add a listening question to that data which could contribute to the current listening research. Answers to a question such as, "Have you ever had any formal training in listening?" could open up a brief conversation about the topic and offer an opportunity for the staff members to promote listening as a competency the speakers might want to come back to work on in the future. Speaker feedback can include a question or two about the consultation experience from a listening perspective. An example of such a question could be, "What behaviors did your consultant use that suggested they were listening?" Data from responses could be collected to further research about listening within the peer tutoring process.

Listening is a central topic for communication centers. For centers that concentrate solely on supporting public speaking competencies, the area of active listening offers a multitude of research possibilities. Faculty members from multiple disciplines often comment that they need to find ways to get their students to listen and pay attention to the presentations of their peers. Advocating for the advancement of the competencies of active listening and audience affirmation would be a good position for these centers to take. Though the potential in this area of research is clear, it remains to be seen whether challenge of researching this new emerging area will be met.

References

Baker, B. T., Watson, K. (2000). *Listen up.* New York: St. Martin's.

Buber, M. (1999). Distance and relation. In J. B. Agassi (Ed.), *Buber on psychology and psychotherapy: Essays, letters and dialogue* (pp. 3–16). Syracuse, NY: Syracuse University Press.

Burley-Allen, M. (1995). *Listening: The forgotten skill: A self-teaching guide* (2nd ed.)

New York, NY: John Wiley & Sons, Inc.

Cissna, K. N., & Anderson, R. (1994). Communication and the ground of dialogue. In R. Anderson, K. N. Cissna, & R. C. Arnett (Eds.), *The reach of dialogue: Confirmation, voice, and community* (pp. 9–30). Cresskill, NJ: Hampton Press.

Cissna, K. N., & Sieburg, E. (1981). Patterns of interpersonal confirmation and disconfirmation. In C. Wilder-Mott & J. Wealland (Eds.), *Rigor and imagination: Essays from the legacy of Gregory Bateson* (pp. 253–282). Skokie, IL: National Textbook.

Cobb, J. B. (2000). Listening within the social contexts of tutoring: Essential component of the mentoring relationship. *International Journal of Listening, 14*, 94–108.

Emery, D. L. (2006). Front and center: Speaking, listening, and assessment in the contexts of communication instruction. *International Journal of Listening, 20*, 62–65.

Ender, S. C., & Newton, F. B. (2000). *Students helping students: A guide for peer educators on college campuses.* San Francisco, CA: Jossey-Bass.

Proctor, R. E., & Wilcox, J. R. (1993). An exploratory analysis of responses to owned messages in interpersonal communication. *Et Cetera: A Review of General Semantics, 50*, 201–220.

Richmond, V. P. (2002). Teacher nonverbal immediacy: Uses and outcomes. In J. L. Chesebro & J. C. McCroskey (Eds.), *Communication for teachers* (pp. 65–80). Boston: Allyn and Bacon.

Rogers, C. R. (1992). The necessary and sufficient conditions of therapeutic personality change. *Journal of Counseling and Clinical Psychology, 60*(6), 827–832.

Stewart, J., & Logan, C. (2002). Empathetic and dialogic listening. In J. S. Stewart (Ed.), *Bridges, not walls: A book about interpersonal communication* (8th ed., pp. 208–229) Boston, MA: McGraw-Hill.

Ward, K., & Schwartzman, R. (2009). Building interpersonal relationships as a key to effective speaking center consultations. *Journal of Instructional Psychology, 36*(4), 363–372.

Wassmer, A. C. (1978). *Making contact: A guide to overcoming shyness, making new relationships, and keeping those you already have.* New York: Dial Press.

Wilde, S. M. (2005). Helping students have more positive experiences in the classroom: Part 1. *The Successful Professor, 1*(4), 3–5.

Yook, E. L. (2006). Assessment as meta-listening at the communication center. *International Journal of Listening, 20*, 66–68.

Chapter 18

Best Practices in Communication Center Training and Training Assessment

Rhonda Troillett and Kristen A. McIntyre

Communication centers have been a campus resource as early as the 1940s (Sapolsky & Byrd, 1986). Often overshadowed by their better-known counterpart the writing center, the existence and function of communication centers has ebbed and flowed with academic trends throughout the years. After reaching the height of their popularity during the 1990s, communication centers are now making a resurgence on college campuses across the nation. Currently, over 50 centers from around the country are registered with the National Association of Communication Centers (NACC) and new centers are in the development process (National Association of Communication Centers, n.d.).These communication centers are once again becoming an integral part of assisting students in their development of effective communication practices.

Peer-to-peer tutoring, made possible by graduate and undergraduate students, serves as the heart of these communication centers. Peer-to-peer tutoring has the ability to develop healthy and productive communication centers (Wilde, Cuny, &Vizzier, 2006). Therefore, the training of communication center staff is vital to not only a center's success but also to the success of the clients they serve. Unfortunately, current literature is limited when it comes to understanding staff training in communication centers. Consequently, this project explored how communication center staff are trained and evaluated in order to highlight current practices as well as to recommend potential best practices in communication center staff training and assessment.

The chapter first presents relevant literature in organizational communication training and specifically communication center training. A brief methodology is then presented and followed by results. The chapter concludes with a discussion of current and recommended best practices in communication center staff training.

Literature Review

Communication centers not only provide a valuable campus service to students, but also provide a student-based staff with a context for experiential learning. Kahl (2010) recommended that in order for students to truly make a difference "they must be engaged in communication scholarship beyond the classroom" (p. 299). In addition to using their communication knowledge to make a difference with their peers, work at the center can also help to prepare student staff for the professional expectations of the workplace. However, this academic and professional development in communication centers is greatly dependent upon the effectiveness of staff training and assessment. Consequently, the following literature review provides an overview of experiential-based organizational training and assessment, as well as recent research on communication center training and assessment.

Organizational Training and Assessment

Beebe, Mottet, and Roach (2004) define training as "the process of developing skills in order to more effectively perform a specific job or task" (p. 5). Training of organization personnel is necessary to empower and equip staff to contribute to the goals of the organization (Olaniyan & Ojo, 2008). Specifically, training provides staff with the knowledge and skills to perform their necessary duties. Undoubtedly, when communication center staff members participate in relevant training, the center's effectiveness is enhanced (Beebe et al., 2004).

At the heart of relevant and meaningful communication center staff training is experiential learning. Influenced by Dewey's (1937) assertion that true learning is based on relevant experience paired with structured reflection, Kolb (1984) offers a cycle of experiential learning, which serves as "a framework for examining and strengthening the critical linkages among education, work, and personal development" (p. 4). Individuals often prefer to learn in different ways, so four adaptive learning modes are used to address these preferences: concrete experience, reflective observation, abstract conceptualization, and active experimentation. Concrete experience requires the learner to fully involve themselves in new experiences (Kolb, 1984). Reflective observation invites the learner to "observe their experiences from many perspectives" (Kolb, 1984, p. 30). In the abstract conceptualization mode, learners "must be able to create concepts that integrate their observations into logically sound theories" (Kolb, 1984, p. 30). The active experimentation mode asks learners "to use these theories to make decisions and solve problems" (Kolb, 1984, p. 30). These four modes transfer into the sample words of feeling, watching, thinking, and doing, respectively. Given the individuality of learning preferences, it is imperative that the cycle is completed, integrating all modes of learning when teaching or training a concept.

Experiential Training Model

Beebe et al. (2004) employ a five-step experiential training model grounded in Kolb's (1984) learning cycle. The first step, tell, requires providing the information needed to learn a new skill (thinking stage). Show is demonstration of the skill, allowing others to model the behavior (watching stage). Invite is participant demonstration of the skill in an experiential activity, such as role-plays, skits, discussions, or simulations (doing stage). Encourage and correct are enacted simultaneously—encourage the things done well, but correct what could be improved. Integrated within the five-step training process is constant debriefing. Debriefing integrates reflection into the process, engaging the participants in application and transference of knowledge and skills developed in the training to professional and personal contexts (thinking and feeling stages) (Beebe et al., 2004).

Using a training model grounded in Kolb's (1984) experiential-based learning cycle for communication center staff training is beneficial for a variety of reasons. First, by rounding the learning cycle, each staff member is guaranteed some component of the training to be in his or her learning preference area, in turn helping staff members to be more open to stepping outside of that learning preference as well as providing multiple opportunities to internalize the knowledge and skills asked of them. Secondly, the learning cycle provides hands-on opportunities via the doing stage to practice and refine the necessary skills required in peer-to-peer tutoring as well as center protocol. Finally, participating in the learning cycle and experiencing the different learning preferences during their own training/learning can help staff members potentially identify and adapt more readily to specific client learning preferences during tutoring sessions.

Training Assessment

Training must be assessed to ensure its efficiency and effectiveness (Beebe et al., 2004). Because communication centers are uniquely situated within the context of higher education, the dual role of students as trainees highlights the increased importance of learning/training assessment. Communication center student staff not only must enact specific center-related learning outcomes but also ideally should be able to connect and apply other relevant inter- and cross-discipline learning outcomes to their communication center experiences.

Beebe et al. (2004) define training assessment as the "systematic process of evaluating training programs to ensure that they meet the needs of the trainees and organization" (p. 239). Additionally, Huba and Freed (2000) provide a more in-depth definition: "Assessment is the process of gathering and discussing information from multiple sources and diverse sources in order to develop a deep understanding of what students know, understand, and can do with their knowledge as a result of their educational experiences; the process culminates when assessment results are used to improve subsequent learning" (p. 8). Praslova (2010) stresses specifically that assessment and evaluation should be measured through a systematic approach, clarity of purpose, and alignment of educational outcomes and methods to inform future trainings. Assessment is a four-step process beginning with the development of intended learning outcomes, followed by selection of direct and indirect assessment measures, then the creation of experiences designed to meet the outcomes, and concluding with the discussion and implementation of assessment results to improve future learning (Huba & Freed, 2000).

First and foremost, in order to accurately assess the success of a specific training, trainings must have clear learning outcomes. Outcomes are explicit expectations of "what students should know, understand, and be able to do with their knowledge" (Huba & Freed, 2000, p. 10). Learning outcomes should be observable, measurable, attainable, and specific (Beebe et al., 2004). Establishing concrete learning outcomes enables trainers to better select training strategies designed to help trainees learn required information and develop necessary skills. Additionally, concrete learning outcomes provide a structured frame for training assessment.

To determine whether or not learning outcomes have been met, direct and indirect assessment methods help us understand what students have learned: "Direct methods prompt students to represent or demonstrate their learning or produce work so that observers can assess how well students' texts or responses fit institution- or program-level expectations" (Maki, 2004, p.158). Direct assessment can be determined by testing knowledge, projects, or presentations. Indirect methods "focus on perceptions of student learning by asking students or others to respond to a set or series of questions" (Maki, 2004, p. 213). Indirect measures can be accomplished by informal observation, self reflection, or survey results.

Feedback is an important method of indirect assessment providing necessary direction in modification of student trainee behaviors (Allen, 2006), as well as assessing trainer effectiveness. DeWine (2001) states that effective "feedback should describe problematic behavior that the receiver can correct" (p. 309). Specifically, there are three types of feedback, according to DeWine, that are helpful for assessing student trainees: evaluative, interpretive, and descriptive. Evaluative feedback critiques someone's behavior, interpretive feedback analyzes the behavior, and descriptive feedback provides feedback on behaviors without evaluating them. All three types of feedback play an important role in training. However, evaluative and interpretive feedback is particularly important in student trainee skill-development as they identify weaknesses and provide suggestions for modifying the performed skill behavior.

Crucial to the assessment process is the use of direct and indirect assessment data to inform future training and learning. Wehlburg (2007) argues that assessing learning

> should produce changes in the curriculum, pedagogy, or in the planned experiences of students; however, it is much less common to discuss the modifications in the outcomes (or perhaps the goals) that result from better or different student learning experiences. This level of reflection moves beyond the point of closing the feedback loop, for it describes what happens after the feedback loop is closed. (p. 1)

Clearly, it is not enough to assess communication center training learning outcomes. Improving learning involves understanding what is and is not effective in a learning or training situation and adapting the design of future learning experiences in the hope of better achieving the intended outcome.

Communication Center Training and Assessment

The communication center student staff training process is not well documented. However, Wilde et al. (2006) described their communication center staff as having the common goal of "fulfilling the center's mission of supporting its clients in their ongoing process of becoming more confident and competent oral communicators" (p. 70). In reaching that mission the center employs specific training. The interns, or "junior staff," are enrolled in a three-hour semester class focused on peer-to-peer tutoring and workshop facilitation and shadow more experienced staff (Wilde et al., 2006).

In reviewing communication center websites listed in the database of the NACC, training information was either non-existent or vague. The majority of training information found mentioned merely that staff was trained. This is not particularly surprising given that the target users of the websites are primarily communication center clients. However, one exception was the University of Delaware: "The Oral Communication Fellows are a specifically trained group of students. Each member of our team is not only a communication major, but has successfully completed an intense public speaking class, gone through an interview and essay application process, and had a semester-long Oral Communication Fellows training program" (University of Delaware, n.d.).

Though research and public information regarding communication center training is sparse, the *Tutor Training and Certification Program,* approved by the National Association of Communication Centers in March, 2010, (Turner & Sheckels, 2010) outlines the recommended procedures for selection, training, and continued evaluation of tutors. However, only three communication centers to date have received certification: Randolph-Macon College, the University of Southern Mississippi, and the University of North Carolina-Greensboro.

In sum, staff training is foundational to a communication center's success. Unfortunately, little is known about the landscape of training in this particular context. Due to the potential academic and professional impact communication centers may have on both their student staff and clients, an understanding of the systematic approach to experiential-based training and assessment of communication center staff is needed.

Method

Participants and Data Collection

Upon receiving Internal Review Board approval, personnel responsible for performing communication center student staff training were invited to participate in an online survey. Participants were recruited via the Commlistserv (devoted to individuals with vested interest in communication centers) and the Basiccc listserv (devoted to individuals with a vested interest in the basic communication course). Of those invited, 29 participants completed the survey. From the 29 participants, 6 indicated a willingness to participate in semi-structured phone interviews. Of those six interviewed, five (83 percent) participants directed or co-directed centers and one (17 percent) served as a communication center graduate assistant.

A variety of center contexts are represented by the participants. The centers represented include four communication centers with paid undergraduate tutors. Of these four, only three provided semester long tutor training; however, one of these would also hire tutors without the training class but provided hours of shadowing experienced tutors. The one center without a specific training class would train tutors by requiring reading of an extensive training manual prior to working, then shadowing of experienced tutors until a level of comfort was developed. The first few tutoring sessions were observed by experienced tutors. The two centers without paid tutors had a credit-bearing course. Both centers required reading of a manual or handbook, as well as an initial training meeting before the semester began.

Data Analysis

Survey data related to communication center training was used quantitatively to provide descriptive statistics. Interview data was approached qualitatively through inductive analysis. Participant responses were broken into units and coded for unique categories. Categories were collapsed and themes were determined by frequency and intensity.

Results

Survey

The survey helped to provide a general overview of communication centers. Historically, the majority of communication centers were founded between 1985 and 2010. Seventy-nine percent of the participants had funded centers with over half of these funded more than $10,000. Most centers had between 1 and 1,000 student visits per semester. The range of services included recording presentations, presentation critiques, outline preparation, access to practice rooms, assistance with online research, departmental and campus workshops, and assistance with departmental assignments.

Results showed that undergraduate students primarily staff the communication centers. Sixty percent of undergraduate staff is paid a stipend. Primary duties of undergraduate staff included presentation video critiques, tutoring other students, providing example presentations for classes, and scheduling client appointments.

Training is provided in 96 percent of the communication centers represented in the survey. Length of training times ranged from twice a year to a semester long course. Center directors are primarily responsible for providing undergraduate staff training. Training focuses on coaching/tutoring students, effective presentation development, critiquing presentation delivery, professionalism, customer service, and PowerPoint creation and integration.

Interviews

Selection of Staff
Forty-four (88 percent) comments reflect an application process for the selection of staff. This process includes all or some of the following: an interview, prerequisite of courses, and other requirements such as a specific GPA, résumé, cover

letter, and/or commitment to stay until graduation. Additionally, five (10 percent) comments mentioned the need of a letter of reference or faculty recommendation.

Training
The major themes related to training of undergraduate staff include experiential activities, informal shadowing, and self-directed training. Fifty-three (32 percent) participant comments express experiential learning as the primary method of staff training. Participants described experiential learning as active engagement in activities using role-play, simulations, practice or engagement, and/or participation in workshops where trainees are given the opportunity to enact the expected behavior.

The second theme, informal shadowing, is reflected in 36 (22 percent) comments. Informal shadowing consists of new staff observing experienced personnel enacting expected behavior to learn, and then new staff practicing the expected behavior are observed by experienced staff. Experienced personnel range from any returning staff, those who have worked a year, tutors who have accomplished a level of training to be deemed ready to tutor, to those who are two semesters out of the training class. A tied second theme includes the use of self-directed training resources and/or materials. Thirty-six (22 percent) participant comments describe self-directed training as using assigned readings, training manuals, guide sheets, and/or training modules to help train center staff.

Evaluation
The evaluation process of center staff is overwhelmingly achieved by evaluative feedback. Evaluative feedback, indicated by 42 (45 percent) participant comments, includes one-on-one meetings, professionalism reports, coaching, and/or corrective procedures. Supervising personnel perform all feedback. In addition to evaluative feedback, participants mentioned the use of staff self-evaluative methods 18 (19 percent) times. Self-evaluation is often represented by reflective journals and/or self-critiques of recorded presentations. Many centers require clients to provide an immediate evaluation of the session with the tutor. Client evaluation using surveys, anonymous comment cards, and workshop participants is mentioned 13 (14 percent) times. All of these methods previously mentioned are achieved through indirect measures. Direct assessment through tests or weekly forms was rarely mentioned in the interviews (5 percent). Only one mention (1 percent) of the use of peer evaluation was reported.

Improving Future Learning
The role of evaluative methods to inform future trainings, though not a strong theme, is reflected in 16 (17 percent) comments. Participants mention the significance of assessing initial training and how that affects the daily practice of helping others, as well as discussing what needs to be changed in training to

make it more effective. However, one participant specifically mentioned that assessment was not used to the extent that it should to improve staff training.

Discussion

The survey and interview data provide valuable information on how communication center training is facilitated and assessed. The following first aligns our findings within the framework of Beebe's et al. (2004) training model and then the requirements for the *Tutor Training and Certification Program* (Turner & Sheckels, 2010).

Training Model Analysis

The steps of Beebe's et al. (2004) training model are present in the data regarding the training of communication center tutors. Specifically, the steps of tell, show, and invite are an integral part of center training. Telling is letting trainees know what it is they need to do. When addressing the tell step of Beebe's et al. model, participants mentioned the use of classes (prerequisite or training classes), online modules, manuals/handbooks, and assigned readings. Each of these approaches work to provide trainees with pertinent information needed in their tutoring experiences.

The next step, show, is accomplished by the demonstration of the skill to be learned. Variations of shadowing are the primary form of showing in center training. The length and type of shadowing varied across centers. One university stated that the process of shadowing occurs until the tutor has a skill level acceptable to be a peer-to-peer tutor as judged by an experienced tutor. However, other universities stated that shadowing ranges from no official shadowing with only indirect observation, or two to three hours to approximately two weeks of shadowing with indirect observation thereafter. The entire process of showing allows the trainee to prepare for the invitation to enact the same behaviors or skill.

The invite step involves practicing the skill. The primary form of skill practice in center training is the use of role-play. Every participant mentioned the use of role-playing to train center staff. Role-plays are particularly useful because they provide the trainee with an opportunity to enact and practice the skill in anticipated situations. Another form of skill development mentioned by participants is the use of discussion. Discussion was commonly associated as a follow-up activity to role-play activities or simulations. Additionally, discussion is also

mentioned as an important component after assigned reading, or within designated times such as meetings, or as a part of the shadowing process.

Beebe et al. (2004) also use the steps of encourage and correct as means to
complete the experiential learning cycle through evaluation. Beebe et al. recommend to "first offer encouragement by pointing out what the trainees are
doing right rather than first telling them what they are doing wrong" (p. 80).
Another part of the encouraging process is to ask the trainees what they see that
they are doing right. This provides an opportunity to suggest specific corrections
for performance improvement.

The reciprocal nature of shadowing lends itself well to the correct step.
Shadowing not only provides the opportunity for a trainee to observe the skill in
action, it also provides the opportunity for an experienced person to observe a
new trainee enacting the skill, and consequently, provides moments for correction. One participant mentioned that for continued correction during a normal
day tutors are evaluated through indirect observation or listening by a more experienced person. This procedure poses an opportunity to ask the tutor, "Why do
you think she or he was having this trouble?" and "How could you have handled
it differently?"

Discussion of performance and/or feedback provides a more direct approach
to the correct step in trainee development (Allen, 2006). With regard to performance evaluation, one center commented on the process of professional reports.
These reports allowed the director (when completed by another supervising person, such as a graduate assistant or other experienced staff member) and tutor to
discuss and know where they stood on the performance of duties and expectations. Additionally, many of the centers commented on immediate feedback. In
one instance, the interviewee stated that when a graduate assistant sees a situation that could have been handled differently, they approach the tutor and discuss with them other ways they could have handled the situation. Another method of evaluation is viewed from the perspective of the client. Many centers
mentioned the immediate completion of a survey detailing how the session went
and if there were any recognized areas of improvement.

Finally, the role of self-reflection was also a strongly mentioned approach
to the correct step in trainee skill development. Participants mentioned the use of
self-reflection in terms of tutoring sessions, recorded presentations, and the use
of the center handbook. Specifically, one participant responded that the self-
evaluation process enables the student tutor to reflect on how a tutoring session
went, as well as things the tutor would like to see changed in the center. Another
participant mentioned that the self-evaluation process helped the tutor refer back
to the handbook when they were not sure of the correct procedure.

Tutor Training and Certification Analysis

The communication center training certification program can be helpful in the development and continued training of center staff. Certification is outlined in three specific categories: selection of staff, training of staff, and continuing evaluation of staff. The following analysis aligns our data with the *Tutor Training and Certification Program* (Turner & Sheckels, 2010).

First, certification requires that center staff be selected through the process of faculty endorsements followed by an interview. The research in this paper found that even though an interview is used in most hiring situations, the endorsement of faculty is not widely used. The certificate program suggests that tutors be "smart, articulate, motivated, sensitive, enthusiastic, and ethical" (Turner & Sheckels, 2010). Though the selection of tutors based on characteristics was not a major theme in the interviews or survey, one interviewee stated that if the reason for applying was to help others, "they are in."

Secondly, the certificate program recommends that tutors have both a significant amount of training and tutoring supervision. Our findings indicate that time spent training tutors varied from institution to institution. Supervision, from the perspective of the certificate, is a form of shadowing. Some centers maintained specific time frames of shadowing, while others modified training times to the individual trainee's competence of modeling appropriate behaviors. Shadowing was often referred to as a reciprocated method. Once the trainee felt a level of comfort in tutoring, the experienced personnel would shadow or observe the tutor in action.

Modes of training mentioned in the certificate are diverse. Some institutions commented on the requirement of courses before being considered for the role of a tutor. Based on the data, the mode of training in most centers is predominantly experiential. Based on the results, experiential training includes the use of role play. However, there are many indirect methods that include sessions with discussion of assigned readings, training manuals, guide sheets, training modules, online instruction, and workshops.

The topics included in the training are too exhaustive to comment on here. However, one of the topics is administrative duties. Almost all the participants mentioned role playing duties such as customer service, scheduling, phones, and working with databases. Interestingly, only one participant mentioned the importance of training in emergency procedures.

Finally, certification requires the continued evaluation of tutors. Our findings suggest center staff is continually evaluated formally and informally in a variety of ways. Specifically, continued evaluation takes the form of meetings aimed to assess performance, reports on professional behavior, and coaching or correction by experienced personnel. Additionally, some participants mentioned the use of client satisfaction surveys to evaluate tutor performance. One institute required tutors to complete a lengthy report at the end of every shift to determine how many clients came in, if shift mates were on time, if there were any problems, or what changes they would like to see at mid-term.

The value of receiving certification from the NACC has several implications. One comment that was frequent among the participants was that the certification program builds community. Explicitly, the certificate program builds community through credibility. The credibility is established through official national recognition that standards of training are acknowledged and implemented in a center. The value to an individual student can be evident through the use of the recognized certification on résumés. Specifically, one participant commented that certification "helps us individually to put on résumés. It boosts our image to students and faculty for our center—to nationally certify."

Best Practices

Though communication centers are diverse, our findings suggest that despite differences in what our centers and staffs look like, there are important experiential-based consistencies in our approaches to staff training and assessment. The following best practices are grounded both in the results of the data as well as key components of the literature review. The promoted practices include valuing explicit learning outcomes, employing experiential learning, developing a guided training process, training for emergency protocols, using assessment data to inform future learning (close the training loop), and recognizing the accomplishments of staff.

Value Explicit Learning Outcomes
Outcomes are necessary to determine that training was successfully accomplished (Huba & Freed, 2000). It is imperative that learning outcomes are stated to all trainees to provide initial expectations of outcomes. The importance of educational or training outcomes was not specifically mentioned in the interviews; however, it is probable that these outcomes are outlined in the handbooks, manuals, or syllabi. The significance of aligning outcomes with the operation of the communication center is pivotal to determine if the training goals meet the expected outcomes. It is important that these outcomes are clearly defined. Outcomes allow confirmation that explicit expectations are met by the training.

Employ Experiential Learning Strategies
Relying solely on printed materials to train staff dramatically limits a tutor's ability to learn fully expected behaviors and does not provide the tutor with the cyclical approach to learning advocated by Kolb (1984). Experiential learning is vital to help center staff experience and learn the necessary skills for their position (Beebe et al., 2004). Specifically, our data emphasizes the varied use of

role-play, simulations, and shadowing to help center staff understand and perform their duties.

Develop a Guided Process
The guided process of training allows trainees to develop a deep understanding of what they should know and how that knowledge functions as the result of their experience (Huba & Freed, 2000). The University of Southern Mississippi employs an exceptional guided approach to staff training. The following is an abbreviated version of their systematic process:

- Debrief about day-to-day process in the center
- Read and discuss literature focused on tutoring
- Discuss the tutoring process
- Shadow an experienced tutor with discussion of the process
- Role play tutoring by watching a speech and providing feedback

The process at the University of Southern Mississippi is more detailed than the steps mentioned and generally takes an entire semester. However, since not all centers have the opportunity to have an entire semester to train tutors it is recommended that this guided process be adapted to a specific center's unique context.

Develop Emergency Training Procedures
Based on the expectations of the certification process, the increase in school shootings across the nation (Gosine, 2008), and the increased awareness of campus crises, it is necessary for communication centers to develop protocol and implement training for emergency procedures. Emergency procedures are standards established to protect and save lives. Consequently, emergency procedures might include, but should not be limited to, campus shooting, earthquake, tornado, fire, health related events, or suicide or personal threats. Staff should understand the significance of each possible emergency. A handbook outlining protocol for managing each situation should be paired with training focused on enacting and practicing the protocol within each context. The impact of these procedures might literally save the lives of our students and staff.

Close the Training Assessment Loop
The evaluation process provides valuable support for the improvement of future trainings. Since the use of assessment data to inform future staff training was not a significant theme in our data, it is important to emphasize the need for a concrete assessment plan that goes beyond the closed feedback loop and instead employs our training assessment "as an upward spiral, still identifying goals and

outcomes, still measuring those outcomes, but with ever-increasing improvement of the quality of student learning as the spiral moves upward" (Wehlburg, 2007, p. 1).

Specifically, careful, varied assessment of learning outcomes should serve to inspire the refinement and elevation of communication center staff training through the continued implementation of innovative experiential learning approaches to reinforce as well as strengthen areas of staff competence. Essentially, if one component of the training is meeting its intended learning outcome, how might revision of the outcome work to elevate staff skill level and what learning activities would now become useful in meeting the new outcome? Conversely, if another component of the training is not achieving its intended learning outcome, what different learning strategies could be employed to help staff meet the outcome? The use of assessment to move past the feedback loop situates staff trainings within a constant state of revisionary opportunities to push staff, and, consequently, communication centers, to reach their greatest potential.

Recognize Staff
Finally, it is always important to remember to honor work well done. Participants emphasized that staff recognition is imperative. Rewards can come in the form of personal rewards, recognition, and/or student appreciation week. Recognition can come in many forms—acknowledging the co-creation of resources, telling them every day how important the work is that they do, or the process of shout-outs in meetings. Shout-outs are a combined staff effort used by one university to appreciate and celebrate all the contributions of individual staff members within the previous week.

Conclusion

While this project focused on understanding the training and training assessment approaches implemented in communication centers, the uniquely situated context of communication centers within establishments of higher learning brings a distinctive complexity to assessing student staff learning. This project focused primarily on understanding the staff/employee component of communication centers. However, it is both important and intriguing to investigate more fully the student aspect of our center staff. Because the center provides an experiential opportunity for students to apply their communication knowledge as well as other college learning, stepping back and understanding how students are making connections between their center experiences, their college curricula, as well as other life experiences could help us to better design training experiences that function in dual capacities—center protocol as well as transference of student skills and knowledge. Additionally, because this study had a modest sample size and took a general approach to understanding the overall approaches to training and training assessment in communication centers, it would be beneficial to conduct a more in-depth study investigating how centers train on specific topics, such as presentation feedback, customer service, and, hopefully, emergency procedures.

Communication centers are important resources for many students on college campuses. These centers often serve their respective departments and campus as a whole. Training, based in evaluative processes, is undoubtedly beneficial to the success of communication centers. In the hope of enhancing existing and new center staff training, this chapter offered six best practices promoting the valuing of explicit learning outcomes, employing experiential training methods, developing a guided process, developing emergency training procedures, closing the training assessment loop, and honoring work well done.

Additionally, this chapter advocates the NACC's *Tutor Training and Certification Program* (Turner & Sheckels, 2010). The certification process is valuable in that it provides a fairly standardized yet adaptable approach to tutor training, creates credibility and community for those centers seeking certification, and aligns well with the best practices advocated in current practice as well as relevant literature. As existing and new communication centers continue to establish themselves as reputable campus resources, consistent staff training, grounded in best practices and certified by the NACC, may do much to help us push through the shadow of our writing center counterpart and validate and elevate not only the credibility of individual centers but also the reputation and visibility of all communication centers.

References

Allen, M. J. (2006). *Assessing general education programs.* Boston, MA: Anker Publishing Company, Inc.

Beebe, S. A., Mottet, T. P., & Roach, K. D. (2004). *Training and development: Enhancing communication and leadership skills.* Boston, MA: Pearson Education, Inc.

Dewey, J. (1937). *Democracy and education: An introduction to the philosophy of education.* New York: The MacMillan Company.

DeWine, S. (2001). *The consultant's craft: Improving organizational communication* (2nd ed.). New York: St. Martin's.

Gosine, S. (2008). Students killing students. *Suite 101 Educational Issues.* Retrieved from http://www.suite101.com/content/students-killing-students-a47304.

Huba, M. E., & Freed, J. E. (2000). *Learner-centered assessment on college campuses: Shifting the focus from teaching to learning.* Boston, MA: Allyn and Bacon.

Kahl, D. H. (2010). Making a difference: (Re)Connecting communication scholarship with pedagogy. *Journal of Applied Communication Research, 38(3),* 298–302.

Kolb, D. A. (1984). *Experiential learning: Experience as the source of learning and development.* Englewood Cliffs, NJ: Prentice-Hall, Inc.

Maki, P. L. (2004). *Assessing for learning: Building a sustainable commitment across the institution.* Sterling, VA: American Association for Health Education.

National Association of Communication Centers. (n.d.). *Directory of Centers.* Retrieved from http://www.communicationcenters.org.

Olaniyan, D. A., & Ojo, L. B. (2008). Staff training and development: A vital tool for organizational effectiveness. *European Journal of Scientific Research, 24(3),* 326–331.

Praslova, L. (2010). Adaptation of Kirkpatrick's four level model of training criteria to assessment of learning outcomes and program evaluation in higher education. *Education, Assessment, Evaluation, and Accountability, 22,* 215–225.

Randolph Macon College. (2008). *Higgins Academic Center: Speaking across the curriculum.* Retrieved from http://www.rmc.edu/offices/higgins-academic-center/SAC/speakingcntr.aspx

Sapolsky, B. S., & Byrd, N. (1986). A survey of communication research centers. *Association for Communication Administration Bulletin, 55,* 46–50.

Turner, K. J., & Sheckels, T. F. (2010). *Tutor training and certification programs.* Retrieved from http://www.communicationcenters.org.

University of Delaware. (n.d.) *Oral communication fellows.* Retrieved from http://www.udel.edu/communication/activities_oralcomm.html

Wehlburg, C. M. (2007). Closing the feedback loop is not enough: The assessment spiral. *Assessment Update, 19(2),* 1–15.

Wilde, S. M., Cuny, K. M., & Vizzier, A. L. (2006). Peer-to-peer tutoring: A model for utilizing empathetic listening to build client relationships in the communication center. *International Journal of Listening, 20,* 70–75.

Index

communicative norms, 91–93, 94, 97–98. *See also* discipline-specific expectations

competence, 4, 58, 206–7

The Competent Speaker evaluation form, 203, 205

complex material, 245–46

computer mediated communication (CMC), xviii, 217–29; advantages of, 219–22; challenges of, 222–28; defined, 187, 188; in use at UNCG, 218–19. *See also* course management systems (CMS); online communication centers

computer-supported learning system (CECIL), 205–6

conferences, xii–xiii

confidence: biology students and, 116–17, 121; communication centers and, 5; effects of space on, 168–70; empowerment and, 47; feedback and, 170; peer tutoring and, 64–65; of tutors, 180

confirmation, 253–54

constructive criticism. *See* feedback

consultants. *See* tutors

consultation report forms, 77, 169

convenience, 190–91, 219, 221

conversations, 13–14, 16–17, 180, 183, 239

course management systems (CMS), xviii, 187–96; benefits of, 190–92; defined, 187, 188; faculty and, 157; incorporation of into communication centers, 192–95; strategies for success with, 195; widespread use of, 188–90. *See also* computer mediated communication (CMC); online communication centers

courses: advanced, 35; basic, 34, 72, 89, 199; communication intensive, 73; delivery in, 26; speaking intensive, 83, 89

course standardization, 45–46, 47–48

Crick, N., 167

critical thinking, xvi, 13–21; advice on, 17–20; biology students and, 128; combined centers and, 183; as conversation, 16–17; defined, 14; in-

creasing emphasis on, 21; oral communication and, 13–16

Cronin, M., & Glenn, P., 27, 35, 73

Cuny, Kimberly, xviii

Curto, Karen, xvii

CXC (communication across the curriculum). *See* communication across the curriculum (CAC/CXC)

Dannels, Deanna, xvii, 31, 35, 74

Darling, A. L., 31, 94

Darling, A. L., & Dannels, Deanna, 34

data collection, 137–39

Davis, Alyssa, xviii

delivery: biology students and, 116–17, 119, 121, 123; discipline-specific expectations and, 77–78; online communication centers and, 206–7; overemphasis on, 26

deMarrais, K. B., & LeCompte, M. D., 43, 47

DePauw University, 56–57, 61, 74

descriptive norms, 134

design departments, 90, 93–94

Dewey, John, 14, 258

DeWine, S., 260

digital natives, 234–35

Dillard, J. P., & Pfau, M., 148

directors of communication centers. *See* administration

disciplinarity. *See* discipline-specific expectations

discipline-specific expectations, 71–85, 87–110; adapting to, 80–82; approaches to education and, 72–75; assignments and, 97–98; challenges of, 91–95; communication centers and, 80–85; CXC and, 88–91; ethnographic approach and, 95–103; faculty support and, 157; liberal arts and, 31; reframing communication center role and, 103–9; at University of Mary Washington, 77–80

Docan-Morgan, T., 33

Downs, E., Boyson, A. R., Alley, H., & Bloom, N. R., 203, 210

Dresner, E., & Herring, S. C., 226, 227

Durkin, K., Conti-Ramsden, G., & Walker, A. J., 221

dynamic activity systems, 99

peer tutors. *See* tutors
The Peer Writing Tutor Alumni Research
    Project, 56
Pensoneau-Conway, Sandra, xvii
perceived barriers, 135, 136
perceived behavioral control, 133, 148–49
perceived benefits, 135, 136
perceived impoliteness, 224–25
perceived need for help, 208
perceived threats, 135, 136
persistence rates, xvi, 6–9
personal lives, 63
persuasion theory, 132–36
persuasive messages, 131–43; develop-
    ment of, 131–32; dissemination of,
    140–41; exposure to, 142; formative
    research and, 137–41; message
    campaign assessment and, 141–42;
    methodologies and, 137–41; persua-
    sion theories and, 132–36
Peters, J. D., 25
Pew Internet and American Life Project,
    217
Pew Research Center, 217, 234
philosophy departments, 78, 79
Piccoli, G., Ahmad, R., & Ives, B., 200,
    201
political science, 77–78
PowerPoint, 237–38, 239–41, 244–46
praise, 226
Praslova, L., 260
preproduction research, 132
presentation software, xviii, 237–38,
    239–41, 243–44, 244–46
Preston, M. M., 26
Prezi (online application), 243–44
privacy, 228
Proctor, R. E., & Wilcox, J. R., 251
production of knowledge, 84–85
production testing, 132

questioning, 105–6, 107–9, 180–81, 252
questionnaires, 138–39, 151–52

radical pedagogies, 42–43, 48–49, 51
Rafoth, B. A., & Rubin, D. L., 178
Ramirez, Artemio, 226
Rao, Anand, xvii
record of consultation forms, 77, 169
recruiting, xvii, 104, 105

reflecting skills, 252–53
reflective listening, 252
reframing: of communication center roles,
    103–9; ethnographic approach and,
    96–103; of tutor/student interaction,
    107–9; of tutor training, 105–7
Reigstad, T. J., & McAndrew, D. A., 178
relational genre knowledge, 98
remediation, 166–68, 172
remix, 166–67, 172
reporting systems, 77, 169, 182–83
research methods, 137
resistance/reluctance, 20, 61, 184
resource gathering, 192–93
respectability of communication field, 83
retention, xvi, 3–10; defined, 6; factors
    affecting, 3–5; persistence rates and,
    6–9
rhetoric, 15–16
Rittschof, K., & Griffin, B., 55
Rogers, C. R., 253
Rogers, E. M., 24–25
role-playing, 265
roles: of communication centers, 103–9; of
    students, 99; in teams, 92; of tutors,
    57–58, 100–103
Romerhausen, Nick, xvii
Roscoe, R., & Chi, M., 55
Rose, N. E., 44

salient beliefs, 150, 159n4
San Jose State University, xii
Santra, T., & Giri, V. N., 219
satisfaction, 202
Sawyer, C. R., & Behnke, R. R., 205
Sawyer, K., 172
Schneider, A., 25
Schramm, Wilbur, 25
scientific presentations, 114–15, 127–28
self-direction, 18–19, 264
self-efficacy, 135
self-reflection: for tutors, 266
shadowing, 58, 264, 265, 266, 267
Shamoon, L. K., & Burns, D. H., 180
shared resources, 176
Sherblom, J. C., 202
Shor, I., 42
Skype, 194
social media, 234
social norms approach, 132, 133–34

About the Contributors

Shawn Apostel is communication coordinator for the Noel Studio for Academic Creativity and teaches public speaking at Eastern Kentucky University. He is a doctoral candidate in rhetoric and technical communication at Michigan Technological University.

Wendy Atkins-Sayre is assistant professor of communication studies and Speaking Center director at The University of Southern Mississippi. Her research interests center on identity as constructed through discourse, both the theoretical study of rhetoric and the pragmatic study of rhetoric through communication centers. She has published in the areas of social movement rhetoric, rhetoric and politics, identity rhetoric, and visual rhetoric. She received her PhD from the University of Georgia in 2005.

Trudy Bayer is assistant professor and coordinator of the Public Speaking Proficiency Program in the Communication Department at Slippery Rock University of Pennsylvania. Before joining SRU in 2007, she was a faculty member in the communication department at the University of Pittsburgh and the founding director of the University of Pittsburgh's Oral Communication Lab. Her research interests focus primarily on science communication, and she has published articles on educational practices to promote oral competencies with science students. She received her PhD from the University of Pittsburgh in 1990.

Russell Carpenter is director of the Noel Studio for Academic Creativity and assistant professor in the department of English and theatre at Eastern Kentucky University. Carpenter received a PhD in texts & technology from the University of Central Florida in 2009.

Rose Clark-Hitt is a doctoral candidate in the department of communication at Michigan State University. For two years she was a communication consultant at the Ernst & Young Accounting Business Communication Center in the Eli Broad College of Business at Michigan State University. Her research interests involve persuasion, social influence, and supportive communication in the contexts of health and organizational communication.

Lynn O. Cooper is associate professor of communication at Wheaton College. Her research interests include listening competency, small group leadership, and organizational communication. She has presented and published articles on the topics of listening theory, interpersonal and workplace competency, nonprofit consulting, educational assessment, and web applications for the basic course. She received her PhD from the University of Illinois in 1991.

Kim Cuny has served as director of The University Speaking Center at the University of North Carolina at Greensboro for 10 years. Kim earned the Communication Centers Section of the National Communication Association's Beth Von Till Newcomer Award and the National Association of Communication Centers Ferguson Research Award. Kim's research interests focus on communication centers, while her creative work is in storytelling and process drama. She received her MFA from the University of North Carolina at Greensboro in 2007.

Karen A. Curto is lecturer in the department of biological sciences at the University of Pittsburgh. Her research interests include teaching and learning in biological science and basic science research on mechanisms of cell signaling and reproductive toxicology. She has published articles on technological support for oral communication instruction to biology students and basic research. She received her PhD from the West Virginia University in 1983.

Deanna P. Dannels is professor and director of graduate teaching assistant development in the department of communication and associate director of the Campus Writing and Speaking Program at North Carolina State University. Her current research explores theoretical and pedagogical frameworks for communication across the curriculum and protocols for designing, implementing and assessing oral communication within the disciplines. Her primary theoretical contributions include the "communication in the disciplines" and "relational genre knowledge" frameworks. She received her PhD from the University of Utah in 1999.

Alyssa Davis is the Online Speaking Center administrator and a graduate assistant at the University of North Carolina at Greensboro's Speaking Center. She is currently working towards her master's degree in communication studies at UNC Greensboro.

Jennifer Butler Ellis is the director of the Ernst & Young Leadership Professional Development Center in the department of accountancy at Northern

Illinois University. Prior to working at Northern Illinois University, Jennifer served as director of the Ernst & Young Accounting Business Communication Center at Michigan State University for over seven years. Her research interests focus on memorable messages, voice, silence, and feedback delivery. She received her PhD from Michigan State University in 2001.

Amy L. Housley Gaffney is assistant professor in the department of communication and division of instructional communication at the University of Kentucky. Her research is focused on instructional communication as well as communication across the curriculum. She recently led a proposal to implement a multimodal communication across the curriculum program at the University of Kentucky, where she also teaches integrated communication (oral, written, visual) in a general education curriculum. She received her PhD from North Carolina State University in 2010.

Michael L. King is a doctoral candidate at The University of Southern Mississippi, has served as a peer consultant at USM's Speaking Center, and was the recipient of the 2011 National Association of Communication Center's Outstanding Peer Consultant Award. His research interests include the study of attitudes toward communication center usage and upward communication within organizational settings.

Luke LeFebvre is director of the Cheyenne, Henderson, and West Charleston Communication Labs and tenure track instructor for the department of communication at the College of Southern Nevada. His research interests include classroom communication and instructional processes, as well as the organizational and relational dynamics of communication centers. He received his PhD from Wayne State University in 2010.

Corey Jay Liberman is assistant professor of communication arts at Marymount Manhattan College. His research interests include the effects of organizational identification on work processes and job satisfaction, organizational and societal communication networks, social influence in interpersonal relationships and during the small group process, and persuasion in the context of health communication. He received his PhD from Rutgers University in 2008.

Casey Malone Maugh is assistant professor of communication studies and Speaking & Writing Center director at the University of Southern Mississippi, Gulf Coast. Her research interests focus on public memory, visual rhetoric, and identity politics of race and gender. She has published work in the areas of visual rhetoric, critical race studies, political rhetoric, and gender studies. She received her PhD from the Pennsylvania State University in 2007.

Kristen A. McIntyre is director of the Communication Skill Center, director of the Basic Communication Course, and assistant professor in the department of speech communication at the University of Arkansas at Little Rock. Her research interests focus on service-learning, basic course assessment, and communication training and development. She received her PhD from North Dakota State University in 2006.

Michelle A. Moreau is the coordinator for the Communication Center at James Madison University, a position she has held for the past six years. She is also a faculty member in the School of Communication Studies. She received her MA from the University of Alabama and is currently in JMU's Assessment and Measurement PhD program.

A. Paige Normand is the Writing and Communication Specialist for the Learning Centers at James Madison University. She consults for both the JMU Communication Center and Writing Center. She is also a faculty member in the School of Media Art and Design. She received her MA from the University of Texas in 2006 where she was the outreach coordinator for the undergraduate Writing Center and taught for the division of rhetoric and writing.

Sandra L. Pensoneau-Conway is assistant professor in the department of speech communication at Southern Illinois University—Carbondale. She received her PhD in speech communication from Southern Illinois University Carbondale in 2006.

P. Anand Rao is associate professor of communication in the department of English, linguistics, and communication, and director of the Speaking Intensive Program at the University of Mary Washington. His research interests include the study of visual rhetoric, public argument, and communication across the curriculum. He received his PhD from the University of Pittsburgh in 1996.

Nick J. Romerhausen is assistant professor and director of Individual Events in the department of communication, media, and theatre arts at Eastern Michigan University. He is a doctoral candidate in communication at Wayne State University.

Alexandra Vizzier Stephenson is a high school teacher of English and oral communication and a forensics coach at a Maury High School in Norfolk, Virginia. She served as a communication consultant at the University of Mary Washington's Speaking Center as an undergraduate and as a graduate assistant at the University of North Carolina at Greensboro's center while in graduate school. She received her MA from the University of North Carolina at Greensboro in 2006.

Rhonda Troillett has worked in the Communication Skill Center at the university for over two years as an undergraduate intern and then as a graduate assistant. She received an MA in applied communication studies from the University of Arkansas at Little Rock in 2011.

Sarah Wilde is an academic advisor at the University of North Carolina at Charlotte and a part-time lecturer at Central Piedmont Community College. Prior to her work in Charlotte, she served as assistant director of the University Speaking Center at the University of North Carolina at Greensboro. She received her MA from the University of North Carolina at Greensboro in 2005.

Susan Wilson is director of the Speaking/Listening Center, associate faculty development coordinator for Speaking and Oral Communication, and professor of communication and theatre at DePauw University. Her research interests focus on the construction of women's identities (particularly motherhood) and performance studies. She received her PhD from Northwestern University in 1988.

Beth Von Till has been the director of the San Jose State Communication Studies Lab for the last 24 years. Currently chair of the SJSU Academic Senate, she has also been the program director for the innovative Chiba Program for students from the Center for Frontier Science, Chiba University, Japan. She has also served as faculty-in-residence for student success in the Center for Faculty Development. Her interests include working with non-native speakers and the intersection of intercultural communication and organizational communication. She received her MA from San Jose State University in 1988.

Eunkyong (Esther) Yook is director of the Speaking Center, director of the Korea Program, and on faculty at the University of Mary Washington. Her research interests focus on the intersections of communication, education, and culture. She has published articles and book chapters on the topics of intercultural communication and communication education, and a book on ESL students in communication classes. She received her PhD from the University of Minnesota in 1997.